New Wine Into Fresh Wineskins

NEW WINE
INTO FRESH
WINESKINS

Contextualizing the
Early Christian
Confessions

RICHARD N. LONGENECKER

HENDRICKSON
PUBLISHERS

© 1999 by Richard N. Longenecker

Hendrickson Publishers, Inc.
P. O. Box 3473
Peabody, Massachusetts 01961–3473

Printed in the United States of America

ISBN 1-56563-098-X

First printing — November 1999

Library of Congress Cataloging-in-Publication Data

Longenecker, Richard N.
  New wine into fresh wineskins : contextualizing the early
Christian confessions / Richard N. Longenecker.
    p. cm.
  Includes bibliographical references.
  ISBN 1-56563-098-X (pbk.)
  1. Creeds in the Bible. 2. Bible. N.T.—Criticism,
interpretation, etc. I. Title.
BS2545.C74 L66 1999
238′.09—dc21
                                     99-046070

To Bruce and Fiona,
with love!

Table of Contents

Preface

This little book has had an extended gestation period. It started long ago with an interest in the early Christian confessions. It later began to take shape as I observed (1) how Paul used early confessional materials in his letters as a basis for his arguments and to structure his presentations and (2) how the canonical evangelists were informed by and supported these confessional materials. The issues, however, came more sharply into focus through discussions at the American Theological Society during the early 1990s that dealt with how to relate Christian theology to the Christian Scriptures. At the ATS sessions of April 2–3, 1993, I presented a paper entitled "In the Beginning Was the Confession," which was my initial attempt at founding Christian theology on the NT confessional materials. During the years following this presentation I have been consumed by issues regarding contextualization of the gospel—both the contextualizations that occur within the NT itself and those that must take place today.

My attempt to deal with these issues picks up on the parabolic statement of Jesus in Mark 2:22, Matt 9:17, and Luke 5:38 that it is necessary to pour "new (νέον) wine into fresh (καινούς) wineskins"—understanding the "new wine" to be the proclamation of the kingdom of God as focused in the teaching and work of Jesus (cf. Mark 1:27, "a new teaching"; Luke 22:20, "the new covenant in my blood") and the "fresh wineskins" to be the forms into which this proclamation was cast in the NT and the diverse contexts into which it needs to be cast today. The underlying assumption is that when either the "newness" of Jesus' teaching and work (which, of course, is also always to be understood in terms of God's redemptive activity of old) or the "freshness" of new situations (whether in the NT or today) is ignored, the result is, as Matthew's Gospel puts it, the perversion of the gospel *or* the spoiling of the situations in which it is proclaimed, or both, but that when both the "new wine" and the "fresh wineskins" are honored—allowing them to interact with one another in a proper fermenting process—"both are preserved" (Matt 9:17).

The caveat to all of this is, as Luke's Gospel states, that such a relationship between the "new wine" and the "fresh wineskins" will be unpalatable to some, who will declare, "The old is better" (Luke 5:39). Nonetheless, as Jesus' statement makes clear, "New wine *must* be poured into fresh wineskins" (Luke 5:38). And it is our task as Christ's followers to bring about this maturing synergism between the "new wine" and the "fresh wineskins."

This book attempts, therefore, to spell out relationships between (1) the "new wine" of the gospel proclamation, which was first expressed by the earliest Christians in the form of confessions, (2) the contextualizations of these confessions into "fresh wineskins" by the NT writers as they addressed particular mind-sets and specific circumstances, and (3) the further contextualizations of these confessions that need to take place in the "fresh wineskins" of the differing circumstances, cultures, subcultures, regions, and ideological contexts of today. Each of these three fields of study is immense. What follows is hardly exhaustive. It is meant to be only a useful primer on the subject, with "primer" understood as both (1) "an elementary textbook" (i.e., with a short *i*) and (2) "a small amount of explosive used to detonate the main charge" (i.e., with a long *i*). The bibliographies are given not only to guide readers to important literature on the subjects treated but also to signal something of my own dependence.

Introduction

Numerous attempts have been made to identify the basic forms and analyze the central features of the earliest Christian gospel—that is, the forms and features of the "new wine" of the earliest Christian message. Martin Dibelius, for example, in his form-critical analysis of the Gospels, argued that "the oldest tradition about Jesus" took two complementary forms: that of the *sermon* ("proclamation"), whose purpose was propaganda and edification, and that of the *parenesis* ("ethical exhortation"), which was directed to both new and mature Christians.[1] In Rudolf Bultmann's view, however, the individual pericopes that lie behind the formation of the Synoptic Gospels were the first steps toward theologizing among the earliest Christians.[2] And C. H. Dodd, investigating Paul's early letters and the speeches of Acts, declared that "in the beginning was the *kerygma* [proclamation], which was followed by the *didache* [teaching]."[3]

None of these scholars was motivated by "primitivist," "restorationist," or "fundamentalist" concerns. Rather, each, in his own way, was attempting to identify the formal beginning(s) of early Christian thought and practice and to suggest that it was from such a start that all succeeding Christian theology and ethics developed. Yet prior to sermons and hortatory materials (Dibelius), prior to individual pericopes that were later brought together to form the Gospels (Bultmann), and prior to kerygmatic statements and teaching collections (Dodd), the earliest believers in Jesus of Nazareth used what can be called *confessions*.

The noun "confession" and the verb "confess" are commonly used today in a legal sense to mean an admission of guilt. In the NT, however, as well as in the church's language drawn from the NT, "confession" and "confess" usually signify a statement of belief that expresses certain basic convictions about God and Jesus—with this statement taking various forms, depending on the particular circumstance in which it came about (such as in worship, prayer, preaching, liturgy, teaching, catechism, and apology).

Part 1 of this book contends (1) that a number of early Christian confessions, whether in whole or in part, were incorporated by the NT authors into their writings, (2) that form-critical analysis can identify many of these confessional portions, and (3) that analysis of such materials highlights the central features of authentic Christian thought and practice—both as confessed by the NT writers themselves and as held by all true believers in Christ Jesus thereafter. Part 2 proposes that by observing how the NT writers used the early Christian confessions in addressing the various issues, circumstances, and mind-sets of their day, we can (1) gain insight into how the gospel was contextualized in the first century and (2) receive direction for contextualizing this same gospel today. Part 3 sets out a philosophy and program for contextualizing the gospel today, seeking always to (1) root this contextualization in the confessional materials contained in the NT, (2) be guided by the contextualizations of these materials by the NT writers themselves, and (3) be sensitive to differences between the various regions, cultures, subcultures, and worldviews of our contemporary world.

My thesis is not that the confessions of the NT contain all that the early Christians believed or affirmed. Rather, I argue (1) that the early Christian confessions contain the central convictions of the earliest believers in Jesus of Nazareth, (2) that these convictions provide the norms for a distinctly Christian theology and the benchmarks for authentic Christian living, and (3) that the various NT contextualizations of these confessions can yield paradigms for further contextualizations of the Christian message today.

During the past century scholars have worked diligently to identify the confessional materials of the NT and study their provenance and content. The task in Part 1, therefore, will be not to break new ground but to lay out the history of the various form-critical investigations, focus attention on important critical analyses, and highlight the significance of the materials in question. Scholars have given much less attention, however, to how the NT writers contextualized the early Christian confessions in the situations that they confronted and how those confessions can be contextualized today. Hence the need for the work undertaken in Parts 2 and 3 of this book.

Since its introduction in 1972 by the staff of the Theological Education Fund, the term "contextualization" has become something of a shibboleth in missiological parlance.[4] It is often equated with "inculturation," "indigenization," "localization," or "cross-cultural theologizing." Although distinctive nuances are sometimes assigned to some of these terms, all of them are used to explicate relations between the Christian gospel and diverse cultures. "Contextualization," however, seems to have won the day as the most adequate term.

Some missiological theorists see the gospel as the basic datum of the discipline and the various cultures as variables. Others derive the essential data from the cultures themselves, using features drawn from the gospel in support. My own use of the term will emphasize the faithful, responsible, and relevant application of the gospel in differing cultural, societal, and ideological situations. Thus, this book starts with the confessional materials that epitomize the Christian gospel and then attends to how this gospel has been and can be contextualized. The intent is to highlight, as Robert J. Schreiter puts it, "the need for and responsibility of Christians [in whatever culture, region, or circumstance] to make their response to the gospel as concrete and lively as possible."[5]

Implied throughout is an important distinction between (1) the central convictions of the earliest believers in Jesus, which can be found in the early Christian confessions, and (2) the cultural, ideological, and circumstantial contextualizations of these convictions, which appear in the writings of the NT authors—and which must take place continually in every type of Christian ministry, whether at home or abroad. The NT writers, we will argue, viewed the *convictions* expressed in these confessions as normative for Christian thought and practice in their day. Furthermore, we believe they need to be taken as normative for Christian thought and practice today. The *contextualizations* of these confessional materials, however, while pertinent for their day, often do not speak directly to our issues and circumstances. This does not mean, however, that they have little contemporary relevance. Rather, they provide paradigms for our own contextualizing of these same convictions in our differing situations today. In terms of J. Christiaan Beker's description of the nature of Paul's theological statements: (1) the identification of the early Christian confessional portions aids us in marking out the "coherent center" of the early Christian message, and (2) study of how the NT writers contextualized these materials reveals something of the gospel's "contingent interpretation" in their day and sets before us paradigms for contextualizing this same gospel in our day.[6]

PART 1

In the Beginning
Was the Confession

T he title of Part 1 is not meant in any way to upstage the Fourth Evangelist in his opening declaration, "In the beginning was the Word" (John 1:1). The primacy of the Incarnate Word is the basic datum of all Christian thought and practice, and we have no desire to distract attention either from God, who sent the Word, or from Christ, who is himself that Word. Rather, what our title means to suggest is that in our human attempts to explicate the meaning of the Christ-event— that is, in our attempts both to think and to act in a Christian fashion, and so to be authentically involved in formulating doctrine and living ethically as Christians—attention must first of all be directed to the early Christian confessional portions that appear in the writings of the NT. The reason is threefold: (1) it is by means of these confessional materials that the earliest believers in Jesus expressed their central convictions, (2) it is from these confessions that the NT writers worked, contextualizing the distinctive Christian proclamation for the particular mind-sets, problems, and circumstances of their addressees, and (3) it is in the NT contextualizations of these early confessions that we see paradigms for our own Christian thinking, living, and ministries today.

CHAPTER ONE

The Identification of the Early Christian Confessions

That the early Christians used various confessions—including single-statement affirmations and more extended compositions—is suggested by references in the Pauline corpus to (1) "the traditions" that Paul conveyed to his converts (cf. 2 Thess 2:15), (2) the elemental truths about Jesus that Paul received and preached in concert with other early preachers (cf. 1 Cor 15:3, 11), (3) "the form of teaching" to which believers were committed (cf. Rom 6:17), and (4) "the good confession" made by Timothy (cf. 1 Tim 6:12). And that the early Christians cast some of these confessions into poetic form and sang them as hymns seems evident from the reference in 1 Cor 14:26 to the singing of hymns in corporate worship ("When you come together, everyone has a hymn") and the exhortations of Col 3:16–17 and Eph 5:19–20 to include "psalms, hymns, and spiritual songs" in the community's devotions. These poetic portions are to be directed in christocentric fashion ("in the name of the Lord Jesus" and "through him") to God the Father.

Outside the Pauline corpus, the existence of such confessional materials is suggested by references in Hebrews to confessing Jesus (3:1), confessing the faith (4:14), and confessing one's Christian hope (10:23), and perhaps also by references in Jude to "the faith" (v. 3) and "the most holy faith" (v. 20). More important, however, are the early hymns and prayers within the NT that both reflect various Jewish nuances and express distinctively Christian ideas. The most obvious of these hymnic prayers or prayerful hymns are the canticles of Mary, Zechariah, and Simeon in the infancy narrative of Luke 1–2 and the songs of praise to God and the victorious Lamb in Revelation 4, 5, 7, and 15. These NT hymns are comparable to the hymns of praise directed to God alone in the Jewish Scriptures (cf. the Song of Moses in Exod 15:1–18, which is echoed in the Song of Miriam in Exod 18:21; the Song of Deborah in Judg 5:1–31; and the "hymns" of Psalms 8, 9, 29, 33, 65, 67, 68, 96, 98, 100, 103, 104, 105, 111, 113, 114, 117, 135, 136, 145–50) and in the writings of Second Temple Judaism (cf. *Judith* 16:1–17; *Sirach* 51:1–12; and the hymns found in the Qumran texts, esp. in 1QH, the so-called *Thanksgiving Hymns*).

Granted, not every rhythmic phrase, poetic expression, balanced statement, and stylistic use of language is formulaic or signals an early Christian confession. The Jewish Scriptures, from which the early Christians drew spiritual nourishment, are full of such literary features. Indeed, the writings of Second Temple Judaism and the Talmud show how common many biblical forms of speech and artistic turns of expression had become. And early Christians retained much of this language in their teaching, preaching, and writing.

Yet the early Christians also originated certain distinctive confessional materials, which are set out in formulaic fashion (the form) and highlight the central core of their deepest convictions as believers in Jesus (the content). Not everyone, it is true, agrees on the precise identification of such early Christian confessional portions. Neither is there agreement on their genre or their provenance. Almost all NT scholars, however, agree that the early Christians used confessional material in some form or fashion. Furthermore, most are convinced that we can identify at least some of this material within the NT.

Three types of early Christian confessional materials are commonly identified in the NT: (1) single-statement affirmations; (2) formulaic prose portions, which are often called *homologiai* (transliterating the Greek term for "confessions"); and (3) poetic portions, which are usually called hymns. But while these three types can be arranged in this somewhat logical, literary order according to form (moving from simple affirmations to more complex literary structures), the history of their identification has proceeded in the reverse order: first hymns, then *homologiai*, and finally single-statement affirmations. This historical order will govern this chapter's treatment of the identification and nature of the confessional materials.

▓ 1. HYMNS (Poetic Portions)

Scholars first became interested in early Christian hymns during the late nineteenth century and the early part of the twentieth century. Johannes Weiss, in an extended article published in 1897, drew attention to various rhetorical features of Paul's letters and identified some of the more prominent hymnic materials in these letters.[1] Eduard Norden in 1898 surveyed "artistic prose" features described in the ancient rhetorical handbooks *(Theorie)* and used in actual writings *(Praxis)* from the Greek classical period to the Renaissance.[2] He discussed the use of poetry and hymns by the ancient Greek, Roman, and humanist writers, but also, in an appendix, pointed to the presence of many of these same features in the NT.[3] Eduard von der Goltz used a similar approach to study prayer among the earliest Christians;[4] and Alfred Seeberg attempted to reconstruct the earliest Christian catechism, focusing on what he called the earliest *Glaubensformel,* or "formula of faith," found in the NT letters and the writings of the early Fathers.[5] Both von der Goltz and Seeberg highlighted various formulaic prose and poetry portions in the NT that contained such features.

It was Norden, however, who contributed the most to the study of the literary features of early Christian prayers and hymns and was the first to formulate criteria for their identification and analysis. In *Die antike Kunstprosa* (1898) he set out basic principles for investigating the early Christian prayers and hymns found in the NT.[6] In *Agnostos Theos* (1913) he elaborated further on these principles—adding principles for identifying early confessional materials—dealing principally with Rom 11:33–36, Col 1:15–20, 1 Tim 3:16b, 1 Cor 15:3b–5, and Matt

11:25–30.[7] Thus, in what could be called a pre-*formgeschichtliche* study of the hymnic and confessional materials incorporated within the NT, Norden proposed the following criteria for their identification: (1) the presence of *parallelismus membrorum* (i.e., parallel structures), (2) the use of second- or third-person singular pronouns at the beginning of such portions, (3) the use of participial predications and relative clauses throughout these materials, and (4) an elevated, celebratory style.

Norden's work on early Christian hymns has, of course, undergone extensive refinement during the past century. Nevertheless, Norden's four criteria have served as the basis for all succeeding attempts to isolate and analyze hymnic materials within the NT. Representative of the various scholars who have taken over Norden's approach and adopted, in the main, his conclusions are the following, listed in chronological order:[8]

1921: Josef KROLL, *Die christliche Hymnodik bis zu Clemens von Alexandreia;* **1926:** Josef KROLL, "Die Hymnendichtung des frühen Christentums" *Antik* 2: 258–81; **1928:** Ernst LOHMEYER, *Kyrios Jesu: Eine Untersuchung zu Phil. 2,5–11;* **1941:** Ethelbert STAUFFER, *Die Theologie des Neuen Testaments;* **1942:** Günther BORNKAMM, "Das Bekenntnis im Hebräerbrief"; **1947:** Lucien CERFAUX, "Hymnes au Christ des lettres de Saint Paul"; **1950:** Ernst KÄSEMANN, "Kritische Analyse von Phil. 2.5–11"; **1951:** Günther BORNKAMM, "Der Lobpreis Gottes: Röm 11,33–36"; **1957:** James M. ROBINSON, "A Formal Analysis of Col 1:15–20" 76: 270–87; **1960:** Stanislas LYONNET, "L'hymne christologique de l'Épitre aux Colossiens et la fête juive du Nouvel An" 48: 93–100; Ralph P. MARTIN, *An Early Christian Confession: Philippians II.5–11 in Recent Interpretation;* **1962:** Gottfried SCHILLE, *Frühchristliche Hymnen;* **1963:** Günther BORNKAMM, "Zum Verständnis des Christus-Hymnus Phil. 2,5–11"; **1964:** Günther BORNKAMM, "Lobpreis, Bekenntnis, und Opfer"; Dieter GEORGI, "Der vorpaulinische Hymnus Phil 2,6–11"; Ernst KÄSEMANN, "A Primitive Christian Baptismal Liturgy"; James M. ROBINSON, "Die Hodayot-Formel in Gebet und Hymnus des Frühchristentums"; Georg STRECKER, "Redaktion und Tradition im Christushymnus Phil. 2,6–11"; **1965:** Reginald H. FULLER, *The Foundations of New Testament Christology;* Jack T. SANDERS, "Hymnic Elements in Ephesians 1–3"; J. SCHATTENMANN, *Studien zum neutestamentlichen Prosahymnus* **1967:** Reinhard DEICHGRÄBER, *Gotteshymnus und Christushymnus in der frühen Christenheit;* N. KEHL, *Der Christushymnus im Kolosserbrief;* Ralph P. MARTIN, *Carmen Christi: Philippians II.5–11;* **1968:** I. Howard MARSHALL, "The Christ Hymn in Philippians 2:5–11"; **1971:** Jack T. SANDERS, *The New Testament Christological Hymns: Their Historical Religious Background;* **1972:** Eduard LOHSE,

Die Einheit des Neuen Testaments, esp.; pp. 276–84; Klaus WENGST, *Christologische Formeln und Lieder des Urchristentums;* **1975:** Morna D. HOOKER, "Philippians 2:6–11"; **1976:** Otfried HOFIUS, *Der Christushymnus Philipper 2,6–11;* **1977:** Werner STENGER, *Der Christushymnus 1 Tim. 3:16: Eine strukturanalytische Untersuchung;* **1978:** Martin HENGEL, "Hymns and Christology"; **1979:** Witmar METZGER, *Der Christushymnus 1 Tim. 3.16;* **1982:** James H. CHARLESWORTH, "A Prolegomenon to a New Study of the Jewish Background of the Hymns and Prayers in the New Testament"; **1984:** William H. GLOER, "Homologies and Hymns in the New Testament"; Stanislav SEGERT, "Semitic Poetic Structures in the New Testament"; **1986:** James H. CHARLESWORTH, "Jewish Hymns, Odes, and Prayers (ca. 167 B.C.E.–35 C.E.)"; **1988:** Joseph A. FITZMYER, "The Aramaic Background of Philippians 2:6–11"; **1990:** Stephen E. FOWL, *The Story of Christ in the Ethics of Paul: An Analysis of the Function of the Hymnic Material in the Pauline Corpus;* **1992:** Ernest BEST, "The Use of Credal and Liturgical Material in Ephesians"; **1995:** Martin HENGEL, *Studies in Early Christology;* **1996:** Robert J. KARRIS, *A Symphony of New Testament Hymns.*

The length of this list—even though only a representative list—should alert the reader to the mass of scholarship from almost every theological quarter in support of Norden's basic approach.

Not every NT scholar, of course, has viewed the quest for early Christian hymns within the NT with equal favor. Some have ignored them. A few have even denied their presence. Nonetheless, that such materials exist within the NT remains a firmly entrenched axiom of critical scholarship. And this fact is attested not only by the monographs and articles cited above but also by the many contemporary critical commentaries on the NT—beginning with Ernst Lohmeyer's *Die Briefe an die Philipper, an die Kolosser, und an Philemon*[9]—that have attempted to deal seriously with these confessional materials.

Scholars have had their own variations and refinements in method. Nonetheless, despite some differences, there is widespread critical agreement on the legitimacy of the following criteria for the identification of early Christian hymns:

1. The presence of parallel structures *(parallelismus membrorum)* that reflect Jewish or Hellenistic poetic conventions;

2. The presence of words and phrases not used elsewhere in an author's writings *(hapax legomena),* or not with the meaning or in the manner found in his other writings—

which suggests that the material in question was probably composed by someone else;

3. A preference for participles over finite verbs, suggesting an original oral provenance;

4. The frequent use of the relative pronoun ὅς ("who") to begin passages;

5. Contextual dislocations: poetic material in a prose section or doctrinal material in an ethical section;

6. The continuance of a portion after its content has ceased to be relevant to its immediate context; and

7. The affirmation of a basic Christian conviction, usually concerning the work or person of Jesus Christ.

There has been somewhat less agreement as to which NT portions are to be identified as early Christian hymns. Some scholars have been quite inclusive; others, more restrictive. Reinhard Deichgräber, however, has fairly well established the major portions that have a high degree of probability of being hymns, whether praising God or extolling Christ.[10] Though at some points I may differ as to whether a particular passage is a hymn or a *homologia*, I will, in the main, accept Deichgräber's identifications.

Of the early Christian hymns in praise of God, the most obvious are Rom 11:33–36 and Rev 15:3b–4. With these words of adoration the hymn of Rom 11:33–36 concludes Paul's discussion of God's dealings with Israel:

> Oh, the depth of the riches, the wisdom and the knowledge of God!
>   How unsearchable his judgments,
>   and his paths beyond tracing out!
> "Who has known the mind of the Lord?
>   Or who has been his advisor [quoting Isa 40:13]?"
> "Who has ever given to God,
>   that God should repay him [quoting Job 41:11]?"
> For from him and through him and to him are all things.
> To him be the glory forever! Amen.

The hymn of Rev 15:3b–4 is that of the victorious saints in heaven. Some interpreters have taken it to be christological, but more likely it should be read as praise directed to God:

Great and marvelous are your deeds,
  Lord God Almighty.
Just and true are your ways,
  King of the ages.
Who will not fear you, O Lord,
  and bring glory to your name?
For you alone are holy.
All nations will come and worship before you,
  for your righteous acts have been revealed.

Deichgräber also notes the presence of hymn fragments in 2 Cor 1:3–4, Eph 1:3–14, Col 1:12–14, and 1 Pet 1:3–5. Likewise, a number of hymnic portions may be scattered throughout the Johannine Apocalypse, though Deichgräber considers the presence of such materials in the Apocalypse too large and involved a subject for inclusion in his treatment.

Of the early Christian hymns extolling Christ, the most commonly accepted are Phil 2:6–11, 1 Tim 3:16b, and 1 Pet 2:22–23. Of these, the one that has seemed the most obvious to most biblical scholars is Phil 2:6–11:

Who, being in very nature God,
  did not consider equality with God something to be grasped.
But he made himself nothing,
  taking the very nature of a servant,
  being made in human likeness.
And being found in appearance in human form,
  he humbled himself
  and became obedient to the extent of death
    —even death on a cross!
Therefore God exalted him to the highest place
  and gave him the name that is above every name.
That at the name of Jesus every knee should bow,
  in heaven and on earth and under the earth,
and every tongue confess that Jesus Christ is Lord,
  to the glory of God the Father.

First Timothy 3:16b has also long been seen as an early Christian hymn in praise of Christ:

Who appeared in a body,
  was vindicated by the Spirit;
was seen by angels,
  was preached among the nations;

was believed on in the world,
was taken up in glory.

And 1 Pet 2:22–23, with its double use of the relative pronoun ὅς ("who") to begin each of its two parts, has been taken to
be an early christological hymn:

"Who committed no sin,
and no deceit was found in his mouth [quoting Isa 53:9]."
Who when they hurled their insults at him,
did not retaliate;
when he suffered,
he made no threats [alluding to Isa 53:7].

The material in Col 1:15–20 is also considered an early
christological hymn by most NT scholars. It could, however, just
as well be seen as a *homologia*, or formulaic confessional portion,
for its lyrical quality and strophic structure are not readily identifiable. This is how Heb 1:3, 4:12–13, and 5:7–9 should probably
be understood as well—that is, as formulaic confessional materials that speak of Jesus "the Son," and not as portions extracted
from earlier hymns. And Deichgräber is probably right to note
that various early christological hymn fragments are incorporated within the ascriptions of Eph 2:14–18 and Col 2:9–15.

■ 2. *HOMOLOGIAI* (Formulaic Prose Portions)

It has not always been easy for scholars to separate their
form-critical studies of early Christian hymns from their form-
critical studies of early Christian *homologiai*. There is a great deal
of overlap between the two categories, and some scholars have
tended to blend them. Yet there have been studies that have focused more on the *homologiai* than on the hymns, making use of
the hymnic materials only when they contained confessional features that paralleled other confessional features found elsewhere.

Alfred Seeberg's *Katechismus der Urchristenheit* (1903) was
probably the first investigation to focus mainly on the confessional aspect of traditional materials in the NT. For while Seeberg was
interested in several types of material used in the proclamation,
worship, and instruction of the early church (including hymnic

material), he was principally concerned with distilling the *Glaub-ensformel* that underlay all of these forms—and which, he argued, served as the basic catechism for all of the NT writers. C. H. Dodd's *The Apostolic Preaching and Its Developments* (1936) also focused on confessional features. But Dodd was primarily concerned with isolating the primitive *kerygma* ("preaching") from Paul's letters (esp. 1 Cor 15:3b–5) and from the sermons of Acts, and so he gave less attention to their form and provenance. Likewise, A. M. Hunter's *Paul and His Predecessors* (1940)[11] surveyed several kinds of early Christian traditional materials in the NT. Much of his discussion is relevant to the study of early Christian *homologiai*. But, like Dodd, Hunter had other interests than the analysis of the confessions themselves, for he mainly wanted to demonstrate that there existed numerous conceptual and theological links between Paul and his Christian predecessors.

Ethelbert Stauffer's *Die Theologie des Neuen Testaments* (1941)[12] is also important here. For in his study of the creeds of the early church he devoted attention to (1) the creedal formulas in the NT (e.g., how they came about, how they appeared in the life of the early church, and how they were adopted) and (2) the christological formulas of the NT (their origin, content, and nature).

Closest to being a purely confessional investigation, however, and probably the most significant of all these studies, is Oscar Cullmann's *Les premières confessions de foi chrétiennes* (1943).[13] Cullmann focused on an analysis of the confessional materials themselves, asking questions about their form, provenance, and content. In Cullmann's form-critical analysis, an important conclusion was his insistence on the diverse and complex circumstances that gave rise to these materials. In his content analysis, his most significant claims were (1) that a twofold acclamation of Christ as the divine Son of God and as exalted Lord underlies all of these portions and (2) that more primitive than even this twofold acclamation was the single confession κύριος Χριστός, "Christ is Lord." Following along the lines of Cullmann's investigations, but correcting his unitary focus on the lordship of Christ, was Vernon H. Neufeld, *The Earliest Christian Confessions* (1963).[14] Much of Cullmann's argument, as corrected by Neufeld, has appeared in various recent commentaries and NT theologies.

New Testament scholars today tend to view early Christian hymns and early Christian *homologiai* as parallel, though somewhat distinguishable, phenomena—or, to use a biological metaphor, as different species within the same family, with similar characteristics but also a number of differing features. The distinction between hymns and *homologiai* was highlighted by Deichgräber, who took pains to show that the *homologia* of 1 Cor 15:3b–5 is formally different from the hymn of Phil 2:6–11.[15] And that distinction has been carried on in most of the succeeding scholarly treatments—as witness, for example, the titles of two relatively recent writings on the subject: Klaus Wengst's *Christologische Formeln und Lieder des Urchristentums* (1972) and William H. Gloer's "Homologies and Hymns in the New Testament: Form, Content, and Criteria for Identification" (1984).[16]

Many of the form-critical criteria used to identify hymns in the NT are also used to identify early formulaic, but nonpoetic, confessional materials:

1. The presence of *parallelismus membrorum,* even though the material is not poetry;

2. The presence of *hapax legomena;*

3. A preference for participles over finite verbs; and

4. An affirmation regarding the work or person of Jesus Christ.

Added to this list have been such other linguistic indicators as

5. The noun ὁμολογία ("confession") to signal the content of such early Christian material, either expressed or implied;

6. The verb ὁμολογέω ("confess") with a double accusative or an infinitive to introduce a direct or an indirect quotation;

7. The word ὅτι (the *hoti recitativum*) to introduce a direct or an indirect quotation;

8. Verbs for preaching (εὐαγγελίζω, κηρύσσω, or καταγγέλλω), teaching (διδάσκω), or witnessing (μαρτυρέω or μαρτύρομαι) to introduce the confessional material; and

9. A participial construction or a relative clause to introduce the material in question.

The most obvious of these early *homologiai* is that found in 1 Cor 15:3b–5. For what Paul "delivers" or "passes on" (παρέδωκα) to his readers in these verses he explicitly says he "received" (παρέλαβον) and other Christian preachers before him have proclaimed (see vv. 3a and 11). Furthermore, the material is introduced by a fourfold use of the *hoti recitativum,* and the two crucial points of death and resurrection are highlighted by the repetition of the *hapax legomenon* expression "according to the Scriptures":

[That] Christ died for our sins according to the Scriptures;
[that] he was buried;
[that] he was raised on the third day, according to the Scriptures;
[that] he appeared to Peter and then to the Twelve.

Colossians 1:15–20 also seems to be one of these *homologia* portions. The passage is set off by the use of the relative pronoun ὅς at the beginning of each of its two main sections (vv. 15 and 18b). Likewise, it is replete with *hapax legomena* (i.e., words or phrases not used elsewhere in an author's writings, or not with the meanings or in the manner of his other writings)—such as the expressions "image" (εἰκών), "firstborn" (πρωτότοκος, used twice), "before all things" (πρὸ πάντων), "the head" (ἡ κεφαλή), "the beginning" (ἀρχή), and "the fullness" (τὸ πλήρωμα). Furthermore, it evidences a carefully constructed and balanced structure, or what is called *parallelismus membrorum.*

Yet this passage does not appear to be set out in poetic fashion; at least, scholars have found it extremely difficult to reconstruct its strophes. Probably, therefore, it should be viewed as a formulaic prose composition of the early church that proclaims (1) the supremacy of Christ's person, both in the cosmos and in the church (vv. 15–18a), and (2) the supremacy of Christ's work, both before God and in the religious experience of his people (vv. 18b–20). Perhaps, judging by the nuances that many of these *hapax legomena* carried in the ancient world, it should also be seen as having been formulated within, or in opposition to, some type of ascetic-mystical piety or gnostic speculation that tended to deemphasize the importance of the person and work of Christ.

But whatever may be postulated as to the earliest provenance of Col 1:15–20, the passage was used christologically by early Christians and Paul to proclaim:

> He ["Who"] is the image of the invisible God, the firstborn over all creation. For by him all things were created: things in heaven and on earth, visible and invisible, whether thrones or powers or rulers or authorities; all things were created by him and for him. He is before all things, and in him all things hold together. And he is the head of the body, the church.

> He ["Who"] is the beginning and the firstborn from among the dead, so that in everything he might have the supremacy. For God was pleased to have all his fullness dwell in him, and through him to reconcile to himself all things, whether things on earth or things in heaven, by making peace through his blood, shed on the cross.

Likewise, the following portions in the letters of the NT have also often been seen as early Christian *homologiai*, whether in whole or in part:

Rom 1:3b–4, which sets out an elemental "two-stage" Christology:

> The one born of the seed of David,
>   according to the flesh;
> the one declared to be the Son of God with power,
>   according to his spirit [or "the Spirit"] of holiness,
>   by the resurrection of the dead.

Rom 3:24–26, which some argue starts at verse 25 and ends somewhere in verse 26, but probably should be seen to begin at verse 24 and to include all of verse 26:

> [We are] being justified freely by his grace through the redemption that is in Christ Jesus, whom God set forth as a sacrifice of atonement through faith in his blood. He did this in order to demonstrate his justice, because in his forbearance he had let the sins committed beforehand go unpunished. He did this to demonstrate his justice at the present time. So as to be just and the one who justifies the person who depends on the faith/faithfulness of Jesus [or "who has faith in Jesus"].

Rom 4:25, which forms a fitting conclusion to the first four chapters of Paul's letter to the Romans, summarizing, in effect, the central affirmations of 3:21–31 with the repetition of a confessional formula in the form of an antithetical parallelism:

> Who was delivered over to death for our sins,
> and was raised to life for our justification.

1 Cor 1:17–18, 23; 2:2, which appear to incorporate various formulaic uses of the expressions "the cross of Christ" and "Christ crucified," with three verbs referring to preaching used to introduce these expressions.

2 Cor 5:19a, which, in context, also appears to be a confessional portion introduced by a *hoti recitativum*. This confession is the linchpin, or central and cohesive feature, in Paul's exposition in verses 18–20 regarding God's initiative in reconciliation, Christ's work of reconciliation, and the Christian's status of being reconciled to God:

> [That] God was in Christ reconciling the world to himself, not counting people's sins against them.

Gal 1:4, which is set in juxtaposition to the mention of "the Lord Jesus Christ":

> The one who gave himself for our sins to rescue us from the present evil age, according to the will of our God and Father.

Gal 3:13, which affirms one aspect of the work of Christ:

> Christ redeemed us from the curse of the law by becoming a curse for us, for it is written: "Cursed is everyone who is hanged on a tree [quoting Deut 21:23]."

Gal 3:26–28, which combines what appears to be an early Christian saying (v. 26) with an early Christian confessional portion (vv. 27–28):

> You are all children ["sons"] of God through faith in Christ Jesus.
>
> As many of you as were baptized into Christ have been clothed with Christ. There is neither Jew nor Greek, slave nor free, male and female, for you are all one in Christ Jesus.

Gal 4:4–5, which is seen by many to incorporate not only themes of eschatology, true humanity, relation to the law, obedience, and redemption, but also an early "sending formula" of the first Christians:

> When the time had fully come, God sent his Son, born of a woman, born under the law, to redeem those under the law, that we might receive adoption as God's children [or "the adoption"; "the full rights of sons"].

1 Thess 4:14a, which by its form, wording, and usage appears to be an early Christian confessional saying:

> [That] Jesus died and rose again.

Heb 1:3, which serves to buttress the author's central thesis of 1:1–2 and to set up all of his following discussion regarding the superiority of "the Son":

> He ["Who"] is the radiance [or "effulgence"] of God's glory and the exact representation [or "imprint"] of his person, sustaining all things by his powerful word. And after he had provided purification for sins, he sat down at the right hand of the Majesty in heaven.

Heb 5:7–9, which seems to be made up of two confessional portions (v. 7 and vv. 8–9) that speak of Christ's earthly obedience:

> Who in the days of his flesh offered up prayers and petitions with a loud cry and tears to the one who could save him from death [an allusion to Jesus' Gethsemane prayer?], and he was heard because of his reverent submission.

> Although he was a son, he learned obedience from what he suffered; and once made perfect, he became the source of eternal salvation for all who obey him.

All of these *homologia* portions will be discussed in chapters 2 and 3, which analyze their contents and study how they have been contextualized in the NT letters where they appear. Perhaps other portions should also be included, particularly expressions used within the lyrical and almost defiant affirmations of Rom 8:33–39. Possibly there are also echoes of confessional materials in Rom 14:9, 1 Thess 1:9–10, and Heb 4:12–13. Suffice it here to say, however, that this study accepts all of the portions presented above as examples of early Christian confessional materials and that it will build on them in what follows.

■ 3. SINGLE-STATEMENT AFFIRMATIONS

In almost all of the studies of early Christian hymns and *homologiai*, various single-statement affirmations regarding Christ have been highlighted as well. Most often these single-statement affirmations ascribe titles to Jesus. Numerous books and articles, in fact, have been written on the titles of Jesus in the NT; some of these titles appear in the poetic and prose confessional portions, and others in separate traditional statements.

One of the earliest studies of a NT christological title was Wilhelm Bousset's *Kyrios Christos* (1913), which removed the title "Lord" from the consciousness of the earliest Jewish believers in Jesus and assigned it to the outlook of later hellenized Christians.[17] But Ernst Lohmeyer's *Kyrios Jesus* (1928) and Ernst von Dobschütz's "Kurios Iesous" (1931) largely exploded Bousset's theory.[18] Since then, many scholars have dealt with the single-statement confessional affirmations of the NT in a more constructive and positive fashion—for example, Jean Daniélou, *The Theology of Jewish Christianity* (ET 1964, which is an extensively revised version of his 1958 French original); Ferdinand Hahn, *Christologische Hoheitstitel: Ihre Geschichte im frühen Christentum* (1963; ET = *The Titles of Jesus in Christology: Their History in Early Christianity*, 1969); Werner Kramer, *Christos, Kyrios, Gottessohn* (1963; ET = *Christ, Lord, Son of God*, 1966); R. H. Fuller, *The Foundations of New Testament Christology* (1965); and Richard N. Longenecker, *The Christology of Early Jewish Christianity* (1970). The most definitive of such christological studies undoubtedly are those of Oscar Cullmann (see particularly *Les premières confessions de foi chrétiennes* [1943, ET 1949] and *Die Christologie des Neuen Testaments* [1957, ET 1959]) and Martin Hengel (see particularly *Between Jesus and Paul: Studies in the Earliest History of Christianity* [1983] and *Studies in Early Christology* [1995]).[19]

Criteria for identifying single-statement confessional affirmations in the NT are much the same as those for identifying *homologiai* and hymns—obviously excluding, however, criteria relating principally to extended prose or poetry portions (e.g., *parallelismus membrorum* and a preference for participles over finite verbs). Certain linguistic features commonly appear in the introductions to quoted confessional materials, such as the use of

1. the verb ὁμολογέω ("confess");

2. other verbs of a kerygmatic, didactic, or confessional nature;

3. the *hoti recitativum*, a double accusative, or an infinitive (often in combination); and

4. a participial construction or relative clause.

Furthermore, single-statement confessional affirmations speak in a distinctive manner about the work or person of Christ. Chief among them are those ascribing to Jesus the titles "Christ," "Son of God," or "Lord."

Passages where the title "Christ" appears in a confessional manner include the following:

Mark 8:29b, par.	Peter's confession: "You are the Christ";
John 1:15–27	John the Baptist's statements in "testifying about" and "confessing" Jesus that include, by implication, nuances about him being the Christ;
John 1:41	Andrew's words to his brother Simon: We have found the Messiah (that is, the Christ)";
John 7:41	Some of the people said of Jesus, "He is the Christ";
John 9:22b	"The Jews had decided that anyone who confessed him [Jesus] to be the Christ would be put out of the synagogue";
John 11:27	Martha's response: "Yes, Lord. I believe that you are the Christ, the Son of God, who was to come into the world";
John 20:31	"These things are written that you may believe that Jesus is the Christ, the Son of God, and that by believing you may have life in his name";

Acts 9:22	"Saul grew more and more powerful and baffled the Jews living in Damascus by proving that Jesus is the Christ";
Acts 17:3b	Paul's preaching in the synagogue at Thessalonica culminated in the proclamation: "This Jesus I am proclaiming to you is the Christ";
1 John 2:22a	"Who is the liar? It is the one who denies that Jesus is the Christ";
1 John 5:1a	"Everyone who believes that Jesus is the Christ is born of God."

Passages that call Jesus "Son of God" in a confessional manner include the following:

Mark 15:39	The centurion's affirmation: "Surely this man was the Son of God"—with Mark (also Matt 27:54) highlighting this statement as being the proper confession, whatever the centurion himself might have meant;
Matt 16:16	Peter's confession (à la Matthew): "You are the Christ, the Son of the living God";
John 1:34	John the Baptist's testimony: "I have seen and testify that this is the Son of God";
John 1:49	Nathanael's declaration: "Rabbi, you are the Son of God; you are the King of Israel";
John 11:27	Martha's response: "Yes, Lord. I believe that you are the Christ, the Son of God, who was to come into the world";
John 20:31	The evangelist's statement: "These things are written that you may believe that Jesus is the Christ, the Son of God, and that by believing you may have life in his name";
Acts 9:20	Paul preached in the synagogues of Damascus "that Jesus is the Son of God" (as well as "that Jesus is the Christ," as in v. 22);

1 John 4:15	"If any confess that Jesus is the Son of God, God lives in them and they live in God";
1 John 5:5	"Who is it that overcomes the world? Only the one who believes that Jesus is the Son of God."

Passages where the confessional title "Lord" is used of Jesus include the following:

Rom 10:9	"That if you confess with your mouth that Jesus is Lord [the *hoti recitativum* is included in B, et al.] and believe in your heart that God raised him from the dead, you will be saved";
1 Cor 12:3	"No one who is speaking by the Spirit of God says 'Jesus be cursed,' and no one can say 'Jesus is Lord' except by the Holy Spirit";
2 Cor 4:5	"We do not preach ourselves, but 'Jesus Christ is Lord,' and ourselves as your servants for Jesus' sake";
Phil 2:11	"and every tongue confess that 'Jesus Christ is Lord,' to the glory of God the Father";
Col 2:6	"So then, just as you received Christ Jesus as Lord, continue to live in him."

Titular ascriptions and single-statement confessions can also be found in the confessional prose materials noted earlier, which speak about the work or person of Christ. Chief among these portions, though hardly an inclusive list, are Rom 1:3–4; 3:24–26; 1 Cor 1:17–18, 23; 2:2; 15:3–5; Gal 1:4; 3:13, 26, 27–28; 4:4–5; 1 Thess 4:14, and Heb 5:7, 8–9.

■ 4. QUESTIONS OF GENRE AND PROVENANCE

While hymns, *homologiai,* and single-statement affirmations are today generally treated separately in the study of early

Christian formulaic materials, questions still persist about exactly what to call these various portions, either individually or collectively. What type of material or literary genre do they represent? Furthermore, questions remain about what branch, stratum, outlook, or situation of early Christianity these portions stem from, either individually or collectively. What place of origin and ideological background (provenance) do they reflect?

Genre

Scholars have often used such terms as "creed," "formula of faith," "kerygma," "paradosis" (i.e., "tradition"), "hymn," "prayer," "confession," "liturgical formulation," "ecclesial tradition," "narrative portion," "story," and/or "saying" when trying to establish a nomenclature for this material. But as Ethelbert Stauffer long ago observed, "Many confessions were hymn-like and many hymns were creed-like."[20] All of these proposed genre classifications seem to overlap.

It is more appropriate, we believe, to give priority to content and classify all these materials under the generic rubric "early Christian confessions"—that is, to speak of them as formulaic statements that express the essential convictions of the earliest believers in Jesus. The noun ὁμολογία was used by Greeks in the classical and Koine periods to mean (1) "agreement" or "acknowledgment" in matters of law, (2) "concession" or "admission" of guilt, and (3) "conformity" to nature. In the LXX, however, the word often took on a distinctly religious sense: (1) "praise" or "thanksgiving" to God or (2) "confession" or "admission" of sin before God. The NT writers, picking up on this religious use, always employed the noun ὁμολογία to mean a formulaic statement of Christian conviction (cf. 2 Cor 9:13; 1 Tim 6:12, 13; Heb 3:1; 4:14; 10:23). And while the verb ὁμολογέω was used, at times, to mean "to confess" guilt or sin (cf. Acts 24:14; 1 John 1:9), it usually connotes "to confess" something about Jesus or something about one's relationship with Jesus (cf. Matt 10:32 // Luke 12:8; John 9:22; 12:42 [also see 1:20]; Rom 10:9; Phil 2:11 [with the preposition ἐκ]; 1 John 2:22–23; 4:2, 3, 15; 2 John 7).

Provenance

A great deal of effort has been directed toward discovering the historical, ideological, and theological matrix (the *Sitz im Leben*) of each of these individual formulaic expressions. Some scholars have focused attention principally on form, believing it to be the best indicator of provenance, and so have set out to determine whether the various affirmations, *homologiai*, and hymns are Jewish or Greek in form, and thus Jewish or Greek in outlook. For example, Jack Sanders finds Hebrew poetry in the hymns of the NT and concludes that all these hymns had their origin in a myth of cosmic reconciliation that Christians took over from the wisdom writings of Second Temple Judaism.[21] Others object to drawing conclusions primarily from form, preferring rather to focus on vocabulary and content. Klaus Wengst, for example, working on the bases of vocabulary and content, assigns the origin of each formulaic confession and hymn to an Aramaic-speaking Jewish church, a Greek-speaking Jewish church, or a Greek-speaking Gentile church.[22]

Today, however, many scholars doubt that we can fit the various early Christian formulaic materials into specific historical, ideological, and theological matrices. Form-critical studies have successfully identified many of these materials and directed us back to a time before our NT writings were composed. But form criticism's promise has exceeded its performance in determining provenance. Thus Deichgräber, whose work is probably the best form-critical treatment of the NT hymns to date, argues that there is virtually no evidence for assigning these poetic portions a *Sitz im Leben* any more specific than simply the worship of the early church[23]— which is the conclusion that Stauffer and Cullmann came to as well.[24]

James Charlesworth essentially agrees, for while highlighting the Jewish features of the NT hymns and prayers, he concludes:

> Obviously, scholars are presently far from a consensus on many key issues. We do not know the exact length of most of the hymns quoted in the New Testament, whether they are complete or fragmentary, or whether they originate with the author, his community, or with an earlier anonymous Jew or Christian. We are

convinced that many—if not most—of the hymns and prayers have been expanded or interpolated, but the extent of such editorial activity is not clear. We have no refined sieve with which to isolate and remove a quoted hymn. Most importantly . . . we have no clear-cut paradigm or set of categories with which to judge if it is originally Jewish or Jewish Christian.[25]

Hengel is probably right to surmise that christological thought developed more in the early church between 30 and 50 CE than between 50 and 700 CE, although that latter period encompasses all seven great ecclesiastical councils.[26] As to the exact provenance of the confessional materials that came to expression in that earlier time, however, the only truly scholarly stance is one of agnosticism. All that can be said historically is that probably most of the confessional materials identified above were formed earlier than Paul's major missionary letters, which are the earliest writings in the NT. And all that can be said religiously is that these early confessions evidently came about through the guidance of the Holy Spirit as the earliest Christians meditated on the work and person of Jesus of Nazareth and as they attempted to express their new faith in their particular circumstances of worship, instruction, and witness.

CHAPTER TWO

The Contents of the Early Christian Confessions

Any thorough analysis of the contents of the early Christian confessions should deal with each confessional portion separately and only then attempt a synthesis. For every single-statement affirmation, every formulaic prose portion (or *homologia*), and every hymnic passage has its own complex of literary features, its own problems of interpretation, and its own history of scholarly treatment—perhaps even its own ideological background. But these are matters that scholars have dealt with extensively. It would take volumes to treat all of the significant passages and all of the issues properly. This study will therefore only refer to the major issues regarding the most prominent confessional materials and offer some informed observations.

Likewise, full treatment of the early Christian confessions should, perhaps, deal with their contents according to their respective types—that is, according to such categories as (1) single-statement affirmations, (2) formulaic prose passages, and (3) poetic passages ("hymns"); or, possibly, rearrange these categories for pedagogical purposes. Here, however, we will present only a précis of the contents of these portions, referring to the various types of material in the process.

Since Paul's letters are the earliest NT writings, the confessional materials found in them—particularly in his earlier letters—

presumably represent some of the earliest Christian confessions. Hebrews, the General Epistles, the canonical Gospels, the Acts of the Apostles, and the Johannine Apocalypse, however, were written later, and so might have made use of confessional portions that were developed later in the church. Furthermore, since in Paul's letters we are dealing with the best-known author and the best-known addressees within the whole of the NT, we are in a position to judge circumstances and usages better in these letters than in any of the other writings of the NT.

The following analysis of the contents of the early Christian confessions will, therefore, normally begin by focusing on the earlier letters of Paul. It will refer to confessional materials elsewhere in the NT as well, but usually only by relating their contents to the analyses of material found in Paul's letters.

▧ 1. THE NATURE OF THE CONFESSIONAL MATERIALS

Before dealing directly with the major themes of the early Christian confessions, we must make a few observations regarding the nature of these confessional materials. Four matters in particular need to be here highlighted.

Devotional Material

In the first place, probably most, if not all, of the early confessional materials in the NT are devotional in nature, expressing the early Christians' praise of God and adoration of Christ in the context of corporate worship. This is hardly surprising. For confessions in the biblical sense are faith expressions, and memorable faith expressions take form most commonly in the context of corporate worship—whether planned or spontaneous. This observation may seem obvious. But interpreters tend to overlook it all too easily. Consequently, they often treat these texts in a manner inappropriate to their nature.

Devotional material, while having a central focus and expressing essential convictions, is frequently rather imprecise. It attempts to inspire adoration, not to explicate doctrinal nuances.

It uses the language of the heart more than that of the mind. It is, therefore, not always philosophically precise, philologically exact, or theologically correct—perhaps, at times, not even logically coherent. Thus in analyzing Phil 2:6–11, for example, one comes up against a host of exegetical questions that have constantly baffled scholars, simply because the text is ambiguous. What exactly do the expressions μορφῇ θεοῦ ("the form of God") and μορφὴν δούλου ("the form of a servant") signify about the status and person of Christ? What does ἁρπαγμός mean when applied to Christ: something he had and chose not to hold on to *(res rapta)*, or something he did not have and did not try to grasp, even though he could have *(res rapienda)*? Should ἑαυτὸν ἐκένωσεν ("he emptied himself") be read literally or metaphorically? Is ἐν ὁμοιώματι ἀνθρώπων ("in human likeness") a docetic expression, and how should it be understood vis-à-vis Paul's statement in Rom 8:3 that God sent his own Son ἐν ὁμοιώματι σαρκὸς ἁμαρτίας ("in the likeness of sinful flesh")? Was Christ obedient to the Mosaic law, to God, or to both? Was Christ's exaltation the reward for or the result of his humiliation? Does the verb ὑπερύψωσεν ("exalted") suggest exaltation to a higher status than formerly possessed (the comparative sense), or is it used simply to designate the loftiest heights (the superlative sense)? What name has God given to Christ? Who are those "in heaven and on earth and under the earth" who are to bow before that name? Furthermore, is a parallel, either literary or conceptual, being drawn between the humiliation and exaltation of Christ, on the one hand, and the attitude and actions of Adam, on the other—or perhaps between Christ and the Servant of Yahweh, or Christ and a personified Wisdom?

Devotionally, Phil 2:6–11 makes its point regarding the humility and obedience of Christ: verses 6–8 depict Christ's attitude as an obedience that extended even to the point of death—with Paul adding his own exclamation at the end of verse 8, "even death on a cross!"—and verses 9–11 express God's vindication and approval of such an attitude. As for the details of this depiction and the exegetical issues involved, however, the hymn is certainly not as explicit or precise as one might like.

Its main point, Christ's humble self-giving and thoroughgoing obedience, is easy to grasp. Paul's interjection, indeed, serves to focus attention on this main point and underscore the extent of Christ's obedience. But we should not to try to wring too much detail out of the passage by way of philosophical or theological speculation, for we are dealing here with devotional material and not a logically constructed argument.

The same can also be said of such hymnic portions as Rom 11:33–36 and Rev 15:3b–4, which speak of God (also the canticles of Luke 1–2 and the theocentric hymns of the Apocalypse), and of the hymnic materials in 1 Tim 3:16 and 1 Pet 2:22–23, which speak of Christ (also the prologue of John's Gospel and the christocentric hymns of the Apocalypse). Likewise, when interpreting Rom 3:24–26, 1 Cor 15:3b–5, Gal 4:4–5, and Col 1:15–20 (probably also Heb 1:3; 5:7, 8–9), one needs to take into consideration the original devotional matrices of such formulaic prose portions as well.

Portions of a Narrative Substructure or Story about Jesus Christ

Second, in their christocentric expressions (as distinct from their purely theocentric expressions) the early confessional materials of the NT reflect a narrative substructure or story in which Jesus Christ is the main character. Each of the confessions, whether poetic or in a prose formulation, narrates a portion of the story about Christ as God's redemptive agent. We cannot say whether or not all the addressees of each NT writing already knew each confessional portion quoted. What can be affirmed, however, is that these confessions—whether cited in whole or in part—were meant to remind them of the basic story about Christ, which they not only knew but also made the foundation of their lives.

Theological reflection does not draw its impetus from ahistorical, universally accepted concepts such as goodness, love, or justice. Rather, life and thought are sustained in all of the world's religions by stories about the way the world has been and is, how it is being redeemed, and how the adherents of the given religion fit into this scenario. Indeed, the vitality of any religion depends on the explanatory power of its underlying narrative—

and especially the relationship of the adherents and their communities to this narrative.

That was, it appears, one of the primary purposes of the NT writers in using early Christian confessional materials in their writings. For by recalling for their readers the basic narrative story of the Christian gospel, they were establishing all that they wanted to say—whether by way of witness, instruction, exhortation, correction, rebuke, or encouragement—regarding what God had done redemptively through Christ.

Functional Portrayals

Third, the early Christian confessions are predominantly functional in their portrayals of God and Christ. This functional emphasis appears throughout the confessional portions of the NT. But it is particularly prominent in the confessions found in Paul's earlier letters, which, as the earliest writings of the NT, presumably incorporate some of the earliest Christian confessional materials. The following are some of the major Christian confessional formulations found in Paul's earlier letters:

Who gave himself for our sins to rescue us from the present evil age, according to the will of our God and Father. (Gal 1:4)

Christ redeemed us from the curse of the law by becoming a curse for us, as it is written: "Cursed is everyone who is hanged on a tree." (Gal 3:13)

When the time had fully come, God sent his Son, born of a woman, born under the law, in order to redeem those under the law, that we might receive adoption as God's children [or "the adoption"; "the full rights of sons"]. (Gal 4:4–5)

That Christ died for our sins according to the Scriptures; that he was buried; that he was raised on the third day according to the Scriptures; and that he appeared to Peter, and then to the Twelve. (1 Cor 15:3b–5)

[We are] being justified freely by his grace through the redemption that is in Christ Jesus, whom God put forward as a sacrifice of atonement [or "an expiation"; "a propitiation"] through faith in his blood. He did this in order to show his justice, because in his forbearance he had passed over the sins previously committed. He did this to show at the present time his justice, so as to be himself just and the justifier of the one who depends on the faithfulness of Jesus [or "who has faith in Jesus"]. (Rom 3:24–26)

Just as Jewish tradition praised appropriate action ("orthopraxis") more than correct theological speculation ("orthodoxy"), the earliest believers in Jesus seem to have given priority to the functional features of their new commitment to Jesus.

Very soon, however, ontological categories began to come to the fore. This can be seen, for example, in such confessional portions as Heb 1:3 ("Who [the Son] is the radiance of God's glory and the exact representation of his being," etc.) and John 1:1–14 ("In the beginning was the Word, and the Word was with God, and the Word was God. He was in the beginning with God," etc.). And this movement from function to ontology seems to be paralleled, to an extent, by the shift from a focus on *the act* of confessing Jesus and one's relation to him, depicted by the use of the active verb ὁμολογέω, which is predominant in the earlier portions of the NT (e.g., Rom 10:9; Phil 2:11; cf. Matt 10:32 // Luke 12:8), to an emphasis on *the content* of the confession, apparent in the use of the noun ὁμολογία in the later writings (cf. 1 Tim 6:12, 13; Heb 3:1; 4:14; 10:23)—though, admittedly, there is some overlap, as witness not only the early use of the noun in 2 Cor 9:13 but also the continued use of the verb in such later writings as John 9:22; 12:42; 1 John 2:22–23; 4:2, 3, 15; and 2 John 7.

Language and Metaphors of the Day

Finally, and perhaps more obviously, the confessional portions that appear in the NT use the language and metaphors of their day in speaking about the work of Christ and its significance. Romans 3:24–26 is a classic example, for it is filled with concepts and expressions that were evidently part and parcel of the theological outlook and vocabulary of the earliest Jewish believers in Jesus—for example, (1) the concepts of "justification," "redemption," and "sacrifice of atonement [or 'an expiation'; 'a propitiation']"; (2) the ideas that God passed over previous sins and that he is both "just" and "justifier"; and (3) the expression "the one who depends on the faith/faithfulness of Jesus [or 'who has faith in Jesus']" (τὸν ἐκ πίστεως Ἰησοῦ, picking up on a Hebrew understanding of faith/faithfulness). Likewise, Col 1:15–20 reflects the religious language and cosmic metaphors current among the addresses, as do also the confessional portions that appear outside the Pauline corpus in Heb 1:3 and John 1:1–14.

Some of the people addressed by the writers of the NT may not have fully understood all of these concepts and terms. For example, Paul's Gentile readers at Rome may or may not have fully understood the cultic term ἱλαστήριον ("sacrifice of atonement [or 'an expiation'; 'a propitiation']" and the idea of God's passing over previous sins (Rom 3:25). Perhaps the addressees of Hebrews had trouble understanding the Son as the "radiance" or "effulgence" (ἀπαύγασμα) of God's glory and the exact "representation" or "impress" (χαρακτήρ) of God's person (Heb 1:3). Likewise, those addressed by the Fourth Evangelist may have struggled with the concept of "the Word" (λόγος, John 1:1). Interestingly, in none of these cases do the concepts and terms used appear elsewhere in the writings in which they are found.

We might conclude, therefore, that while the NT writers used early Christian confessional materials in order to establish contact with their addressees, and while these materials employed the language and metaphors of the day, some of the concepts and terms found within these confessions were evidently somewhat difficult for certain readers to understand. And, indeed, much of this language continues to be difficult, if not impossible, for modern readers. Such concepts and terms often require considerable translation into modern parlance if they are to be understood today.

▓ 2. MAJOR THEMES IN THE CONFESSIONAL MATERIALS

It is not difficult to identify a number of themes in the early Christian confessional materials. Some receive special emphasis in particular writings; others appear a number of times in various contexts. The trick is to sort out major themes from minor themes. The following are nine major themes that are emphasized and appear repeatedly. Often the themes are so interrelated that it becomes difficult to speak of any one of them as more important than any other. We will present them here in a roughly logical order, recognizing at all times their interdependence.

God Is the Initiator, Sustainer, and Ultimate Agent of Redemption

All of the early Christian confessions reverberate with the theme of God as the initiator, sustainer, and ultimate agent of redemption, whose salvific purposes for humanity and all creation come to focus in the work and person of Jesus Christ. For though there is a decidedly christocentric emphasis throughout the NT, there is never anything approaching a "Unitarianism of the Second Person" or a "Jesus Only" perspective—as though only Christ were important or God should be seen as standing passively on the sidelines. Rather, the portrayals of Christ's work and person in the early Christian confessions are constantly presented in the context of theology, with God the Father identified throughout as the One who (1) originated and sustains all of the factors involved in redemption, (2) was at work in the ministry of Jesus to effect salvation, and (3) is the ultimate agent in the reconciliation of all people and all creation to himself.

A number of the early confessions explicitly highlight God's initiative, purpose, grace, activity, and glory when they speak about the redemptive work of Christ:

> [Christ's redemptive work was] according to the will of our God and Father. (Gal 1:4)

> God sent his Son. (Gal 4:4–5)

> God was in Christ reconciling the world to himself. (2 Cor 5:19)

> [We are] being justified freely by his [God's] grace... God presented him [Christ] as a sacrifice of atonement. . . . He did this to demonstrate his justice . . . He did it to demonstrate his justice at the present time, so as to be just and the one who justifies those who depend on the faith/faithfulness of [or, have faith in] Jesus. (Rom 3:24–26)

> God exalted him [Jesus Christ]... and gave him the name that is above every name... Every tongue [will] confess that Jesus Christ is Lord, to the glory of God the Father. (Phil 2:6–11)

> God was pleased to have all his fullness dwell in him [Christ], and through him to reconcile all things to himself. (Col 1:15–20)

So conscious, indeed, were the early Christians of God's purposes, presence, and activity expressed in the redemptive work of

Christ that they also composed confessional hymns that were predominantly, if not entirely, theocentric—as is evident in the confessional materials of Rom 11:33–36 and Rev 15:3b–4, as well as the canticles of Luke 1–2 and the theocentric hymnic portions of the Apocalypse.

Jesus Is Israel's Messiah (the Christ)

The basic conviction of the earliest believers about Jesus of Nazareth was that he is Israel's Messiah ("the Anointed One").

Though subject to nationalistic and political misunderstandings, and therefore requiring redefinition in order to be serviceable, the conviction about Jesus as Israel's Messiah laid the foundation for the church's very existence, and thus for all of its thought and practice. So fundamental, in fact, was the messiahship of Jesus in the consciousness of the earliest believers that they uniquely associated the Greek term for Messiah, Χριστός ("Christ"), with the person of Jesus, first as a title and then as a proper name, and eventually made it the basis for their own self-identification in the ancient world, Χριστιανοί ("Christ followers").

Questions regarding Jesus' own messianic consciousness have received a great deal of scholarly attention. Indeed, many modern questions regarding Jesus may be difficult to resolve. But Paul clearly begins on the premise that Jesus is the Christ, as can be seen at many places in his letters and from Luke's accounts of Paul's conversion in Acts 9, 22, and 26. Most often Paul used Χριστός in his letters as a proper name and not as a title—probably because Gentiles might have taken "the Anointed One" to mean someone medicinally anointed for a sickness or rubbed with oil in preparation for an athletic contest. Usually, therefore, he spoke of "Jesus Christ," "Christ Jesus," or simply "Christ," with the title ascribed being that of "Lord." Yet a number of Paul's references to Christ reflect a Jewish understanding of messiahship. Such a titular use of Χριστός comes to the fore most clearly in Rom 9:5, at the conclusion of Paul's list of Israel's advantages: "From them [the people of Israel] comes the Christ [ὁ Χριστός, 'the Messiah'], according to the flesh."

Equally pertinent, however, are the many places outside the Pauline corpus where the identification of Jesus as Israel's Messiah is found in a confessional statement or portion. The most obvious is Peter's confession, reported in Mark 8:29 par.: "You are the Christ." Also significant is the confession "Jesus is the Christ," which appears in John 1:20; 7:41; 9:22; 11:27; 20:31; Acts 9:22; 17:3; and 1 John 2:22; 5:1. Throughout Matthew, John, Hebrews, and the Johannine Apocalypse, in fact, Χριστός appears commonly as a title rather than as a name. And where it appears as a title in these writings, it is always connected with the single name "Jesus," thereby further signaling that the title has a confessional history

The Eschatological Age of Redemption Has Been Inaugurated

Associated with the identification of Jesus as Israel's Messiah is the recognition that something new has taken place in the unfolding of the ages, as those "ages" or "times" have been established by God: that the eschatological age of redemption has dawned—or, better, has been inaugurated. This is declared in a fairly straightforward manner in the confession of Gal 4:4–5, which begins with the words "when the time had fully come" and ends with the affirmation of "adoption as God's children" as being now the status of believers in Christ. The recognition of a new age comes to the fore also in 1 Cor 15:3b–5 in the twice-repeated statement "according to the Scriptures," which is ascribed to both Christ's death and his resurrection; and it is implied in the contrast set out in Rom 3:24–26 between God's action "beforehand" and his actions "at the present time."

It is also inherent in the application of Isaiah 53 to Jesus' experience in the confession of 1 Pet 2:22–23, which first quotes verse 9 of that Servant of Yahweh passage ("Who committed no sin, and no deceit was found in his mouth") and then alludes to verse 7 in the words that follow ("Who when they hurled their insults at him did not retaliate; when he suffered, he made no threats"). Likewise, such a recognition of the dawning or inauguration of the final eschatological age underlies all of the other NT confessional portions—for example, Martha's response to Jesus in John 11:27: "Yes, Lord, I believe that you are the Christ, the Son of God, who was to come into the world."

It is doubtful that the earliest Jewish believers in Jesus would ever have adjusted their eschatological outlook had they not been convinced that Jesus was Israel's true Messiah. But once they made such a radical identification, their eschatological perspective changed radically as well. For now, proclaiming that "Jesus is the Christ," they also proclaimed that the eschatological age of redemption had dawned or been inaugurated. No longer was the eschatological experience reserved only for the future. Rather, now believing that Jesus of Nazareth was Israel's Messiah, their lives were given a new eschatological context and meaning.

Jesus Is God's Obedient Son

Important as well among the single-statement affirmations of the NT are those declaring that "Jesus is the Son of God" (Mark 15:39 // Matt 27:54; Matt 16:16; John 1:34, 49; 11:27; 20:31; Acts 9:20; 1 John 4:15; 5:5; cf. Matt 26:63 and Luke 4:41; the inclusion of "Son of God" in Codex Sinaiticus and a few minor manuscripts at Mark 8:29 is certainly a scribal error). Earlier, many history-of-religions scholars had asserted that "Son of God" was imported into the NT from current Hellenistic polytheism. But owing to the appearance of "Son of God" in some of the writings of Second Temple Judaism in connection with Jewish messianic expectations (cf. 4Q*Florilegium* on 2 Sam 7:14; *1 Enoch* 105:2; *4 Ezra* 7:28–29; 13:32, 37, 52; 14:9), its application to Jesus in the NT is today viewed as a functional Jewish Christian way of indicating Jesus' unique relationship with God and obedience to the Father's will. For just as Israel was understood to be uniquely God's "son" among all the people of the earth, and Israel's anointed king to be God's "son" in a special manner—with both pledged to a relationship with God of loving obedience—so also Jesus, who exemplified unparalleled obedience to God, was seen to be the Son of God par excellence.

The confessional materials quoted by Paul carry forward this concept of the sonship and obedience of Christ. Philippians 2:8 is the prime example. For at the very heart of the Christ hymn of 2:6–11, and undoubtedly its main point, is an affirmation regarding the complete obedience of Christ: "He humbled himself and became obedient unto death—even death on a cross!" This obedience was not just expressed "in death," as is so often mistakenly assumed. Rather, it characterized Christ's entire life and extended "even to the inclusion of death," as the preposition μέχρι ("unto") suggests in its emphasis on degree, measure, or extent.

The formulaic material incorporated in Gal 4:4–5 is also significant here: "When the fullness of time had come, God sent his Son, born of a woman, born under the law, in order to redeem those under the law, so that we might receive adoption as God's children [or 'the adoption'; 'full rights as sons']." Central to this confessional portion is the stress on Christ as God's Son, which in a Jewish Christian context expressed not so much his ontological status as his attitude of loving obedience. And though Christians may have adopted the statement "God sent his Son" from Jewish Wisdom literature in order to associate Wisdom with Christ (cf. 1 Cor 1:24, 30), as Eduard Schweizer has argued,[1] the confession itself focuses its attention on Christ not only as truly human ("born of a woman") but also as offering perfect obedience to God the Father ("the Son . . . born under the law") on behalf of all those "under the law," that is, all Jews.

Perhaps Rom 1:3–4 should also be considered here. For most NT scholars believe that after speaking about "his [God's] Son" in verse 3a, Paul goes further in verses 3b–4 to present a two-stage understanding of "Son of God" drawn in whole or in part from an early Christian confession:

> The one born of the seed of David,
>   according to the flesh;
> the one declared to be the Son of God with power,
>   according to his spirit [or "the Spirit"] of holiness
>   by the resurrection of the dead.

The first part of the couplet identifies Christ as David's descendant. The second part, however, speaks of what God declared Christ to be—certainly by raising him from the dead, as the last phrase plainly declares, but also κατὰ πνεῦμα ἁγιωσύνης. This latter phrase may mean either (1) in line with the character of Jesus' earthly life ("the spirit of holiness" referring to Christ's own obedience and righteousness, as in the NRSV) or (2) by the witness of the Spirit (capitalizing "Spirit," referring to the Holy Spirit's activity, as in the NIV). In the former case, the title "Son of God" would be highlighting the obedience of the Son more than his ontological status—although, of course, such an affirmation would fit well into later christological speculations.

One further confessional portion in Paul's letters should also be mentioned, although its form and content have been the subjects of extensive debate. This portion appears at the close of the thesis paragraph of Rom 3:21–26. Rudolf Bultmann, Ernst Käsemann, and others have argued that the confessional portion is composed of verses 24–26, starting with the participle δικαιούμενοι ("being justified"). Eduard Lohse and others, however, have claimed that it comprises verses 25–26, starting with the relative personal pronoun ὅν ("who"). On the basis of an analysis of structure, style, *hapax legomena,* and theological content, I believe that both parties are correct in seeing here an early Christian confessional portion, but that Bultmann and company are right in viewing it as starting with the participle δικαιούμενοι.

Yet however we bracket off the material, the important point to note is that everything said in the passage about God's salvific activity is based on the final statement of the confession, which serves as the climax of the whole passage: "In order that God might be just and the justifier of those who have faith in Jesus [ἐκ πίστεως Ἰησοῦ]"—or, better, "those who are based on the faith/faithfulness of Jesus" (reading ἐκ πίστεως as a genitive of source and Ἰησοῦ as a subjective genitive, in keeping with the scholarly opinion of many today about the phrase πίστις Χριστοῦ). The confession of Rom 3:24–26 thus concludes its recital of God's salvific activity through Christ with the statement that God, who is just, is the One who justifies those basing their hopes and lives on the faith/faithfulness of Jesus—that is, on his loving obedience to God the Father.

Outside the Pauline corpus, the theme of the obedience of Christ comes to the fore in Hebrews in two passages that many believe were drawn from early Christian confessional material. The first is 5:7, which speaks of Jesus' "reverent submission" during the days of his "life on earth." The second is 5:8–9, which reads, "Although he was a son, he learned obedience from what he suffered; and once made perfect, he became the source of eternal salvation for all who obey him." The writer to the Hebrews seems to have been far more interested in ontology than was Paul—as witness, for example, the poetic material he quotes in 1:3, which speaks of the Son as "the radiance of God's glory and the exact representation of his being," and the catena of passages he sets out in 1:5–13, which support the superiority of the Son over angels. Yet though he uses the concept of Christ's sonship in a more ontological manner throughout his writing, taking pains to identify features of the Son's *being* and *status,* the writer also speaks in a functional manner of the Son's obedience. Indeed, he even states that this obedience was "learned from what he [the Son] suffered" (5:8) and refers to factors of *becoming* and *process* (cf. 2:10; 7:28).

Jesus Is Humanity's Redemptive Lord

The sermon of Peter at Pentecost concludes with this assertion: "Therefore let all the house of Israel assuredly know that God has made him both Lord and Christ, this Jesus whom you crucified" (Acts 2:36). In the Acts of the Apostles the two major titles used of Jesus are "Christ" and "Lord." At times "Lord" appears first when these two titles are brought together, as in Peter's sermon. In the non-Pauline NT writings authored by Jewish believers in Jesus, however, the title "Christ" usually takes ascendancy and is more common—although "Lord" is also used.

There is little question today that "Lord" was an early designation for Jesus. The title was used with reference to Jesus both (1) as a term of respectful address (e.g., Mark 7:28; Matt 8:25; 17:4, 15; 20:31, 33; Luke 18:41; cf. the synoptic parallels in each case, where other titles are used in an equivalent manner) and (2) as a worshipful acclamation (cf. the Aramaic expression μαράνα θά, "Come, O Lord!" which Paul repeats in 1 Cor 16:22) used by believers in Jesus prior to the ministry of Paul. It also appears as a worshipful acclamation in some of the earliest confessional statements (e.g., Rom 10:9; 1 Cor 12:3; 2 Cor 4:5; cf. Col 2:6) and portions (Phil 2:11) that Paul incorporates into his letters.

Cullmann has rightly observed that "nothing indicates better . . . how vital was the present lordship of Christ in early

Christian thought" than the repeated quotation of Ps 110:1 in the NT: "The Lord says to my Lord: 'Sit at my right hand until I make your enemies a footstool for your feet.' "[2] No other passage is quoted or alluded to as often by the writers of the NT (cf. Mark 12:36, par.; 14:62, par.; Acts 2:34–35; 5:31; 7:55; Rom 8:34; 1 Cor 15:25; Eph 1:20; Heb 1:3; 8:1; 10:12–13; 1 Pet 3:22; Rev 3:21). And none, once it was interpreted by Jesus in a messianic fashion (cf. Mark 12:35–37 par.), expresses the idea of the Son's supremacy more clearly or asserts the lordship of Christ more forcefully.

The True Humanity of Jesus

Also connected to concepts of sonship, obedience, and faithfulness was the early believers' conviction regarding the true humanity of Jesus, the one sent by God. This is declared in poetic fashion in verses 7–8a of the Christ hymn of Philippians 2: "He emptied himself, taking the very nature of a servant, being born in human likeness; and being found in appearance as a man, he humbled himself." It is also referred to in the confessional phrase of Gal 4:4, "born of a woman"—a Jewish locution for being human (cf. Job 14:1, "Man born of woman is of few days and full of trouble"; Matt 11:11 // Luke 7:28, "Among those born of women there has not arisen anyone greater than John the Baptist"; see also Josephus, *Antiquities* 7.21; 16.382). Most explicitly, however, the full humanity of Christ, and so his true incarnation, is declared in the confessional formula of 1 Tim 3:16, which begins with the words "he [ὅς] appeared in a body [ἐν σαρκί]," and in the confessional statement of 1 John 4:2, "Jesus Christ has come in the flesh [ἐν σαρκί]."

Christ's Redemptive Death on a Cross

A prominent theme of the early Christian confessions is, of course, that of Christ's redemptive death on a cross. Philippians 2:6–11, as we have seen, focuses on the fact that Christ was "obedient unto death—even death on a cross!" (v. 8). First Corinthians 15:3b–5 begins with the statement "Christ died for our sins" and then underlines this statement with the first of its two uses of the phrase "according to the Scriptures." Galatians 3:13 proclaims that "Christ redeemed us from the curse of the law by becoming a curse for us, as it is written: 'Cursed is everyone who is hanged on a tree.'" Romans 3:25 says that "God put him [Christ] forward as a sacrifice of atonement through faith in his blood," and Col 1:20 closes the confessional portion of 1:15–20 with the affirmation that Christ reconciled all things to God "by making peace through his blood, shed on the cross." So prominent, in fact, was the theme of Christ's redemptive death on a cross in the consciousness of the early Christians that at many places in the NT the terms "death" and "cross" appear in metonymous fashion for all the work of Christ in accomplishing human redemption.

The great problem for the earliest Jewish Christians, when speaking of Christ's death on a cross, was that Deut 21:23 declares that "anyone who is hung on a tree is cursed by God." The verse originally had reference to the exposure of a criminal executed for a capital offense, whose dead body was hung on a tree for public ridicule. But it came to be understood among Jews as referring also to the impalement or crucifixion of a living person on a pole or cross (the pole and cross understood as parts of a tree). Paul reflects the general Jewish repugnance to the idea of a crucified Messiah when he speaks in Gal 5:11 and 1 Cor 1:23 of the "scandal" of Christ put to death by crucifixion on a cross.

Jewish believers in Jesus, however, resolved the problem of a crucified Messiah by viewing God's curse of Christ on the cross as "an exchange curse,"[3] as stated in the confession of Gal 3:13 ("Christ redeemed us from the curse of the law by becoming a curse for us") and as reflected in Paul's words in 1 Cor 5:21 ("God made him who had no sin to be sin for us, so that in him we might become the righteousness of God"). Thus Christ's death on the cross was interpreted as not punitive but redemptive.

Christ's Resurrection/Exaltation to New Life

Also prominent in the early confessions is the theme of Christ's resurrection. It is referred to in terms of exaltation in Phil 2:9–11, where it completes the humiliation-exaltation pairing of that early Christian hymn. It is also paired with Christ's death in 1 Cor 15:3b–5, where both "death" and "resurrection" are highlighted by the inclusion of the repeated phrase "according to the Scriptures." It is affirmed in the confessional statement of 1 Thess 4:14, "Jesus died and rose again." And it is proclaimed in the second part of the confessional portion of Rom 1:4, "The one declared to be the Son of God . . . by the resurrection of the dead."

In materials that can be dated somewhat later than the major Pauline letters, the theme of Christ's resurrection comes to expression in terms that seem to reflect gnostic nuances in Col 1:18b—"He [Who] is the beginning [ἀρχή], the firstborn [πρωτότοκος] from the dead"—which commences the second half of this confessional portion. It also appears in the closing statement of the formula of 1 Tim 3:16, "He [Who] . . . was taken up in glory." Outside the confessional materials of the Pauline corpus, the theme is found in the confession of Heb 1:3 in terms of exaltation ("After he had provided purification for sins, he sat down at the right hand of the Majesty on high"). Included in all of these confessional portrayals are allusions to Christ's new life after death, whether cast in the imagery of exaltation (as in Phil 2:9–11; 1 Tim 3:16; Heb 1:3) or in terms of resurrection (as in 1 Thess 4:14; 1 Cor 15:4; Col 1:18b).

New Relationships Established through the Work of Christ

Two passages in Paul's Letter to the Galatians have been seen, of late, to incorporate early Christian confessional materials that explicitly refer to new relationships as established through the work of Christ. The first is Gal 3:26–28, which is made up of at least one, though probably two, pre-Pauline confessional fragments: (1) a confessional saying in verse 26 ("You are all children [sons] of God through faith in Christ Jesus") and (2) a formulaic, *homologia* portion in verses 27–28 ("As many of you as were baptized into Christ have clothed yourselves with Christ. There is no longer Jew or Greek, slave or free, male and female, for you are all one in Christ Jesus"). The second passage is Gal 4:4–5, which states that God sent his Son "that we might receive adoption as God's children [or 'the adoption'; 'full rights as sons']"—which directly suggests that a new relationship has been established. Likewise, 2 Cor 5:19 contains a confessional statement that highlights a change of relationships: "God was in Christ reconciling the world to himself."

Other confessional portions within the NT may also carry implications regarding the new relationships brought about through the work of Christ. But here in Gal 3:26–28; 4:4–5 and 2 Cor 5:19 we have rather explicit statements regarding the new relationships—both spiritually (i.e., "children of God," "clothed with Christ," "one in Christ Jesus," "adopted as God's children," and "reconciled to God") and societally and culturally (i.e., "no longer Jew or Greek, slave or free, male and female").

Taking, then, Gal 3:26–28, 4:4–5 and 2 Cor 5:19 to contain early confessional materials—whether drawn from one, two, or three preexisting portions; whether quoted in whole or in part—we may posit that the early Christians, even before Paul's ministry, proclaimed that "all" who respond to Christ "through faith" and are "baptized into Christ" have thereby come into a whole new set of relationships, both with God and with others. What the Christians proclaimed in principle may not always have worked out well in practice, particularly concerning the triad of couplets that speak about Jew-Greek, slave-free, and male-female relations. And they may not always have expressed in their lives what it means to be now reconciled, both to God and to one another. Nonetheless, using these three couplets and laying stress on the concept of reconciliation, the early believers in Jesus proclaimed not only a gospel that countered the dominant divisions of their day and put an end to existing antagonisms, but also one that set a new tone of reconciliation for all of their theological and ethical reflections.[4]

PART 2

The Contextualization
of the Confessions in the
New Testament

The NT is no textbook of theology. Nor is it a compendium of ethical theory. Neither the Jewish Scriptures (the Old Testament, in Christian parlance) nor the Christian Scriptures (both OT and NT) set out their message in the form of pure theological statements or abstract ethical maxims. Many people read the Bible as a book of theological and ethical axioms, and so view biblical study as consisting only of gathering together the Bible's various statements and putting them into some larger basket of truth. Others, however, recognizing the gap that exists between the Bible's proclamation, on the one hand, and the formulation of theology, on the other, have despaired of any correlation between the Christian Scriptures and contemporary Christian theology or ethical practice.

A better approach, and the one that gives direction to what follows, is to see the Scriptures (both Jewish and Christian) as setting out (1) *functional portrayals* of who God is and what God has done redemptively for his people, as well as for all people and his created world, and (2) *prophetic interpretations* of what such divine, redemptive activity means for the lives of God's people in their particular circumstances and for all people living in God's created world. In particular, the essential portrayals of divine redemption in the NT are couched principally in the form of confessions, which contain the "new wine" of the Christian message. The interpretations, however, are presented in various forms—in letters, Gospels, sermonic tractates, accounts about the life of the church, and apocalypses—all of them used to convey applications suitable to the situations being addressed. In effect, these forms are the "fresh wineskins" of the NT authors' contextualization of the gospel in their day.

The major confessions of Second Temple Judaism were (1) the Shema ("Hear, O Israel: The Lord our God, the Lord is One!" [Deut 6:4]), which defines God as a unity contra all forms of polytheism; (2) the "First Word" (which is not just the preamble) of the ten "Words of Instruction," the so-called Ten Commandments ("I am the Lord your God, who brought you out of Egypt, out of the land of slavery!" [Exod 20:2; Deut 5:6]), which identifies God in a relational manner and declares that in the exodus God acted redemptively on behalf of his people; and (3) the Shemoneh Esreh (the Eighteen Benedictions [or Blessings, or Prayers]), which speaks of who God is, God's love for his people, and his people's obedience to his instructions. The confessions incorporated within the NT, however, while building on the theocentric confessions of Judaism, focus on the redemptive work and revelatory person of Jesus of Nazareth. And what is avowed about his work and person underlies all that is proclaimed and taught by the various NT authors.

Such christocentric confessional materials were presumably widely known among the early Christians, even though not every believer may have been able to identify each individual confession in its particulars. So when early Christians in their worship services heard the reading of a letter, a Gospel, a sermonic tractate, an account of the life of the church, or an apocalypse—materials now included in the NT—they were able, knowing the basic story line of the Christian proclamation, to recognize the confessional portions that had been derived from the gospel's narrative substructure. They expected their teachers to provide (1) applications of these confessions to their own situations (as in the letters and sermonic tractates), (2) portrayals of how these confessions had been enacted and exemplified in the ministry of Jesus (as in the Gospels) and the mission of the church (as in the Acts), and (3) indications of what they should expect for the future (as in the eschatological portions and ethical exhortations of the letters, Gospels, and sermonic tractates generally, and the Johannine Apocalypse in particular).

The writings of the NT took the place of the actual presence of the writers and were meant to contextualize the early Christian confessions in the experience of the readers in much the same way as the writers would have done in person. We modern readers may have difficulty identifying the confessions from which they worked, possibly because we have lost the thread of the original narrative substructure—or, perhaps, because we have become dependent on formal indicators such as quotation marks or indentations to mark off the quoted material. More likely, however, it is because we have never heard the confessions repeated in the liturgy of corporate worship and therefore cannot recognize them when we come across them in the NT. So many early confessions have remained unidentified in the NT.

In what follows, we will survey how the NT writers contextualized the church's early confessions in speaking to the issues their addressees faced and the circumstances they encountered. Probably there are other confessional materials in the NT that we have missed. But a number of single-statement affirmations, prose *homologia* portions, and poetic-hymnic passages of a confessional nature have been identified during the past century (see Part 1), and it is instructive to observe how they have been contextualized in the NT. In so doing, we will deal first with the Pauline corpus and the other so-called letters of the NT (ch. 3), then with the Synoptic Gospels and the Acts of the Apostles (ch. 4), and finally with the Fourth Gospel and the Johannine Apocalypse (ch. 5).

CHAPTER THREE

The Pauline Corpus
and the Other Letters

A number of passages in the Pauline corpus and the other letters of the NT contextualize early Christian confessions. Some of these are in ethical contexts; others in theological contexts. But since these categories are often intertwined, this study will treat the contextualizations in the NT letters not in terms of "ethical usages" and "theological usages" but simply according to the letters in which they are found, beginning with the Pauline writings that most clearly evidence such contextualizations, and then moving on to the other letters.

My primary thesis is twofold: (1) that underlying all that the NT writers wrote were certain central convictions about God and Jesus, which took the form of confessions, and (2) that Paul and the other writers of NT letters and sermonic tractates contextualized these basic confessional materials in a number of ways when addressing the problems and needs of their readers. Sometimes they used confessional materials to establish rapport with their readers. At other times they used them to summarize the essence of their presentations, thereby capping off and showing the validity of their arguments. More often, however, they used confessional materials as the basis of their arguments, working from what was commonly accepted to what yet needed to be said. They also seem to have used confessional materials most frequently when writing expositionally (in sustained teaching) or polemically (when countering false teaching), and not usually when writing something more expressly apologetic (in a defensive response to a personal attack).

■ 1. THE PAULINE CORPUS

Philippians

The Letter to the Philippians is probably the most appropriate place to begin, since the Christ hymn of 2:6–11 is one of the most readily identifiable confessional portions in Paul's letters. Furthermore, it is used by Paul to ground all of the exhortations of the letter.

The exact nature of the situation addressed in Philippians is difficult to determine. We can infer with confidence from the letter itself, however, whether viewed as a single letter or a collection of two or three letters, (1) that Christians at Philippi were experiencing some kind of hostility, which Paul believed called for instruction on how to live under such conditions, and (2) that certain Christian teachers were opposing Paul in some manner, so that he needed to tell his converts how to respond to them. These two matters—hostility against Paul's converts and opposition to Paul himself—seem to have been related, for intertwined throughout Philippians are ethical teachings for Christians who find themselves in a hostile environment (cf. 1:27–2:18; 3:12–4:9) and statements about Paul's opponents (cf. 1:15–18; 3:2–11).

Paul uses the Christ hymn of 2:6–11 as the basis for his pastoral instructions and the paradigm for his converts' thinking and acting. To show them how to live in the face of hostility, Paul holds up the example of Christ. For though Christ possessed equality with God, he willingly humbled himself in the incarnation and became obedient throughout his earthly ministry, even to the extent of death (vv. 6–8)—and his attitude and action were approved by God, who then exalted him to the highest of positions (vv. 9–11).

In the exhortations that immediately precede and follow this hymn, Paul urges believers at Philippi to adopt Christ's attitude of humility, steadfast obedience, and concern for others. Thus, on the basis of the confession of 2:6–11, he exhorts his converts, "Do nothing out of selfish ambition or vain conceit" (v. 3a); be humble and "consider others better than yourselves" (v. 3b); "look not only to your own interests, but also to the interests of others" (v. 4); continue in a life of obedience (v. 12a); "continue to work out your salvation with fear and trembling" (v. 12b); "do everything without complaining or arguing" (v. 14); "hold on to the word of life" (v. 16a); and "be glad and rejoice with me" (v. 18). He also implies, on the basis of this confessional portion, that God will vindicate them for their steadfast adherence to the gospel in the midst of hostility, for God has set the precedent by vindicating Christ.

Paul goes on to show how this pattern of humility, obedience, and concern for others was being exemplified in the ministries of two of his coworkers, who were also well known to his addressees: Timothy, whom he characterizes as one who "takes a genuine interest in your welfare" and "has served with me in the work of the gospel" (vv. 19–24), and Epaphroditus, whom he describes as the one "you sent to take care of my needs" and who "almost died for the work of Christ" (vv. 25–30). Furthermore, he declares his desire to reflect the pattern of Christ's life in his own life (3:10–11). Then he presents certain features and motivations of his ministry—which he believes reflect the paradigm given by Christ—as a further example for his converts to follow (3:12–21). And he concludes by reminding the Philippians how this pattern of humility, obedience, and concern was expressed in their repeated financial support of him, for which he thanks them and assures them of God's blessing (4:10–19).

Notable, as well, is the fact that in dealing with the Christian teachers who oppose him, Paul also makes use of the main themes of the hymn of 2:6–11. When compared with the attitudes and actions of Christ, the selfish ambitions and feigned sincerity of these teachers (1:15–18)—possibly also their activities as "mutilators of the flesh" (3:2–3)—come off quite badly. Implied throughout the Philippian letter, in fact, are requests (1) for the opposing teachers to measure themselves by the attitudes and actions of Christ rather than react enviously to Paul, and (2) for the Philippian believers to judge these teachers by how they model Christ's pattern of humility and obedience, not by their pretensions or claims.

1 Corinthians

After Philippians, the next most obvious letter for observing how Paul contextualizes early Christian confessional materials is 1 Corinthians. In the first two chapters of this letter Paul repeatedly refers to the content of his message as being "the cross" and "Christ crucified" (1:17, 18, 23; 2:2), with the presence of confessional material signaled by the verbs "announce good news" (εὐαγγελίζω, 1:17), "preach" (κηρύσσω, 1:23), and "proclaim" (καταγγέλλω, 2:1) and the noun "proclamation" (κήρυγμα, 2:4). Furthermore, in chapter 15 there appears the formulaic confessional material of verses 3b–5 that speak of Christ's death, burial, resurrection, and appearances.

Using these two sets of confessional materials (chs. 1–2 and 15:3b–5), Paul presents what appear to be the two major items on his own agenda when writing 1 Corinthians. Although he also responds to rumors that were generally circulating (chs. 5–6) and answers questions asked by the Corinthians themselves (chs. 7–14), Paul seems most concerned about divisions within the church, which he deals with in chapters 1–4, and denials of the physical resurrection of believers, which he counters in chapter 15. To address these matters, he builds first on the confessional phrase "Christ crucified" and statements about the cross (1:17, 18, 23; 2:2), then on the confessional formula regarding Christ's death, burial, resurrection, and postresurrection appearances (15:3b–5).

Having heard reports from members of Chloe's household about divisions within the Corinthian congregation and about believers flaunting human wisdom over against an emphasis on the cross (cf. 1:11–17), Paul begins his argument in 1 Corinthians on the basis of the confessional phrase "Christ crucified." This message, he acknowledges, is "a scandal to Jews and foolishness to Gentiles" (1:23). And although he speaks about a number of topics in the first four chapters, they all concern the polarities of human "wisdom" and "talk," on the one hand, and "the cross" and God's "power," on the other (cf. particularly his concluding words in

4:19–20). All his arguments in these chapters, in fact, are in some manner based on and explicate what the confession "Christ crucified" means for the circumstances of believers at Corinth.

After dealing with rumors about incest among believers at Corinth and about Christians taking their disputes before pagan courts for settlement (5:1–6:20), and after answering specific questions about marriage, food sacrificed to idols, women's decorum in worship, the Lord's Supper, and spiritual gifts (7:1–14:40). Paul then turns to a matter that was very much on his mind and that he believed was important for Christians at Corinth: a proper understanding of the resurrection of believers (15:1–58). This subject, it may be conjectured, did not arise because of reports, rumors, or questions, and so its appearance in 1 Corinthians reflects not someone else's concerns, but rather Paul's own agenda—though, of course, he evidently thought it a topic of great importance for his converts as well.

What needs to be noted here, however, is that in his rather extensive treatment of the resurrection of believers in chapter 15, Paul bases all of his arguments on the fact and prototypical nature of Christ's resurrection as declared in the confessional materials of verses 3b–5. He probably knew that some Christians at Corinth were claiming that a future, personal, corporeal resurrection of believers in Jesus was (1) *irrelevant*, since the eschatological hope of the gospel was already fulfilled in a believer's present, spiritual experience; (2) *impossible*, since in Greek religious thought the physical body was excluded from divine redemption (the Corinthians may also have been reacting to Jewish ideas about the resurrection as merely revivification, or resuscitation; and (3) *unnecessary*, since believers already possessed an immortal soul, which, now redeemed by Christ, made any further action by God superfluous. Countering such assertions, Paul in chapter 15 sets out (1) the *fact* of a Christian's future, personal, corporeal resurrection in verses 12–34 (signaled by ὅτι, "that," twice in v. 12), (2) the *manner* of a Christian's resurrection in verses 35–49 (signaled by πῶς, "how," in v. 35), and (3) the *necessity* of a Christian's resurrection in verses 50–58 (signaled by δεῖ, "it is necessary," in v. 53).

Throughout, all of 1 Corinthians 15 Paul bases his arguments on the confessional statement about Christ's resurrection in verse 4 (cf. also v. 12). He does this explicitly in declaring the fact of a future and personal resurrection of believers (vv. 12–34), by analogy to argue for the corporeal nature of their resurrection (vv. 35–49), and by implication to assert the necessity of their resurrection if they are ever to be clothed with immortality (vv. 50–58).

Thus, in the two major expositional and polemical sections of 1 Corinthians where the apostle seems to be expressing his most urgent personal concerns, Paul can be seen contextualizing early Christian confessional materials. He does this first by focusing on confessions that speak of "the cross" and "Christ crucified," using these confessional materials as the basis for all that he argues in the first four chapters. Then at the close of the letter he again contextualizes confessional materials by focusing on the formulaic confession of 15:3b–5, which informs all that he writes in chapter 15.

Galatians

Paul's Letter to the Galatians also contains a number of portions and phrases that have been seen as outcroppings of early Christian confessional materials. Two major themes in these materials are highlighted: Christ's redemptive death on a cross (1:4; 3:1; 3:13) and the establishment of new relationships because of Christ's redemptive work (3:26, 27–28; 4:4–5). Also to be noted is the theme of God's salvific purpose having been accomplished in what Christ did (cf. 1:4; 4:4–5). In fact, Paul argues his case against the Judaizers and their message primarily on the basis of these confessional materials.

The first of these themes appears in the salutation of the Galatian letter at 1:4, which speaks about Jesus Christ as "the one who gave himself for our sins in order that he might rescue us from this present evil age, according to the will of our God and Father." The portion begins with the substantival participle τοῦ δόντος, "the one who gave" (cf. 1:1b in its use of τοῦ ἐγείραντος, "the one who raised," with regard to "God the Father," which may also be a reflection of early Christian language about God). It highlights the affirmation "Christ gave himself for our sins," which is both similar to the confession "Christ died for our sins," cited by Paul in 1 Cor 15:3, and different from Paul's usual way of identifying the referents of Christ's death (cf. Rom 5:6–8; 1 Cor 1:13; 11:24; Col 1:21–22). Furthermore, the verb ἐξέληται, "he might rescue," is a Pauline *hapax legomenon*. Paul elsewhere in his letters uses σῴζω, "save," ῥύομαι, "deliver," ἐλευθερόω, "set free," and ἐξαγοράζω, "redeem," as verbs of deliverance, but not ἐξαιρέω, "rescue" (from which ἐξέληται, "he might rescue," is derived)—though the verb is common in the LXX in this sense and is reported by Luke in Acts to have been used in the early church (cf. Acts 7:10, 34; 12:11; 23:27; 26:17). Likewise, the phrase ὁ αἰὼν ὁ ἐνεστώς (from ἐνίστημι), "this present age"—which is equivalent to the Hebrew expression *ha 'olam hazzeh*, "this age," as contrasted with the Hebrew *ha 'olam habba*, "the age to come"—is a NT *hapax*. And although the evil character of this age is assumed elsewhere in Paul's writings (cf. Rom 12:2; 1 Cor 1:20), only here is the adjective πονηρός, "evil," attached to αἰῶν, "age."

The theme of Christ's redemptive death on a cross also comes dramatically to the fore at Gal 3:13: "Christ redeemed us from the curse of the law by becoming a curse for us, for it is written, 'Cursed is everyone who is hanged on a tree.' " The content of this verse has often been argued to stem from some early Jewish Christian source—either directly from an early Jewish Christian confession (e.g., H. D. Betz[1]), more indirectly from a Jewish Christian midrash based on the Akedah (e.g., H. J. Schoeps, N. A. Dahl, G. Vermes[2], who also often include v. 14), or derivatively from an underlying "narrative substructure" held in common among the early Christians (e.g., R. B. Hays[3]). Likewise, the theme surfaces in allusive fashion at the beginning of Paul's theological argument in 3:1: "You foolish Galatians! Who bewitched you, before whose eyes Jesus Christ was clearly portrayed as having been crucified?"

It would take too long to present and evaluate all of the stylistic and content arguments put forward for the thesis that the above passages in Galatians stem from early Christian confessional materials.[4] But assuming such a thesis to be true, the important point here is that in the first part of his Galatian letter Paul contextualizes the theme of Christ's redemptive death on a cross in a manner that puts an end to all stray thoughts about Gentile believers either being justified before God by observing the Jewish law (i.e., legalism) or pleasing God by their keeping of that law (i.e., nomism). Indeed, as 3:1 shows, Paul is at a loss to know how his converts could ever have failed to see the significance of "Christ crucified"—the message he had openly and clearly proclaimed to them—for issues of both legalism generally and nomism in particular

The second of the major confessional themes in Galatians is the establishment of new relationships through the work of Christ. This theme comes to expression particularly in 3:26–4:11. The section begins with a thesis statement: "For you are all children [sons] of God through faith in Christ Jesus." The postpositive connective γάρ ("for") has both explanatory and continuative functions, and so probably should be translated "for, you see."

The statement itself, "You are all children [sons] of God through faith in Christ Jesus," has been aptly argued to be a "Sayings" statement drawn from an early Christian confession.[5] It could have been used by Jewish Christians within their own assemblies in a number of ways: (1) with a stress on "all" whenever there was division in a congregation, without any thought regarding possible Gentile believers; (2) with an emphasis on "children [sons] of God" to heighten their own self-understanding, without any thought to how Gentile Christians should be viewed as related to Abraham; (3) with a focus on the article "the" with the noun "faith" (τῆς πίστεως) to highlight the importance of personal faith (i.e., "your faith"), without any thought to how faith and Torah observance are to be related among the Gentiles; and (4) with the phrase "in Christ Jesus" to signal the distinctive object of this faith over against Judaism generally, without becoming more precise regarding the relationship between Christ and Torah. Whatever its possible past use in other contexts, however, Paul uses this confessional statement in connection with his argument for the freedom of Gentile Christians. And so he proclaims that new relationships have been established by Christ—ringing the changes by means of the expressions "all," "children [sons] of God," "the faith," and "in Christ Jesus" in a way decidedly applicable to the problems faced by his Gentile converts.

Paul does likewise in his quotations of two other confessional portions found in his discussion of new relationships—3:27–28 and 4:4–5, both of which have undergone, during the past decades, extensive form-critical analyses demonstrating their pre-Pauline confessional nature.[6] In 3:27–28, without any development of the latter two couplets ("slave or free" and "male and female") of the confessional triad, Paul picks up on "no longer Jew or Gentile" to argue that distinctions between Jews and Gentiles have come to an end for believers in Christ—thereby undercutting a major premise of the Judaizers. In 4:4–5 he highlights the theme of full family membership ("adoption as God's children") for all believers because of God's action and Christ's work, arguing that Gentiles as well as Jews have been redeemed not only from the curse but also from the supervision of the law—thereby undercutting another major premise of the Judaizers.

At the start of his discussion about the new relationships established by Christ, therefore, Paul lines up two confessional portions that speak of such new relationships (3:27–28 and 4:4–5) and places both under the heading of a Sayings statement that does likewise (3:26). Then he contextualizes their messages for the situation at hand in the Galatian churches by what he says thereafter in the letter.

Romans

Romans may very well be the "mother lode" of early Christian confessional materials. The letter only awaits a proper form-critical mining—particularly in its epistolary body of 1:16–15:13 (or perhaps commencing at 1:13 or 1:18). Identified to date as confessional portions are (1) the hymn of praise to God in 11:33–36; (2) the formulaic christological portions of 1:3–4, 3:24–26 (or perhaps 3:25–26) and 4:25; and (3) the single-statement affirmation of the lordship of Christ in 10:9. Parts of the lyrical and almost defiant affirmation of 8:33–39 should probably also be seen as confessional in nature. And echoes of such material may also be present in 9:5b ("Who is God over all, forever praised! Amen") and 14:9 ("Christ died and returned to life so that he might be the Lord of both the dead and the living").

Of particular interest for a structural analysis of Romans is the fact that three of these confessional portions appear as the final items of their respective sections, and so serve to summarize and conclude these sections. Romans 4:25 ("Who was delivered over to death for our sins, and was raised to life for our justification") seems to function in this manner, summarizing the central statements of 3:21–31 and bringing to a climax the whole presentation of 1:16–4:24. Likewise, the forceful affirmations of 8:33–39, which probably include a number of early confessional statements, summarize and bring to a dramatic conclusion all that is said in chapters 5–8. And while it may be debated whether the beginning portion of chapters 9–11 includes a confessional doxology at 9:5b, certainly the majestic hymn of praise to God in 11:33–36 is confessional and provides a fitting climax to these three chapters.

Paul seems to be using early Christian confessional materials to close off each of the three main theological sections of his letter (chs. 1–4, 5–8, and 9–11). And with addressees who did not regard Paul as their spiritual father but looked elsewhere for their traditions and support,[7] this was undoubtedly a strategic move on his part. For in concluding his three main theological sections with confessional materials that were presumably known and accepted by his addressees—or that his addressees would at least have recognized as echoing such materials—Paul ensured their acceptance of his presentations.

Three or four confessional portions are also used by Paul in his theological arguments of chapters 1–4 and 9–11 and his exhortations of 12:1–15:13. These other confessional materials are to be found in: (1) 1:3–4, which presents a two-stage understanding of Christ ("The one born of the seed of David, according to the flesh; the one declared to be the Son of God with power, according to his spirit of holiness [or 'the Spirit of holiness'], by the resurrection of the dead"); (2) 3:24–26, which depicts God's salvific activity through the work of Christ in terms of "justification," "redemption," and "expiation-propitiation" and in a manner not quite Pauline; and (3) 10:9, which incorporates the confession "Jesus is Lord." Likewise, 14:9 has seemed to many to be also an early Christian confessional portion ("Christ died and returned to life so that he might be the Lord of both the dead and the living").

Each of these portions has a strategic place in the overall argument of Romans. First, 1:3–4 appears in the salutation, which Paul uses to highlight a number of the themes that he intends to develop later in the letter. Similarly, 3:24–26 is included in what most commentators take to be a major thesis paragraph of the letter, 3:21–26—though it may be debated whether the paragraph sets out the thesis of the whole letter, of the first eight chapters, or of only the first four chapters. And 10:9 appears at the heart of Paul's discussion of the gospel and Israel in chapters 9–11, while 14:9 is central in his exhortations regarding the weak and the strong in 14:1–15:13.

In addressing, therefore, a predominantly Gentile Christian audience at Rome—whom he considered within the orbit of his Gentile mission, but who he knew did not trace their spiritual heritage back to his preaching—Paul uses early Christian confessional materials in at least two ways: (1) to summarize and bring to a climax his presentations in the three main theological sections of his letter, as in 4:25, 8:33–39, and 11:33–36, and (2) to support and focus his arguments, as with the materials of 1:3–4, 3:24–26, 10:9, and 14:9. Also of significance is the fact that Paul builds bridges of commonality with his addressees by using these materials, which were presumably familiar to them.

1 Thessalonians

Almost all modern commentators point out at least one confessional portion in 1 Thessalonians, the statement in 4:14a: "Jesus died and rose again." The verb ἀνίστημι, "rise again," suggests a confessional formulation, for elsewhere Paul usually uses ἐγείρω, "rise" (some forty times, and normally in the passive) when speaking about Christ's resurrection or the resurrection of believers. Most of the apparent exceptions are found where the apostle is quoting: Rom 15:12 (citing Isa 11:10); 1 Cor 10:7 (citing Exod 32:6); and Eph 5:14 (using expressions drawn from Isa 26:19 and 60:1 in a proverbial manner). Another exception is found two verses later in 1 Thess 4:16, where he cites a "word of the Lord" (probably an *agraphon*, or "unrecorded word" of Jesus not included in the canonical Gospels).

Likewise, his use of the name Jesus alone supports such a view, for usually Paul speaks of "Jesus Christ," "Christ Jesus," or simply "Christ." Only rarely does he use "Jesus" alone—in Rom 8:11, 2 Cor 4:14, 1 Thess 1:10 (which may also be part of an early Christian confession, as noted below), and the latter part of our verse here (4:14b), whose phraseology is conditioned by the confessional language of the first part of the verse (4:14a). Furthermore, the ὅτι introducing the statement "Jesus died and rose again" seems to be used as a *hoti recitativum*, and so further suggests that Paul here is quoting an early Christian confessional portion.

In 4:15–17, the three verses that follow the confession "Jesus died and rose again," Paul quotes a "word of the Lord" regarding the eschatological coming of Christ. Exactly what is meant by ἐν λόγῳ κυρίου, "by a word of the Lord," and how this teaching came to Paul have been hotly debated. The options are usually narrowed down to three: Was this "word" a revelatory teaching from the exalted Jesus? Was it an *agraphon*? Or was it a deduction drawn by Paul himself from teachings now recorded in our canonical Gospels? With Joachim Jeremias, I think the second option to be the most probable.[8]

But whatever the specifics of the case, it is clear that in 4:13–5:11, when Paul speaks about a believer's resurrection hope and exhorts his converts to preparedness, he does so first on the basis of an early Christian confession (4:14) and then on the basis of Jesus' own teachings (4:15–17). Speaking to those who needed to be encouraged (cf. 4:18; 5:11) and reminded (cf. 5:1–2; also 2 Thess 2:5) about the gospel's proclamation concerning the resurrection of Christian believers, Paul contextualizes two traditional portions: (1) an early Christian confession that proclaimed that "Jesus died and rose again" (4:14) and (2) a teaching of Jesus, somehow retained within the memory of the church, about what will take place at the time of resurrection (4:15–17).

The wording of 1:9–10 ("you turned from idols to serve the living and true God, and to wait for his Son from heaven, whom he raised from the dead—Jesus, who rescues us from the coming wrath") may also incorporate expressions drawn from earlier confessional materials, as some have argued. Its theological and christological content, its rather formal presentation, and its use of the name Jesus alone all seem to point in such a direction, though little more can be said beyond that.

Colossians

The exact nature and provenance of Col 1:15–20 are disputed. Almost everyone recognizes that the passage quotes material from some earlier source. This is because of its balanced structure, its use of the relative pronoun ὅς at the beginning of each of its two parts (vv. 15a and 18b), and its numerous *hapax legomena*—many of which seem to have some affinity with various ascetic-mystical or gnostic concepts. But numerous questions remain, such as these: Was this some type of ascetic-mystical or gnostic hymn that had been "disinfected" and "rebaptized" by the early Christians to become an appropriate hymn to Christ, and then used by Paul? Or should this material be seen more as a Christian formulaic prose portion than a hymn, with its terminology employed to counter certain ascetic-mystical or gnostic ideas then current? Or did Paul just pick up bits and pieces from earlier Christian confessional materials, some of whose expressions had been used originally by Christians in contradistinction to certain pagan or gnostic ideas? Furthermore, what exactly is the nature of the problem confronted in the Letter to the Colossians?

Clearly, the letter argues for the lordship of Christ not only religiously but also cosmically, and so presents one of the loftiest christological portrayals in the NT. And that it presents the Christian life as complete "in Christ," both now and in the future, is also clear. But was the error of the false teacher whom it combats (note the singular pronoun τις in 2:8; cf. 2:16, 18, etc.) some form of ascetic-mystical piety that pervaded much of the ancient world, or some form of Greek gnosticism, or some form of Jewish apocalyptic speculation—or some eclectic amalgamation of two or more of these perspectives?

Such matters have been debated extensively and cannot be resolved here. Nor need their consideration detain us from our present purpose. The point here is that the confession that Christ is the supreme source of "all fullness" by virtue of his preeminence in "all things" provides the basis for Paul's arguments against the false teacher, who wanted the Colossian Christians to adhere to certain beliefs and practices that he claimed would give them a fuller experience of God.

The false teacher at Colossae may very well have claimed to accept the lordship of Christ in the religious sphere of a believer's life. But his teaching seems also to have asserted that the acceptance of such a lordship was only a preliminary step in Christian commitment. The false teacher seems to have been proposing that a much greater understanding of Christ's lordship and a much greater experience of relationship with God await those who move beyond this first stage into a more cosmic understanding of lordship—a more advanced stage achievable only by adherence to the teacher's doctrines.

Paul, however, insists that Christ's lordship extends over everything that can be thought of—whether conceived of religiously or cosmically—and that God has fully reconciled all things to himself and has effected final peace through Christ's death on the cross. And Paul uses the confessional materials of 1:15–20 as the basis for his arguments.

Nothing more, therefore, needs to be added to the experience of believers "in Christ." Christians who were "once alienated from God and enemies" are now "reconciled" to God "by Christ's physical body through death" and will be presented before God "holy in his sight, without blemish and free from accusation" (1:21–22). Concerning Christ's person, "all the fullness of the Deity resides in bodily form in him" (2:9). And concerning the Christian believer's experience, "you have this fullness in him, who is the head over every power and authority" (2:10)—with "this fullness" spelled out in the directives that follow in the rest of the letter vis-à-vis the teaching and practice advocated by the false teacher. The basis for such claims, Paul seems to be saying, can be found in the confessions of the early church, which use some of the very terms and expressions that the false teacher evidently took pride in.

1 Timothy

What has been said regarding the contextualization of Col 1:15–20 can also be said regarding 1 Tim 3:16. The confessional formula of 3:16—"He [Who] appeared in a body, was vindicated by the Spirit, was seen by angels, was preached among the nations, was believed on in the world, was taken up in glory"—serves as the basis for countering the demands of certain false teachers who were advocating some form of ascetic mysticism. Furthermore, these two confessions of Col 1:15–20 and 1 Tim 3:16—which appear in somewhat later NT writings—begin to focus more on ontological issues than on strictly functional matters (also those of Heb 1:3 and 5:7, 8–9, to be discussed below). Such an observation, of course, raises questions about the development of the confessional materials themselves during the first Christian century. But these are questions that go far beyond our immediate purpose, which is only to highlight the fact and manner of the contextualization of the early Christian confessions in the epistolary writings of the NT.

2 Corinthians

The last Pauline confessional portion to be considered is 2 Cor 5:19a. Our rationale for dealing with this portion last is not any supposed lateness of date or possible disjunction from the rest of the Corinthian correspondence, but rather because the formal criteria for identifying confessional materials are somewhat less evident here. Furthermore, treating 2 Corinthians last highlights what seems to be a pattern in Paul's letters: that confessional materials appear frequently in contexts that are primarily expositional (i.e., a sustained teaching) and polemical (i.e., an aggressive explication against some false teaching), but are relatively absent in passages that are more expressly apologetic in nature (i.e., a defensive response to personal attacks). This pattern is not surprising, since confessional materials beg to be explicated, which is what occurs in expositional and polemical contexts. On the other hand, being highly theological in nature, they would seem rather inappropriate in the context of a personal defense.

Second Corinthians is often viewed as a collection of Paul's letters that have somehow been brought together to form one letter (e.g., the "lost letter" of 6:14–7:1 [cf. 1 Cor 5:9]; the "severe letter" of 10:1–13:14; the "conciliatory letter" of 1:1–7:16 [with or without 6:14–7:1]; and one or two letters on ministry and giving in chs. 8 and 9). But however 2 Corinthians came about, it is obvious that in most of its seemingly disparate sections Paul is responding in apologetic fashion to attacks on his person, his apostolic authority, and his ministry. It may not be surprising, therefore, that very few, if any, confessional materials have been found in 2 Corinthians.

Nonetheless, 2 Cor 5:19a has often been seen as an early Christian confession: "God was in Christ reconciling the world to himself, not counting people's sins against them." In all probability that judgment is correct. The statement evidences a certain balance of structure, seems to be formally introduced by a *hoti recitativum*, and focuses on both God and Christ. As a confessional portion, it serves as the linchpin of Paul's defense of his apostolic ministry. For not only did God take the initiative in the redemptive work of reconciliation, not only did Christ effect this work, and not only is the work being realized in the reconciliation of the world and its people to God (as the confession states), but, in addition, God commissioned Paul to be Christ's ambassador (in line with the intent of this confession). And so Paul declares, applying the confession to the situation at hand, that he has been commissioned as an apostle to carry out a ministry of reconciliation for the sake of the Corinthians.

■ 2. THE OTHER EPISTOLARY WRITINGS

Less scholarly effort has been expended on identifying early Christian confessions in the non-Pauline epistolary writings of the NT—in particular, in the General Epistles and Hebrews. Nevertheless, confessional portions have been identified in some of these writings, and these portions are contextualized by their authors in both theological and ethical ways.

1 Peter

After its epistolary salutation, 1 Peter begins in 1:3–5 with what appears to be a hymn of praise to God—or, at least, words of praise that incorporate several hymnic fragments of a Christian confessional nature:

Praise be to the God and Father of our Lord Jesus Christ!
In his great mercy he has given us new birth into a living hope,
    through the resurrection of Jesus Christ from the dead,
and has brought us into an inheritance that can never perish,
spoil, or fade,
    which is kept in heaven for you.
Through faith you are shielded by God's power,
    unto the salvation that is prepared,
    which will be revealed in the last time.

Thus, at the very start of his letter to believers in Jesus, who are identified as being the true remnant of Israel and living in various provinces of Asia Minor ("To God's elect, strangers in the world, scattered throughout Pontus, Galatia, Cappadocia, Asia, and Bithynia"), the writer expresses praise to God with what appears to be an early Christian confessional formulation. He seems to use this formulation to (1) form a bond with his addressees in the expression of their common praise, thereby opening the way for their reception of what he has to say, and (2) lay a theological basis for his exhortations to perseverance in the face of persecution and suffering. A confessional hymn (or a collection of hymnic fragments), therefore, stands at the beginning of the writer's ethical exhortations, providing a theocentric context for his addressees' attitudes and actions.

Yet while rooted in the redemptive plan and purposes of God, the ethical exhortations of 1 Pet 1–2 also look to Jesus Christ for guidance as to how Christians should think and act when persecuted and suffering. On how Christian slaves should relate to their masters, the example of Christ is cited in 2:22–23—with Christ's example presented in the form of a confessional hymn:

"Who committed no sin,
    and no deceit was found in his mouth" [quoting Isa 53:9].
Who when they hurled their insults at him,
    he did not retaliate;
when he suffered,
    he made no threats [alluding to Isa 53:7].

Like the Christ hymn of Phil 2:6–11, the Christ hymn of 1 Pet 2:22–23, which picks up on the imagery of the Servant Song of Isaiah 53, presents the attitude of Jesus in his afflictions and suffering as the paradigm for a Christian's attitude amidst persecution and suffering. Thus the quotation of confessional materials in 1:3–5 and 2:22–23, which were probably both originally set in hymnic form, encourages the addressees to recognize that their sufferings are within the plan and purposes of God and challenges them to take Christ himself as the exemplar for their attitudes and actions.

Hebrews

Commentators have often noted the confessional nature of 1:3 and 4:12–13 in the so-called Letter to the Hebrews. Likewise, 5:7–9 has been seen to be either one long confessional passage or two confessional portions that have been joined together into one (some taking v. 10 to be also included). Balanced structures, use of *hapax legomena,* and introductions by the relative pronoun ὅς ("who") strongly support this identification for 1:3 and 5:7–9— and perhaps also for 4:12–13.

The material of 1:3 functions in a very significant manner for all of Hebrews. After stating the central thesis of the letter in 1:1–2—"In the past, God spoke to our ancestors through the prophets at many times and in various ways, but in these last days he has spoken to us by his Son, whom he appointed heir of all things, and through whom he established the ages"—the writer supports this statement with what appears to be an early Christian confessional portion, which highlights both the cosmic and the redemptive significance of the Son:

> He [Who] is the radiance [ἀπαύγασμα, effulgence] of God's glory and the exact representation [χαρακτήρ, imprint] of his person, sustaining all things by his powerful word. And after he had provided purification for sins, he sat down at the right hand of the Majesty in heaven. (1:3)

But more than just buttressing the thesis statement of 1:1–2, the writer's quotation of this confession sets up the argumentation of all that follows. It does this for the rest of chapter 1 by its allusion to Ps 110:1 ("he sat down at the right hand of the Majesty in heaven"), which anchors the catena of christologically interpreted passages in verses 5–6 and 8–13. More importantly, it does this for the whole of the letter by its proclamation of Christ's exaltedness, which is then transposed by the writer into an emphasis on the Son's superiority.

The confessional materials of 4:12–13 and 5:7–9—if, indeed, that is what they are—also function in strategic ways in the writing. With a climactic set of statements, 4:12–13 concludes the writer's opening discussions on the superiority of the Son over angels, both in his exaltation and his humiliation (1:4–2:18), and the superiority of the Son over Moses, Joshua, and Israel's entrance into the land (3:1–4:13):

> The word of God is living and active. Sharper than any double-edged sword, it penetrates even to dividing soul and spirit, joints and marrow; it judges the thoughts and attitudes of the heart. Nothing in all creation is hidden from God's sight. Everything is uncovered and laid bare before the eyes of him to whom we must give account.

And 5:7–9 concludes the writer's treatment of the superiority of the Son over the Levitical-Aaronic priesthood (4:14–5:9) with an emphasis on his "reverent submission," his "obedience," his "suffering," his "perfection," and so his perfect redemption:

> Who, in the days of his flesh, offered up prayers and petitions with a loud cry and tears to the One who could save him from death [an allusion to Jesus' Gethsemane prayer?], and he was heard because of his reverent submission.

> Although he was a son, he learned obedience from what he suffered; and once made perfect, he became the source of eternal salvation for all who obey him.

The argument of Hebrews rises with increasing intensity until it reaches the double crescendo of the superiority of the Son over the Melchizedek priesthood (5:10–7:28) and the superiority of the Son over the sacrifices, tabernacle, and covenant of the OT (8:1–10:39). But before he comes to these final climaxes of his argument, the writer clinches his presentations of the subjects discussed in 3:1–4:13 and 4:14–5:9 by the inclusion of the confessional materials of 4:12–13 and 5:7–9, respectively.

CHAPTER FOUR

The Synoptic Gospels and Acts

Many reasons can be given as to why the Synoptic Gospels and the Acts of the Apostles were written. Redaction criticism has highlighted various theological reasons, which stem from the distinctive interests and purposes of the respective evangelists, the particular problems and concerns of their addressees, and the various ministries of the early church. Form criticism has shown how some portions within these writings were probably liturgically conditioned—whether originally composed by the early Christians for their worship or adapted for such use.

There were also, however, historical reasons for the writing of these materials. One reason had to do with external outreach: they were written to provide accounts of the origin and development of the Christian religion for inquiring persons—whether Jews or Gentiles; whether inclined to belief or not—in terms that their intended audiences could understand. Another reason was purely internal: they were written to support and strengthen the life of the church by providing narratives of the origins and growth of the Christian faith, presenting the stories of Jesus and the nascent church in ways that believers from various backgrounds would appreciate.

Speaking of the origins of the Synoptic Gospels, Werner Kümmel has stated that the "main concern" of the evangelists was "to evoke faith and to strengthen it":

> Jesus' words and deeds are brought together from out of his life and reproduced in the form of a simple narrative in order to show to the early Christian church the ground of its faith and to provide firm support in its mission for preaching, instruction, and debate with its opponents.[1]

"To evoke faith" and "to strengthen it" are complementary motivations, with extensive areas of overlap. Also complementary are the desires "to show to the early Christian church the ground of its faith" and "to provide firm support in its mission for preaching, instruction, and debate with its opponents." In both cases, whether to evoke faith within those who might be interested or to support and strengthen faith among those who already believed, the Gospels were written "out of faith and for faith."

The Greco-Roman world was not interested in foreign religions just making their sacred texts available for others to read. The Jews did that by translating their Scriptures from Hebrew (and Aramaic) into Greek and producing the LXX of 250–100 BCE. But this translation was largely ignored by both Greek and Roman thinkers. As Arnaldo Momigliano has observed, "The Greeks expected the Jews, not to translate their holy books, but to produce an account of themselves according to the current methods and categories of ethnography."[2] Momigliano points out, "This was an old practice in the Greek world," one carried on by various foreign writers from the fifth century BCE on and by such Jewish authors as Demetrius in the third century BCE and Eupolemus and Aristobulus of Paneas in the second.[3]

Josephus, the Jewish military general, historian, and apologist, provided such an account for his Roman clients in his *Jewish Antiquities*. In twenty books he set out in narrative form a history of the Jewish people and their religion from the creation of the world up to "the thirteenth year of Domitian" (i.e., through the latter years of the emperor Domitian's reign, to about 93–94 CE)—using a number of sources at his disposal, but also putting his own spin on these materials in line with his own proclivities and the perceived interests of his readers. He did much the same in his earlier *Jewish War* (written toward the end of Vespasian's reign, sometime between 75 and 79 CE), in his later autobiographical *Life* (written during the reign of Trajan, early in the second century), and, though in a much more apologetic manner, in his *Against Apion* (also written early in the second century). The Greco-Roman world also wanted something along these lines from the Christians—and the Synoptic Gospels and the Acts were written, in large part, to provide it.

More important, however, was the evangelists' internal rationale for writing. For congruent with their own theological interests and perspectives, as well as with their desire to speak to the concerns and problems of their addressees, was the need to set out the essential features of the story that constituted the church's very existence in order to support and strengthen the church's life, worship, and ministry. As C. F. D. Moule has argued, the early believers in Jesus, both in their worship and in their proclamation, "recognized that their faith stood or fell with the sober facts of a story, and that it was vital to maintain the unbroken tradition of those facts."[4] So, recognizing that "the plain story of what happened in the ministry of Jesus"[5] was foundational to all that they believed and proclaimed, the synoptic evangelists attempted to produce this story in a manner that would be true both to the ethos of the story itself and to the methods of the day—with each evangelist giving his own spin to the narrated events in terms of his own interests and his perception of his addressees' outlook and concerns. Especially important here, however, is the fact that each evangelist sets out his story not only in support of the church's worship and witness but also in support of the church's basic confessions.

Such an understanding of the relationship between the Synoptic Gospels and Acts vis-à-vis the early Christian confessions involves, of course, a hermeneutical circle. On the one hand, the confessions are grounded in the historical events of Jesus' life, ministry, death, and resurrection, which are narrated in the Gospels; while on the other hand, the evangelists' narration of those events is conditioned by the theological understanding of those events that the confessions already embody. This reciprocity highlights the dual—that is, both historical and theological—character of the Synoptic Gospels and Acts.

One important way to approach the writings of the evangelists, therefore, is to view their compositions as both (1) inspired and shaped by the central confessions of the earliest believers in Jesus and (2) attempting to set out the basic story line that supports those confessions. This approach is particularly significant for an understanding of the Synoptic Gospels and Acts, which speak rather directly about origins and developments. So this chapter will treat the Synoptic Gospels in this way, dealing with each of the three in terms of (1) their introductory materials, (2) their portrayals of Jesus' ministry, and (3) their passion narratives and resurrection accounts. The following chapter will deal with the Fourth Gospel and the Johannine Apocalypse, which, in their own more interpretive and expansive fashions, depict origins and developments as well.

▨ 1. MARK'S GOSPEL

The Gospel according to Mark is the appropriate place to begin. For not only was Mark, in all likelihood, the first of our canonical Gospels to be written, it also was most clearly motivated by the central confessions of the early Christians and sets out most directly the underlying story line that supports those confessions.

Many modern studies treat Mark's Gospel as a document that expresses, in the main, the theology of the Christian community where it was written, with a minimum of attention given to the factuality of the events that it purports to relate. Some also argue that the Gospel must be seen as reflecting the liturgy used in the worship of that community. But it is a mistake to characterize Mark as only the expression of a community's theology or a reflection of its liturgy, even though redactional features that sprang from the life of the author's community and his own perspectives are certainly present.

Comparing Mark's Gospel and Paul's Letter to the Romans, C. F. D. Moule has pointed out that although Mark was evidently composed in the matrix of believers "who would know what was meant by trusting Christ (Rom 3:22), by having access through Christ to God (Rom 5:2, 11), by being baptized into his death and fused with him in a death and resurrection like his (Rom 6:1–11), by being a single body in union with Christ (Rom 12:5), and by being possessed of and by the Holy Spirit (Rom 8)"—assuming, of course, a Roman provenance for Mark's Gospel—none of these doctrinal features comes to the fore in any clear manner in Mark. One would, however, expect a clearer expression of these features had the Gospel been written principally as an expression of the theology of the Christian community at Rome or a reflection of its liturgy.[6] Rather, as Moule argues, it is much more likely that Mark was written as an "explanation of 'how it all started' " and that its purpose was to provide support for the teachings and practices of the early Christians by recounting "the story of how it [the good good news of the Christian proclamation] came [about]" in the life and ministry of Jesus.[7] In fact, Moule even calls Mark's Gospel an "exercise of reminiscent reconstruction."[8]

More particularly, and without disputing Moule's thesis, we propose (1) that the evangelist was motivated by such early Christian confessions as "Jesus is the Christ [Messiah]," "Jesus is the Son of God," "the eschatological age of redemption has been inaugurated," "Christ's death on the cross is redemptive," and "new relationships have been established through the work of Christ." (2) Moreover, the evangelist sought to support these confessions by a narration of Jesus' ministry. Furthermore, not only does Mark's Gospel set out the basis for these confessions, it also seeks to show how Jesus' earliest disciples came to believe what they confessed.

The Caption (1:1), Beginning (1:2–13), and Unfolding Structure

In the very first sentence of his Gospel, Mark declares that what he is presenting is "the good news" (or "gospel") that has as its focus the story about "Jesus," who is identified as both "Christ" (i.e., "Messiah") and "Son of God" (1:1). "The beginning" of this good news includes the ministry of John the Baptist (1:2–8), the baptism of Jesus by John (1:9–11), and the temptation of Jesus by Satan (1:12–13). The first half of the Gospel (1:14–8:30) then recounts selected incidents in the ministry of Jesus that expressed his authority, caused amazement and fear in the people, and gave rise to questions about his identity. Its high point is reached with the acclamation of Peter: "You are the Christ!" (8:29). The second half (8:31–15:47)—through depictions of Jesus' passion predictions (8:31–10:52), events at Jerusalem (11:1–13:37), and the passion narrative proper (14:1–15:47)—spells out the nature of Jesus' messiahship as entailing suffering. It climaxes with the affirmation of the Roman centurion: "Truly, this man was the Son of God!" (15:39). Mark thus not only focuses attention on Jesus as the content of the gospel's proclamation, he also highlights the two confessional formulations "Jesus is the Christ" and "Jesus is the Son of God."

What impressed the centurion (Mark 15:37–39; cf. Matt 27:50–54; Luke 23:46–48) and what he meant by calling Jesus "Son of God" may be debated, for the centurion was a Gentile and so probably used the title in a polytheistic manner (in the sense of a quasi-divine offspring of a deity, a "son of God"). It is doubtful that he had in mind anything like the Jewish concept of "one who is in loving obedience to God the Father." Nonetheless, Mark seems to have considered that the centurion spoke better than he knew. Therefore Mark makes the point that, in calling Jesus "Son of God," the centurion used the proper title, whatever he might have meant by such an honorific outburst. For in both his life and his death, as expressed particularly in Gethsemane and on the cross, Jesus' response to God was, indeed, one of loving obedience par excellence.

The Portrayals of Jesus' Ministry (1:14–13:37)

After presenting matters concerning "the beginning of the good news" in 1:1–13, Mark sets out two vignettes that serve to signal the significance of all that he will later portray from the ministry of Jesus and support the confession that the eschatological age of redemption has been inaugurated. The first focuses on the proclamation of Jesus himself in 1:14–15: "The time has come [i.e., temporally in the divine program]. The kingdom of God is near [i.e., spatially in Jesus' ministry]. Repent and believe the good news!" The second vignette depicts Jesus calling four

Galilean fishermen in 1:16–20: "Come, follow me!"—with the additional words, "I will make you fish for people!"

The evangelist seems to have viewed both of these vignettes as of great importance, for together they serve to introduce his accounts about Jesus' ministry in Galilee and in Jerusalem. Certainly the announcement that the kingdom of God is temporally present ("has come") and spatially near (in Jesus' ministry) sets the tone for all that the evangelist says about the fulfillment of the eschatological age of redemption in the ministry of Jesus. Likewise, the call to Galilean fishers to join with Jesus to "fish for people" produces all sorts of eschatological reverberations. For many Jews of the Second Temple period expected that in the final days of eschatological redemption God, through his appointed representatives, would "fish for people."[9]

After these two vignettes, Mark presents a number of episodes depicting various aspects of the divine authority expressed by Jesus during his ministry. Thirty or more portrayals of Jesus' authority are given, principally in the first half of the Gospel. All of them elaborate the theme set by the two introductory vignettes of 1:14–20 and highlight the fact that the eschatological age of redemption has dawned in the ministry of Jesus. In almost staccato fashion, Mark presents a series of events in Jesus' ministry that sound a distinctive note of authority: in teaching (1:21–22; 6:1–6, 34), in casting out demons (1:23–27, 32–34, 39; 3:11–12, 22–30; 5:1–20; 7:24–30), in healing the sick (1:29–31, 32–34; 3:9–10; 5:25–34; 6:5, 54–56), in cleansing a leper (1:40–45), in restoring the paralyzed and deformed (2:1–12; 3:1–5), in doing various other miracles (4:35–41; 6:35–44, 47–52; 7:31–37; 8:1–10, 22–26), in declaring his presence to take precedence over Jewish tradition (2:18–20, 23–28; 7:1–8), in raising the dead (5:21–24, 35–43), and in forgiving sins (2:5–7)—with "the Twelve" commissioned to act with similar authority (3:13–19; 6:6b–13). When these episodes are understood as elaborations of the theme set by the two vignettes of 1:14–20, we see that the evangelist's accounts of Jesus' ministry, particularly in the first half of his Gospel, support the confession that the eschatological age of redemption has been inaugurated.

NEW WINE INTO FRESH WINESKINS

Furthermore, Mark presents (1) three parables of Jesus that compare the kingdom of God to "seed" in 4:1–34 (two of these parables are repeated and five more added by Matthew in his section on the parables of the kingdom) and (2) Jesus' teaching on what "clean" and "unclean" mean vis-à-vis a Jewish traditional understanding in 7:14–23. These presentations, too, should, in all likelihood, be understood primarily as supporting the confession that the eschatological age has been inaugurated. For Mark's purpose in reporting the teaching of Jesus was not so much to set out *what* Jesus taught as to point out *that* he taught with authority. He thereby portrays Jesus as the eschatological agent of redemption whose teaching corrected misunderstandings about what was to happen in the eschatological age.

The Passion Narrative (14:1–15:47) and Resurrection Account (16:1–8)

The passion narratives of all four canonical Gospels clearly support the confession regarding Jesus' redemptive death on a cross. The greatest degree of agreement between the four Gospels, in fact, is found in their passion narratives (Mark 14:1–15:47; Matt 26:1–27:66; Luke 22:1–23:56; John 18:1–19:42). This agreement might not be considered too surprising for the Synoptic Gospels, for they represent, in the main, a single tradition regarding the events of Jesus' passion—one that Mark used as the basis for his Gospel, which both Matthew and Luke essentially followed. It is somewhat surprising, however, that John's account of Jesus' passion is remarkably similar, for the Fourth Gospel is quite different from the Synoptic Gospels in its portrayal of the ministry of Jesus. In fact, of the roughly 6 percent of material in John's Gospel that is comparable to that contained in the Synoptics, almost all is found in John's passion narrative.

Such a commonality suggests that the events of Jesus' passion, more than any other part of the Jesus story, were relatively fixed in the minds of the earliest believers and in the traditions of the early church. This does not mean, however, that the passion narratives of the four Gospels are identical. Certainly that of the Fourth Gospel, while comparable in its overall presentation, is different from the others in its selection, arrangement, and wording of material. And the Synoptic Gospels, to some extent, differ among themselves on such matters as well. Nor should it be assumed that the four evangelists interpreted the events of Jesus' passion in exactly the same way.

For Mark, Jesus' death was a sacrifice on behalf of others; features related to suffering, sacrifice, the cross, and human redemption are prominent in the Markan passion narrative. Thus, in Mark's portrayal, Jesus (1) characterizes his ministry as one in which he is "to give his life a ransom for many" (10:45; cf. Matt 20:28); (2) views his anointing by a woman at Bethany as an act that "has anointed my body beforehand for burial" (14:8; cf. Matt 26:12); (3) says at the Last Supper, "This is my blood of the covenant, which is poured out for many" (14:24; cf. Matt 26:28); (4) interprets the events of his death in terms of Zech 13:7, "I will strike the shepherd, and the sheep will be scattered" (14:27; cf. Matt 26:31); and (5) endures willingly the awful agonies of the cross (14:35–36, etc.). In this way, the evangelist presents the bases for the church's confession that Jesus' death on the cross is redemptive.

Mark's account of Jesus' temptation in 1:12–13, compared to those of Matthew (4:1–11) and Luke (4:1–13), makes little of the theme of Jesus' obedience. Yet in his passion narrative, Mark includes in 14:36 that great expression of obedience voiced by Jesus in his prayer in Gethsemane:

> Abba, Father, everything is possible for you. Take this cup from me. Yet not what I will, but what you will! (cf. Matt 26:39; Luke 22:42; also John 12:27)

Thus there is a solid basis in Mark's Gospel for the confession that Jesus is God's obedient Son—though, admittedly, support for this affirmation appears more extensively in Matthew's Gospel.

More distinctly Markan is the evangelist's support for the confessional theme that new relationships have been established through the work of Christ. For in a manner that may well have shocked many of his contemporaries, Mark highlights the role of women in his passion narrative. He begins his account of Jesus' passion with the story of a woman who expressed a beautiful act of loving concern by anointing Jesus with expensive perfume before

his crucifixion (14:3–9, which is sandwiched between two accounts of treachery: that of the "chief priests and scribes" in
14:1–2 and that of Judas Iscariot in 14:10–11). Jesus declares in
response, "Wherever this gospel is preached throughout the
whole world, what she has done will also be told, in memory of
her" (14:9). And Mark closes his passion narrative with references
to the many women who witnessed Jesus' death (15:40–41) and to
the two women who saw where he was buried (15:47). In addition,
in his resurrection account women are the first to see the empty
tomb and the first commissioned to give testimony to the fact of
Jesus' resurrection (16:1–8).

The testimony of women carried little weight in Judaism.
Josephus expresses the general Jewish attitude: "From women let
no evidence be accepted, because of the levity and temerity
of their sex" (*Antiquities* 4.219). Even the confession of 1 Cor
15:3b–5 makes no mention of women as witnesses to the events of
Jesus' death, burial, resurrection, or postresurrection appearances—in all likelihood because of an earlier, engrained Jewish
attitude. But such an attitude, it seems, did not become entrenched among the early Christians. Mark's Gospel speaks of
the witness of women regarding Jesus' death, burial, and resurrection. Thus Mark's inclusion of their testimony at the beginning and end of his passion narrative serves to support one
feature of the early church's developing convictions: that new relationships, both with God and with others, have been established
through the work of Christ—in particular, new attitudes toward
women because of Christ's redemptive work and our common relationship with him.

■ 2. MATTHEW'S GOSPEL

The Gospel according to Matthew is considerably more
complex in its structure, its design, and its working out of its basic
themes than Mark. "Matthew," as Graham Stanton has observed,
"is undoubtedly the supreme literary artist among the four evangelists," and despite extensive investigation, "the precise relationship between his literary skill and his theological intentions is
not at all easy to determine."[10]

Yet though it differs in many respects from Mark in its structure, design, and development of presentation, Matthew's Gospel should also be read as inspired and shaped by the central confessions of the earliest believers in Jesus and as attempting to set out the story line that supports those confessions. Throughout the Gospel at least four early Christian confessions reverberate: "Jesus is Israel's Messiah [the Christ]," "Jesus is God's obedient Son," "the eschatological age of redemption has been inaugurated," and "Jesus is humanity's redemptive Lord"—with attention also directed, in the later parts of the Gospel, to the themes of the Messiah's redemptive death on a cross and his resurrection to new life.

The Genealogy (1:1–17) and Infancy Narrative (1:18–2:23)

Matthew's carefully contrived genealogy of 1:1–17, with its three sets of fourteen generations covering the time from Abraham through David to "the Christ," is obviously designed to show that Jesus has the proper pedigree to be Israel's Messiah. Likewise, the evangelist's stress on Jesus as a "son of David" in verses 1, 6, and 17—perhaps even the mere fact of his triple use of the number fourteen, which has in Hebrew the numerical value of David's name (ד = 4; ו = 6; ד = 4)—seems rather patently meant to support Jesus' messiahship. For the most prominent expectation of Jews during the Second Temple period was that God's agent in bringing about the messianic age would be one who could be identified as a "son of David."

The infancy narrative of 1:18–2:23 has often been called an "infancy gospel," simply because it contains a number of features that appear throughout the rest of the Gospel: (1) explicit declarations that Jesus is "the Christ" (1:18; 2:4), (2) clear suggestions that Jesus is uniquely God's Son (1:20–21, 22–23; 2:15), (3) affirmations that Scripture is fulfilled in the events of Jesus' birth (1:22–23; 2:5–6, 15, 17–18, 23), (4) statements that he is "the king of the Jews" and "the ruler and shepherd of Israel" (2:2, 6), and (5) an announcement that his mission is "to save his people from their sins" (1:21). In addition, it includes material highlighting the differences of opinion, which existed from the very beginning, regarding Jesus' person—particularly the opposition of Herod and the Jewish leaders (2:1–12, 16), on the one hand, and the worship of the Magi (2:9–11), on the other. All of these features of the first two chapters present the major christological confessions that the evangelist highlights throughout the rest of his Gospel.

Granted, nowhere in the Matthean infancy narrative is Jesus directly called the Son of God. But there can be no doubt that this is what was intended by (1) the angel's statement that Mary's male child had been conceived by the Holy Spirit (1:20–21), (2) the use of Isa 7:14 in connection with his birth, together with calling him Immanuel, which means "God with us" (1:22–23), and (3) the application of Hos 11:1, "Out of Egypt have I called my son," to his residence in Egypt. Likewise, nowhere in Matthew's infancy narrative is Jesus called Lord or expressly hailed as humanity's redemptive Lord. But redemptive lordship is implied by (1) the name Jesus, which means "Savior" (1:21b), (2) his mission, corresponding to his name, that he was "to save his people from their sins" (1:21c), and (3) the quotation of Mic 5:2 not only to signal his place of birth but also to highlight his function as "the ruler and shepherd of my people Israel" (2:6).

Matthew, however, seems not content with portraying Jesus as the Lord only of Israel. The story of the Magi worshiping Jesus (2:1–12) carries the suggestion of Jesus' lordship over even Gentiles and anticipates other stories in Matthew that depict the submission of Gentiles to Jesus—for example, the Roman centurion who came to Jesus on behalf of his paralyzed servant (8:5–13) and the Canaanite woman who came to him on behalf of her demon-possessed daughter (15:21–28). Furthermore, in the final pericope of this Gospel Jesus is presented as declaring, in strikingly universal terms, "All authority in heaven and on earth has been given to me. Therefore go and make disciples of all nations" (28:18–19; ἔθνη, "nations," which is the word used also for "Gentiles").

The Portrayals of Jesus' Ministry (3:1–25:46)

Moving beyond the genealogy and the infancy narrative, the early Christian confessions regarding Jesus' messiahship, sonship, and lordship all appear, as well, in the portrayals of

Jesus' ministry throughout chapters 3–25: (1) the opening events of his ministry (John the Baptist's testimony, the baptism of Jesus, and the temptation of Jesus in 3:1–4:11), (2) his ministry in Galilee (4:12–18:35), (3) his ministry in Judea (19:1–20:34), and (4) his final ministry in the city of Jerusalem (21:1–25:46). These chapters between the infancy narrative and the passion narrative are based almost entirely on the narrative of Mark's Gospel. But they are not just a reproduction of Mark's account, for they evidence Matthew's own redactional spin on the Markan narrative and include many additional events and large blocks of Jesus' sayings (logia or Q material). Also, throughout these portrayals appears the theme that the messianic age of redemption has been inaugurated, particularly in the repeated references to the fulfillment of Scripture and in the typological allusions.

Jesus as Israel's Messiah (the Christ)

Although Matthew, following Mark, records Peter's confession that Jesus is "the Christ" (16:16), the climactic significance of that confession is somewhat diminished in Matthew, compared with Mark. For Matthew has already presented John the Baptist pointing to Jesus as the Messiah of Israel's expectation (3:3) and being reassured that Jesus is, indeed, "the coming one" of Israel's hopes (11:2–6)—with the rest of that the latter passage also comparing the works of John and the works of Jesus to show that Jesus' works qualified him to be accepted as Israel's Messiah (11:7–19; cf. 17:10–13). Then, after Peter's confession, through the three explicit passion predictions of 16:21, 17:22–23, and 20:17–19 (as also in Mark's Gospel), Matthew portrays Jesus as a suffering Messiah. In addition, throughout his depictions of Jesus' ministry, Matthew's repeated references to Jesus as the messenger of wisdom (11:19, 25–30), the son of David (9:27; 12:23; 15:22; 20:30, 31; 21:9, 15; cf. 22:42, 43, 45), and the nation's eschatological king (21:5; 25:34, 40) identify Jesus as Israel's Messiah.

Jesus the Son of God

The theme of Jesus as God's obedient Son appears far more frequently in Matthew than in Mark, and with a somewhat different nuance. At the very beginning of Jesus' public ministry—at his baptism—Matthew portrays Jesus as declaring that his purpose is "to fulfill all righteousness" (3:15). And in response to such a symbolic act of obedience, God the Father declares, "This is my Son, whom I love; with him I am well pleased" (3:16–17).

In contrast to Mark, where the Father's voice seems to be heard by Jesus alone ("*You are* my Son, whom I love; *with you* I am well pleased"), in Matthew the voice is directed openly to John the Baptist and its message is meant for him (and presumably also for Matthew's readers) as well as for Jesus: "*This is* my Son, whom I love; *with him* I am well pleased". This change of wording becomes highly significant in the context of Matthew's portrayals. For whereas Mark presents Jesus' divine sonship as something hidden from humans until the centurion's affirmation of 15:39 ("Truly, this man was the Son of God"), Matthew presents the sonship of Jesus as a fact that was recognized by others (here by John the Baptist) from the outset of his ministry. This knowledge of Jesus' sonship in Matthew's Gospel is, of course, still a revealed knowledge (cf. 11:25–27; 16:17), but it is more public than in Mark's Gospel.

Likewise, Matthew's account of Jesus' temptations in 4:1–11 (an account derived from Q and absent in Mark) depicts Jesus as the obedient and faithful Son of God. Three times Satan tempts Jesus in his capacity as the Son of God. All three temptations are based on the premise of the divine sonship of Jesus; twice, in fact, they begin with the words "If [i.e., 'Since'] you are the Son of God" (vv. 3, 6). The temptations are depicted as the antitypes of those experienced by Israel in the desert. But whereas God's son Israel broke faith with God, Jesus resists Satan's temptations and is shown to be the Son of God par excellence.

Not only Satan knows that Jesus is God's Son. The demons also recognize his divine sonship, though, of course, their acknowledgments do not amount to any confession of faith. Matthew records only one of Mark's stories in which demons declare that Jesus is "the Son of God" (8:28–34; cf. Mark 5:1–20). The evangelist, it appears, chose to omit Mark's other accounts in which demons recognize Jesus (cf. Mark 1:21–28, 34; 3:11) evidently because he did not have the same interest in Jesus' activities as an exorcist. But Matthew heightens the disciples' awareness of Jesus' filial relationship with God, for he presents them as truly exhibiting faith in Jesus as God's Son. Thus, whereas Mark's account of Jesus walking on the water ends with the disciples in a state of complete confusion and misunderstanding (Mark 6:51–52), Matthew portrays them as worshiping Jesus, saying, "Truly, you are the Son of God" (14:33). And whereas in Mark's Gospel Peter confesses Jesus to be "the Christ," Matthew adds to Peter's lips the words "the Son of the living God" (16:16; cf. Mark 8:29).

The Eschatological Age of Redemption Has Been Inaugurated

The concept of fulfillment, which underlies the early Christian confession "the eschatological age of redemption has been inaugurated," characterizes virtually all that Matthew says about Jesus. This idea comes to the fore in Matthew's ten fulfillment formula quotations of 1:23; 2:15, 18, 23 (in his infancy narrative); 4:15–16; 8:17; 12:18–21; 13:35; 21:5 (in his portrayals of Jesus' ministry); and 27:9–10 (in his passion narrative). Even more expressly, Jesus' declaration "I have not come to abolish [the law or the prophets] but to fulfill them" in 5:17, together with the antitheses he sets up in 5:21–48 between the Mosaic traditions and his own teaching, demonstrate that a new era of fulfillment has arrived.

Similarly, when Jesus is asked why his disciples do not fast like the Pharisees, he says, "How can the guests of the bridegroom mourn while he is with them? The time will come when the bridegroom will be taken away from them; then they will fast" (9:14–15). This comment about a new time is then reinforced by sayings about the impossibility of a "new patch" being sewn on an old garment or of "new wine" being poured into old wineskins (9:16–17)—which sayings proclaim the presence of a new age of fulfillment in the ministry of Jesus, a new age that cannot just be equated with the old age.

Somewhat obliquely—though nonetheless integrally in support of the confessions regarding Jesus' obedient sonship and inauguration of a new age of fulfillment—Matthew parallels the life and ministry of Jesus, on the one hand, and the experiences of the

nation Israel and Israel's leader Moses, on the other. Throughout his
Gospel, particularly in the first half, the evangelist depicts Jesus as
the Jew who recapitulates the experiences of the nation, but now as
the obedient Son/Messiah in contrast to disobedient Israel—even,
in certain sections, as the "new Moses" who saves his people in a new
way. The following portrayals of Jesus have often been seen as significant in paralleling the OT portrayals of Israel and Moses:

(1) Jesus as a child of promise	1:18–23; cf. Gen 12:3; 18:1–19; 21:1–7
(2) Jesus delivered from Herod's slaughter	2:1–18; cf. Exod 1:15–2:10
(3) Jesus called out of Egypt	2:15; cf. Hos 11:1; also 2:19–21; cf. Exod 4:19–20
(4) Jesus passing through the waters	3:3–17; cf. Exod 14:10–31
(5) Jesus entering the wilderness for testing	4:1–11; cf. Exod 16:1–17:7; 24:18; 32:1–35; 34:28; Deut 6:13, 16; 8:3
(6) Jesus calling out the "twelve sons of Israel"	4:18–22; cf. Num 1:1–16
(7) Jesus giving the law from the mountain	5:1–7:29; cf. Exod 19:1–23:33; 34:1–28
(8) Jesus performing ten miracles	8:1–9:38; cf. Exod 7:1–12:51
(9) Jesus sending out twelve disciples to "conquer" the land	10:1–42; cf. Num 13:1–25
(10) Jesus feeding the multitudes with "manna" from heaven	14:15–21; 15:32–39; cf. Exod 16:1–36
(11) Jesus transfigured before his disciples	17:1–13; cf. Exod 24:12–18; 34:29–35

Many interpreters have sketched out such parallels.[11] Not all of the parallels proposed, however, are equally evident or compelling. But the general similarities between Jesus and the experiences of the nation of Israel, which appear mainly in the first half of Matthew's gospel, cannot easily be dismissed. And this parallelism goes a long way in support of the confessions "Jesus is God's obedient Son" and "the eschatological age of redemption has been inaugurated."

Jesus as Lord

The evangelist uses "lord" (κύριος; κύριε in the vocative) in a number of ways: (1) as an honorific title for God, (2) as a description of a character in a parable or of some anonymous "master," (3) as a polite form of address ("sir") for Jesus, and (4) as an honorific title for Jesus connoting divine authority or majesty. More important for this discussion of the confession "Jesus is humanity's redemptive Lord," however, is the fact that whereas in Matthew's Gospel strangers and opponents (and later Judas Iscariot) usually address Jesus as "Teacher" (διδάσκαλε) or "Rabbi" (ῥαββί), but not as "Lord" (κύριε), the disciples and those who come to him for healing never address him as "Teacher" or "Rabbi" but always as "Lord." This linguistic usage has led Günther Bornkamm to declare that "the title and address of Jesus as *kyrios* in Matthew have throughout the character of a divine Name of Majesty."[12]

Bornkamm may have somewhat overstated the case. For it is not always easy to determine whether Matthew intended the vocative κύριε, when ascribed to Jesus, to signify merely a polite form of address ("sir") or some type of honorific "confession" regarding Jesus' person or authority. It is not clear, for example, just how those who came to Jesus for healing viewed him when they addressed him as "Lord" (cf. 8:2–4; 8:5–13; 9:27–31; 15:21–28; 17:14–18; 20:29–34).

With the disciples, however, the situation is quite different. They are portrayed in Matthew's Gospel as "transparent" examples for Christians in the evangelist's own time, and so their address of Jesus as "Lord" should be seen as signaling a confessional stance. Thus, according to Matthew, true disciples of Jesus call him Lord—even in 8:21, where "another man, one of his disciples," responds, "Lord, first let me go and bury my father."

Elsewhere in portraying Jesus' ministry, the evangelist certainly uses the title "Lord" (κύριος) of Jesus in a manner that reflects something of a confessional stance: (1) in 3:3, where the Isaian phrase "Prepare the way for the Lord!" is used to epitomize the preaching of John the Baptist about Jesus; (2) in 12:8, where Jesus speaks of himself as "Lord of the Sabbath"; and (3) in 21:3, where Jesus instructs his disciples to tell anyone who asks about their taking a donkey and her colt to Jesus, "The Lord needs them." Furthermore, in three eschatological passages Jesus is ascribed the title "Lord" in an honorific sense: (1) in 7:21–22, with its twice-repeated cry of "Lord, Lord" by those who desire to enter the kingdom of heaven but cannot; (2) in 24:42, with its exhortation to believers to "keep watch, because you do not know on what day your Lord will come"; and (3) in 25:37, 44, where both the righteous (the "sheep") and the wicked (the "goats") address the glorified Son of Man, the eschatological king who sits in judgment, as "Lord."

Perhaps the most significant text in Matthew's Gospel on Jesus' lordship is 22:41–46. This account also appears in Mark 12:35–37 (and Luke 20:41–44), but Matthew has added a postscript: "No one could say a word in reply, and from that day on no one dared to ask him any more questions" (v. 46). In this passage, which appears at the end of a number of actions, parables, and controversies in chapters 21–22 that pit Jesus against the Jewish leaders, Jesus asks them, "What do you think about the Christ? Whose son is he?" The Pharisees answer, "The son of David!" Jesus, however, arguing on the basis of Ps 110:1, insists that he should be thought of in terms of "Lord."

Matthew 22:41–46, with its synoptic parallels, undoubtedly depicts a historical incident, for it reflects the kind of opposition that Jesus often must have met. More than that, it (1) presents a new interpretation of Psalm 110, (2) proposes a new understanding of messiahship, and (3) suggests a new appreciation of Jesus as humanity's promised Lord. From Matthew's later perspective, it also seems to support the early Christian confession "Jesus is humanity's redemptive Lord."

The Passion Narrative (26:1–27:66) and Resurrection Account (28:1–20)

Matthew's passion narrative continues many of the confessional themes seen earlier in his portrayals of Jesus' ministry. For example, "Jesus is the Christ" culminates in Matthew, as it does in Mark, with Jesus' affirmative response to the high priest's adjuration ("Tell us if you are the Christ, the Son of God"): "You have so said" (26:64). Likewise, that the confession "Jesus is Lord" is the proper acclamation of true disciples, as opposed to those who are only strangers or opponents, is nowhere more evident than in Matthew's account of the Last Supper (26:17–30). For after Jesus declares that one of the Twelve will betray him, the disciples say one after another, "Surely not I, Lord!" (v. 22; cf. Mark 14:19, "Is it I?"; no parallel in Luke). But Judas Iscariot says, "Surely not I, Rabbi!" (v. 25; no parallel in Mark or Luke).

The prayer voiced by Jesus in Gethsemane, which occurs in all three Synoptic Gospels (Mark 14:36; Matt 26:39; Luke 22:42)—as well as in the Fourth Gospel (John 12:27)—is the most significant support for the confession "Jesus is God's obedient Son," a theme that has resonated throughout Matthew's presentations of the ministry of Jesus. None of the evangelists, of course, have included the title "Son of God" in their accounts of this Gethsemane experience. But certainly ideas about Jesus' filial relation to God and his faithful obedience to the Father's will feature prominently in the Gethsemane prayer: "My Father, if it is possible, may this cup be taken from me. Yet not as I will, but as you will!" (Matt 26:39).

Matthew has his own emphases in his Gospel. And here, although the depictions of Jesus' Gethsemane experience in Mark and Matthew are similar, Matthew goes his own way by repeating the essence of Jesus' words the second time he prays (26:42; Mark 14:39 has only "saying the same words") and then by stating that the third time "he prayed . . . saying the same words" (26:44; no parallel in Mark). Thus Matthew has, by repeating Jesus' prayer, laid greater stress on the agony felt by Jesus and highlighted, at least to a degree, the concepts of divine sonship and faithful obedience.

Furthermore, three references to Jesus as the "Son of God" appear explicitly in Matthew's portrayal of Jesus' crucifixion. The first is on the lips of "those who passed by": "Come down from the cross, if you are the Son of God!" (27:40). The second is ascribed to "the chief priests, scribes, and elders": "Let God now rescue him if he wants him, for he said, 'I am the Son of God'" (27:43). These two taunts are contrasted with a third statement, that of the Roman centurion, which parallels Mark's account: "Truly, this [man] was the Son of God" (27:54; cf. Mark 15:39).

The centurion's response in Matthew, however, follows on the heels of a number of references to natural and supernatural occurrences—the veil of the temple being torn in two, an earthquake, tombs being opened, "the bodies of many holy people" being raised, and those who were resurrected going into Jerusalem and appearing to many people (27:51–53). The centurion is terrified at "all that had happened" (27:54). So, whereas in Mark the centurion's confession is directly linked to Jesus' death, in Matthew this correlation with Jesus' death is, to an extent, somewhat blunted, for in Matthew's portrayal the confession is made in the context of a whole series of events at the time of Jesus' crucifixion.

Concerning the confession about Jesus' redemptive death on a cross, Matthew generally continues the emphases set out by Mark. Matthew's three passion predictions of 16:21–28, 17:22–23, and 20:17–19 are largely comparable to those of Mark, although Matthew has dislocated and altered Mark's second passion prediction (18:1–5; cf. Mark 9:33–37). Likewise, the events of Jesus' passion in Matthew's Gospel are presented in a similar fashion and with similar emphases as in Mark's Gospel.

Of greater significance, perhaps, is Matthew's addition to Jesus' words of institution at the Last Supper: "This is my blood of the covenant, which is poured out for many *for the forgiveness of sins*" (26:28). The phrase "for the forgiveness of sins"—which was omitted in Matthew's report of the preaching of John the Baptist (cf. 3:2; note its inclusion in Mark 1:4 and Luke 3:3)—is here associated by Matthew with Jesus' death. It appears, therefore, that Matthew wanted his readers to understand that forgiveness of sins was only possible through the death of Christ, not just through John's baptism. Thus, in so formulating the words of institution, Matthew has provided further support for the confession regarding Christ's redemptive death on a cross: it is only through Christ's "blood of the covenant, which is poured out for many," that "forgiveness of sins" is possible.

■ 3. LUKE'S GOSPEL AND ACTS

Luke's Gospel and Acts were written as two volumes of a single work, and therefore they must always be considered together. Probably the work was written by a Gentile Christian, whom early Christian tradition has identified as Paul's associate Luke. It is addressed to a Gentile named Theophilus (Luke 1:3; Acts 1:1), apparently a recent convert who, in order to understand better his new faith, needed an account of how the Christian faith began and how it developed: "It seemed good to me also to write an orderly account for you, most excellent Theophilus, so that you may know the certainty of the things you have been taught" (Luke 1:3–4). Evidently Theophilus was expected not only to read the two volumes himself but also to circulate them among other Gentiles of his acquaintance—among Gentiles who were already believers in Jesus, among Gentiles who were only interested, or among both.

As an account written by and for Gentiles, and therefore styled and nuanced along the lines of Gentile interests, Luke's Gospel must be seen to be (1) more removed from the events narrated than those of Mark or Matthew; (2) more interested in a broader range of issues and topics than Mark or Matthew; and (3) presenting a more developed understanding of the Christian movement than the other Synoptic Gospels. Though neither an eyewitness of the ministry of Jesus nor one of the earliest believers, Luke declares that he has "carefully investigated everything from the beginning" (Luke 1:3a). And it is his careful use of sources, which has preserved the basic thrust of the materials on which he depended, that allows an investigation of the Lukan writings with respect to the confessional materials of early Christianity.

The Preface (1:1–4), Infancy Narrative (1:5–2:52), and Prologue (3:1–4:13) of the Gospel, with Attendant Themes in Acts

As a Gentile writing to Gentiles, Luke may be presumed to have had wider interests than those of a Jew writing to Jews. And this seems to be the case. For example, his prologue of 3:1–4:13 in his first volume (1) speaks of John the Baptist's ministry as taking place during the reigns of the Roman rulers Pontius Pilate in Judea, Herod in Galilee, Philip in Ituraea and Trachonitis, and Lysanias in Abilene, as well as during the time of the high priests Annas and Caiaphas at Jerusalem (3:1–2a); (2) extends the quotation of Isa 40:3 to include "every valley," "every mountain," and "all flesh" as affected by "the salvation of God" (3:5–6); and (3) traces Jesus' lineage back through seventy-seven generations to God himself (3:23–38; cf. Matt 1:1–17, which begins with Abraham, goes through David and the Jewish deportation to Babylon, and ends with the Messiah).

God as the Initiator, Sustainer, and Ultimate Agent of Redemption

The infancy narrative of 1:5–2:52, particularly in its three canticles and its depiction of praise by the "heavenly host," not only incorporates this wider scope of Luke's interests but also lays stress on God as the initiator and ultimate agent of redemption. For not only do these materials hint at a broader application of God's salvation than was often visualized by Jews (cf., e.g., 2:31–33, "which you have prepared in the sight of all people, a light for revelation to the Gentiles and for glory to your people Israel"), they also identify God as the one who has originated and brought to completion all that is proclaimed in the Christian gospel. And in so doing, they both reflect and support one of the major confessions of the early church, that "God is the initiator, sustainer, and ultimate agent of redemption."

This theme is prominent in Mary's Magnificat, which, reflecting Hannah's hymn of praise (1 Sam 2:1–10) and OT language generally, speaks of "God my Savior" who "has done great things for me" (1:46–55). It appears more explicitly in Zechariah's Benedictus:

> He has come and has redeemed his people. He has raised a horn
> of salvation for us . . . salvation from our enemies . . . to remember
> his holy covenant . . . to rescue us from the hand of our enemies . .
> . to give his people the knowledge of salvation through the for-
> giveness of sins because of the tender mercy of our God. (1:68–79)

It appears also in Simeon's Nunc Dimittis:

> My eyes have seen your salvation, which you have prepared in the
> sight of all people, a light for revelation to the Gentiles and for
> glory to your people Israel. (2:29–32)

And the Gloria in Excelsis of the angelic host says much the same
thing: "Glory to God in the highest, and on earth peace to people
whom he has favored" (2:14).

In the speeches of Acts the theme of God as the initiator,
sustainer, and ultimate agent of redemption is prominent as
well. Peter, for example, explains the unusual phenomena at
Pentecost:

> God has raised this Jesus to life, and we are all witnesses of the
> fact. Exalted to the right hand of God, he has received from the
> Father the promised Holy Spirit, and has poured out what you
> now see and hear. . . . Therefore let all Israel be assured of this:
> God has made this Jesus whom you crucified both Lord and
> Christ. (2:33, 36)

Similar words are attributed to Peter in his temple sermon
(3:12–26) and his speeches before the Jewish Sanhedrin (4:8–12;
5:29–32). And Paul, too, highlights the initiative and redemptive action of God in his speeches (cf. 13:16–41, esp. 32–39;
17:30–31).

Regardless of what might be thought regarding the origin
and composition of the speeches of Acts, the important point
here is that they portray God as the initiator and ultimate agent
of redemption. Thus they serve to support a major confession of
the early Christian church.

The Inauguration of the Eschatological Age

Luke's infancy narrative also contains support for the
confession "the eschatological age of redemption has been
inaugurated." All of the above passages regarding God as the

agent of redemption apply here as well. In addition, the annunciation to Zechariah of John's birth includes the statement "he will
go on before the Lord, in the spirit and power of Elijah, to turn
the hearts of the fathers to their children and . . . to make ready a
people prepared for the Lord" (1:17). This clear allusion to the
eschatological prophecy of Mal 4:5–6 suggests that with John the
Baptist the penultimate stage of history has arrived.

Also to be noted is the announcement to Mary about the
birth of Jesus: "He will be great and will be called the Son of the
Most High. The Lord God will give him the throne of his father
David, and he will reign over the house of Jacob forever; his kingdom will never end" (1:32–33). Here is a direct statement that the
time of eschatological fulfillment will be inaugurated by the ministry of Jesus.

Furthermore, at the beginning of Luke's prologue, when
John begins his ministry of "preaching a baptism of repentance
for the forgiveness of sins," the words of Isa 40:3–5 are quoted in
3:4–6—words that speak of preparing the way for the Lord and
assert that all humanity will see God's salvation. The application
of this messianic testimonium to John's ministry signals that the
final age of redemption has been inaugurated.

Jesus as Christ, Lord, Son of God, and Savior

The infancy narrative of Luke's Gospel also refers to Jesus
as Israel's promised Messiah. In 2:11 an angel announces to the
shepherds the good news about Jesus: "A Savior has been born to
you, who is Christ, the Lord." In 2:26 Luke tells his readers that it
had been revealed to Simeon that he would not die before seeing
"the Lord's Christ." Furthermore, the angel's announcement of
Jesus in 2:11, which proclaims him to be the "Christ" (Χριστός),
also calls him "Savior" (σωτήρ) and "Lord" (κύριος).

Both Luke's infancy narrative and his prologue speak of
Jesus as the Son of God. In the infancy narrative Jesus' divine
sonship is revealed to Mary from the time of conception by the
announcement that her child "shall be called the Son of the
Highest" (1:32) and "the Son of God" (1:35). When the twelve-
year-old Jesus calls the Jerusalem temple "my Father's house"
(2:49), it underlines his special filial relationship to God (2:49).

Likewise, in his prologue Luke repeats from Mark's Gospel the words of the heavenly voice at Jesus' baptism: "You are my Son, the Beloved. With you I am well pleased" (3:22; cf. Mark 1:11). But whereas this attestation is presented in Mark as a private epiphany to Jesus, in Luke it seems to have been a public manifestation, for Luke takes pains to mention that "all the people" were present (3:21) and that "the Holy Spirit descended on him in bodily form like a dove" (3:22). And in the Lukan temptation account, which was evidently derived from Q, Satan premises his challenge with the same words as appear in Matthew: "If [i.e., 'Since'] you are the Son of God" (4:3, 9; cf. Matt 4:3, 6).

The Portrayals of Jesus' Ministry (4:14–21:38), with Attendant Themes in Acts

A number of early Christian confessional themes are interwoven in Luke's portrayals of Jesus' ministry (in his Gospel) and the church's ministries (in his Acts). Often they are presented in a more developed and homogenized fashion than in Mark or Matthew, though with the various strands still somewhat distinguishable. And often they are presented with a slightly different spin from that found in the other Synoptic Gospels.

The Inauguration of the Eschatological Age

In his Gospel, Luke rarely uses fulfillment language for Jesus' ministry. The verb "fulfill" (πληρόω), which appears twice in Mark (1:15; 14:49) and fourteen times in Matthew (1:22; 2:15, 17, 23; 3:15; 4:14; 5:17; 8:17; 12:17; 13:35; 21:4; 26:54, 56; 27:9), appears only twice in Luke—in 4:21 and 24:44 (though the verb τελέω in this sense is used also in 18:31; 22:37). The first instance occurs in the Nazareth pericope (4:16–30), which functions in Luke's writings as the "frontispiece," the "programmatic prologue," or the "main pillar" for all that the evangelist writes in his two volumes. Here Luke, alone among the synoptic evangelists, reports that after Jesus had read Isa 61:1–2a in his hometown synagogue, he declared, "Today this scripture is fulfilled in your hearing" (4:21). Jesus was thereby asserting that the messianic age was being inaugurated in his ministry. And in his recording of Jesus' words, Luke was evidently seeking to support the early church's confession that "the eschatological age of redemption has been inaugurated."

In Acts, as in his Gospel, Luke does not often use explicit fulfillment language (πληρόω, in the sense of fulfilling the Scriptures, is present only in Acts 3:18; 13:27, 33; τελέω, in 13:29). Yet the notion that the age of fulfillment has been brought about by Jesus runs throughout the speeches attributed to Peter (2:14–36; 3:12–26; 4:8–12; 5:29–32; 10:34–43; 11:4–17), Stephen (7:2–53), James (15:13–21), and Paul (13:16–41; 14:14–17; 17:22–31; 22:3–21; 26:2–23). In Acts 2, for example, a sense of fulfillment pervades the whole of Peter's Pentecost sermon. More pointedly, the concept of a presently inaugurated eschatological age comes to expression in his argument that Christ's resurrection and exaltation to God's right hand are the factors that have brought about the Holy Spirit's presence among Christians (vv. 22–35), which event is also depicted as the fulfillment of Joel's prophecy regarding "the last days" when God will pour out his Spirit on all people (vv. 16–21).

Likewise, the idea of an eschatological age that has been presently inaugurated is clearly expressed in Peter's sermon of Acts 3, particularly in verses 22–26:

> Moses said, "The Lord your God will raise up for you a prophet like me from among the people; you must listen to everything he tells you. Anyone who does not listen to him will be completely cut off from among his people" [quoting Deut 18:18–19].
>
> Indeed, all the prophets from Samuel on, as many as have spoken, have foretold these days. And you are heirs of the prophets and of the covenant God made with your ancestors. He said to Abraham, "Through your offspring all people on earth will be blessed" [quoting Gen 22:18; 26:4]. When God raised up his servant, he sent him first to you to bless you by turning each of you from his or her wicked ways.

Also, Paul's sermon in a synagogue at Pisidian Antioch, as reported in Acts 13:16–41, repeats some of these same themes (e.g., the significance of David, the fulfillment of the prophets' words, and the resurrection of Jesus), which are culminated concisely in the sermon's closing proclamation of verses 32–33: "We tell you the good news: What God promised our fathers he has fulfilled for us, their children, by raising Jesus from the dead."[13]

Jesus as Israel's Messiah (the Christ)

The confession "Jesus is Israel's Messiah" is reflected a number of times in Luke's Gospel, though without the emphasis given it in either Mark or Matthew. In the main, Luke only repeats the confession from Mark's Gospel, principally in his account of Peter's confession (9:20, "[You are] the Christ of God"; cf. Mark 8:29), but he also clarifies the demons' reaction to Jesus from simply "they knew who he was" (Mark 1:34) to "they knew he was the Christ" (Luke 4:41). Likewise, Luke includes all four of Mark's references to Jesus as the "son of David" in 18:38, 39 and 20:41, 44. And his reference to Jesus as "king" in 19:38, quoting Ps 118:26, evidently derives from Mark as well.

All of these titles in Luke's Gospel have a messianic content, for "son of David" was virtually synonymous with "Christ" among the Jews and "king" points to an expectation that the Messiah would be of royal descent and a kingly deliverer of Israel. Yet though the theme of Jesus' messiahship was important for Luke, and so repeated from his Markan source, Luke's emphasis in portraying the ministry of Jesus in his Gospel appears not to have been on Jesus as simply *Israel's* Messiah.

In the speeches of Acts, however, there is a particularly strong emphasis on Jesus as the Messiah. Early Christian proclamation, as Luke presents it, made the messiahship of Jesus the focus of its message—particularly in proclaiming the good news to Jews. This is evident in the following representative texts from Acts:

2:36	Let all Israel be assured of this: God has made this Jesus whom you crucified both Lord and Christ.
3:18–20	But this is how God fulfilled what he had foretold through all the prophets, saying that his Christ would suffer. Repent, then, and turn to God, so that your sins may be wiped out, that times of refreshing may come from the Lord, and that he may send the Christ, who has been appointed for you—even Jesus.
5:42	Day after day, in the temple courts and from house to house, they never stopped teaching and proclaiming the good news that Jesus is the Christ.

8:5	Philip went down to a city in Samaria and proclaimed there the Christ.
9:22	Saul grew more and more powerful and baffled the Jews living in Damascus by proving that Jesus is the Christ.
17:2–3	Paul went into the synagogue, and on three Sabbath days he reasoned with them from the Scriptures, explaining and proving that the Christ had to suffer and rise from the dead.
18:5	Paul devoted himself exclusively to preaching, testifying to the Jews that Jesus was the Christ.
18:28	[Apollos] vigorously refuted the Jews in public debate, proving from the Scriptures that Jesus was the Christ.
26:22–23	[Paul declared before Agrippa II, who was a benefactor of the Jews and knowledgeable about their traditions] I am saying nothing beyond what the prophets and Moses said would happen—that the Christ would suffer and, as the first to rise from the dead, would proclaim light to his own people and to the Gentiles.

Jesus as the Son of God

In his portrayals of Jesus' ministry in 4:14–21:38—that is, in the material between his infancy narrative and prologue, on the one side, and his passion narrative and resurrection account, on the other—Luke retains the same passages and much the same emphasis on Jesus as the Son of God as do his sources, Mark and Q. In 4:41 the demons' acclamation "You are the Son of God" is here added to Mark 1:34, but it is included later in Mark 3:11 in a similar situation. In 8:28 the Gerasene demoniac cries out, "Jesus, Son of the Most High God," exactly as in Mark 5:7. In 9:35 the heavenly voice at Jesus' transfiguration proclaims, "This is my chosen Son; listen to him!"—which is only a slightly altered version of the proclamation in Mark 9:6, "This is my beloved Son; listen to him!" In 22:20, at his trial before the Sanhedrin, Jesus is asked, "Are you, then, the Son of God?," which is a reformulation of the question in Mark 14:61, "Are you the Messiah, the Son of the Blessed One?" Furthermore, Luke's depiction of Jesus' Father-Son language in 10:22 and 20:13 reproduces, almost exactly, the materials found in Q (cf. Matt 11:27) and Mark (cf. Mark 12:6; Matt 21:37). Three conclusions may be drawn from this data: (1) that in his portrayal of Jesus as "the Son of God" in 4:14–21:38 Luke depended completely on his sources; (2) that he was quite traditional in his treatment of this christological theme, without further nuancing or emphasis; and (3) that by retaining this feature he was, in effect, like his sources, supporting the early Christian confession "Jesus is the Son of God."

In Acts the declaration that Jesus is the Son of God is not nearly as prevalent as the proclamation that Jesus is the Messiah. Two passages, however, speak of Jesus as God's Son. The first, in 9:20, reports that after his conversion Paul "began at once to preach in the synagogues that Jesus is the Son of God," and then adds two verses later, in 9:22, that he also proclaimed that "Jesus is the Christ." The second, in 13:33, presents Paul, in a speech to Jews in the synagogue at Pisidian Antioch, as quoting Ps 2:7 in support of his preaching about Jesus' resurrection: "You are my Son; today I have become your Father." This latter verse, as does also the confession of Rom 1:3–4, associates Jesus' sonship with an acceptance of his resurrection. Such an association seems to have been the original context for the earliest believers' affirmation that "Jesus is the Son of God." By Luke's time, however, the divine sonship of Jesus was being also traced back through various events in Jesus' ministry (as seen in the first half of Matthew's Gospel)—even to his conception (as noted earlier in Luke 1:31–35).

Taking an overall look at Luke's references to Jesus as "the Son" or "the Son of God," we can make two points about the evangelist's redactional treatment. First, Luke understood "Son of God" in a messianic sense—or, to put the matter somewhat better, he conceived of the titles "Messiah" and "Son of God" as somehow joined in meaning. Ideas about Jesus' messianic status and his divine sonship are linked at a number of places in Luke's writings: (1) in the annunciation to Mary, where the angel declares that Jesus "will be called Son of the Most High" and will receive

"the throne of his father David" (Luke 1:32–33); (2) in Jesus' baptism, where his sonship is proclaimed and he receives a kind of
messianic investiture (Luke 3:21–22); (3) in Jesus' confrontation
with demons, where, although they shout out, "You are the Son
of God," Jesus rebukes them "because they knew he was the
Christ" (Luke 4:41); (4) in Peter's confession, which Luke formu-
lates to read, "The Christ of God" (Luke 9:20; cf. Mark 8:29; see
also Luke 23:35 for the same wording as in 9:20); (5) in the transfiguration scene, where the heavenly voice declares Jesus' sonship and Moses and Elijah talk with Jesus about the messianic
sufferings that he "was about to accomplish at Jerusalem" (Luke
9:31; cf. 9:22, 43–45; 18:31–34); (6) in Jesus' trial before the Sanhedrin, where, according to Luke's reformulation, the Sanhedrin
asks the double question "If you are the Messiah, tell us!" (an implied question) and "Are you, then, the Son of God?" (Luke
22:67–70); and (7) in the report of Paul's early preaching, which
highlights the two confessional themes "Jesus is the Son of God"
and "Jesus is the Christ" (Acts 9:20, 22).

In view of this linking of "Messiah" and "Son of God," it
may seem somewhat strange that Luke, in his Gospel, never puts
the title "Son of God" on the lips of the disciples or others, with
the exception of the question posed by the Sanhedrin in 22:70
(contrast the centurion's statement in Mark 15:39, the disciples'
acclamation in Matt 14:33, Peter's confession in Matt 16:16, and
the taunts of the crowd, the Jewish leaders, and others at Jesus'
crucifixion in Matt 27:40–44). But this omission probably only
serves to show, as suggested above, that for Luke the concept of
Son of God is subsumed under that of Messiah. Thus in Luke the
confession of Peter, "[You are] the Christ of God," explicitly proclaims Jesus' messianic status but does not speak of the Messiah
as the Son of God, although certainly ideas about Jesus' sonship
were implied by this confession. The two concepts, however, are
not just juxtaposed by Luke, as in the Gospels of Mark and Matthew; rather, in Luke's writings "Messiah" has the pride of place
and "Son of God" is subsumed under it. Perhaps such an explanation also accounts for the fact that only twice in Acts is "Son of
God" mentioned in connection with the early preaching, whereas
"Messiah" is central and climactic.

A second point can also be made about Luke's redactional treatment of the title "Son of God": the evangelist tends to emphasize in his usage a heightened sense of the intimacy of Jesus' relation with God his Father. This feature of intimacy is evident in the Gospel's reports about Jesus' growth (2:40, 52), in its story about Jesus as a boy in the Jerusalem temple (2:49), in its reproduction of Jesus' Father-Son language (10:22; 20:13; cf. also 22:29 and 23:46 in the passion narrative and 24:49 in the resurrection account), and in its depictions of Jesus' prayer life (3:21; 6:12; 9:18, 28; 11:1; 22:42), particularly—to anticipate a later discussion—his Gethsemane prayer (22:39–45).

In sum, Luke in his two volumes presents the confessions "Jesus is the Messiah" and "Jesus is the Son of God" in a fairly traditional manner, though also with some of his own redactional spin. He does not juxtapose the titles "Messiah" and "Son of God," as did Mark and Matthew. Rather, he seems to think of the former as the preeminent title, with the latter subsumed under it and implied. Furthermore, more than either Mark or Matthew, Luke tends to emphasize the feature of intimacy in the relation of the Son with the Father.

Jesus as Lord

"Lord" as a designation for Jesus appears frequently in Luke's two volumes—about forty-two times in his Gospel, compared with four times in Mark and nineteen times in Matthew, and some fifty-three times in Acts. But since "Lord" is used for both God and Jesus, it is not always easy, particularly in Acts, to determine exactly when it refers specifically to Jesus. Furthermore, since the term signals both respectful address ("sir") and worshipful acclamation ("Divine Sovereign"), with various shades of meaning between these two extremes as well, it is not always easy to precisely identify its significance.

Luke's Gospel, however, offers little support for the view that Jesus was acclaimed by anyone, whether disciples or others, as Lord in a worshipful sense *before* his resurrection. In the Lukan portrayals of Jesus' ministry, the vocative "Lord" (κύριε) appears nineteen times on the lips of others addressing Jesus, and "Master" (ἐπιστάτα), a synonym for "Lord," seven times on the lips of

Jesus' disciples. But the fact that "Teacher" (διδάσκαλε) takes the place of "Lord" or "Master" in eleven similar situations in Luke's Gospel suggests that "Lord" and "Master" had no special significance in addressing Jesus during his ministry beyond that of respectful address—often, of course, profound respect, but not necessarily worshipful acclamation.

The synoptic parallels to Luke's vocative uses of "Lord" and "Master" seem to confirm the fact that in "triple tradition" passages they are not to be seen as having special significance: (1) ἐπιστάτα in Luke 8:24, but διδάσκαλε in Mark 4:38 and κύριε in Matt 8:25; (2) ἐπιστάτα in Luke 9:33, but ῥαββί in Mark 9:5 and κύριε in Matt 17:4; (3) διδάσκαλε in Luke 9:38 and Mark 9:17, but κύριε in Matt 17:15; and (4) κύριε in Luke 18:41 and Matt 20:31, 33, but ῥαββουνί in Mark 10:51. Only in Mark 7:28 and Matt 15:27, in the response of a Gentile woman from Syrian Phoenicia ("Yes, Lord, but even the dogs under the table eat the children's crumbs"), is there a rather clear acclamation of Jesus in the Synoptic Gospels that uses the vocative κύριε. But though Jesus interpreted her response as worshipful acclamation (cf. Mark 7:29; Matt 15:28), it is uncertain what she herself actually intended. Furthermore, it needs to be noted that Luke did not include this pericope in his Gospel.

Yet Luke's Gospel frequently uses "the Lord" (ὁ κύριος) for Jesus, though the title appears only in certain non-Markan narrative portions of the Gospel. This pattern of usage probably reflects Luke's own more developed christological terminology. The only exception to this pattern is found in 19:31, 34 (cf. Mark 11:3; Matt 21:3), where Jesus instructs his disciples what to say to those who object to their loosing and taking the donkey: "The Lord has need of him." It may be debated, however, whether Jesus here had himself in mind as the referent of the title or, as seems more likely, he meant "God has need of him."

But even if it is claimed that Jesus spoke of himself as "the Lord" in 19:31, he is represented in 22:11 (cf. Mark 14:14; Matt 26:18) as referring to himself as "the teacher" (ὁ διδάσκαλος) in a similar set of instructions on preparations for the Passover. This suggests, perhaps, that these two titles could be used interchangeably. And going beyond Luke's portrayals of Jesus' ministry in his Gospel, the title "Lord" appears on the lips of others as a christological ascription only in the report of the two from Emmaus to the Eleven at Jerusalem: "The Lord is risen indeed!" (24:34). But this is an acclamation voiced by followers of Jesus *after* his resurrection.

The title "the Lord," as distinct from the vocative "Lord," was not, it seems, used of Jesus in Luke's sayings source, Q. Furthermore, it is found only once, as noted above, in his narrative source, that is, Mark 11:3, where Jesus instructs his disciples to say "the Lord has need of him" when questioned about taking the donkey—which is a debatable identification, as already mentioned. It thus appears that in presenting the teachings and activities of Jesus, Luke has not changed his sources in his use—or, better, his nonuse—of the title "the Lord" for Jesus during his ministry.

Nonetheless, "the Lord" as a christological title is used twelve times in non-Markan narrative portions of Luke's portrayals of Jesus' ministry, where it appears as an equivalent to the name Jesus (cf. 7:13, 19; 10:1, 39, 41; 11:39; 12:42; 13:15; 17:5, 6; 18:6; 19:8; see also later in 22:61 [twice] and 24:3). Thus, whereas Mark and Matthew almost never designate Jesus as "the Lord" in their narrative portions—the single exception possibly being the saying "The Lord has need of it" in Mark 11:3; Matt 21:3 (also Luke 19:31, 34), which is disputed as referring to Jesus—the identification of Jesus as "the Lord" is so frequent in the distinctive narrative material of Luke's Gospel as to be characteristic of the evangelist.

Furthermore, in Luke's infancy narrative Elizabeth's identification of Mary as "the mother of my Lord" (1:43) is striking, especially in a context where "Lord" otherwise refers to God (cf. 1:28, 32, 38, 45). Similarly, in both the infancy narrative and the prologue, references to John's work of preparing "the way of the Lord" (1:76; 3:4) apply an OT reference to God in a new way to Jesus. Finally, the resurrection account reports that the women did not find the body of "the Lord Jesus" (24:3).

Throughout Luke's telling of the gospel story, therefore, there seem to be two features running side by side without becoming entwined—except, perhaps, in Jesus' instructions of 19:31. The first is that in Luke's portrayal of *what the characters in the story know* about Jesus, they confess him as Lord only *after* his resurrection.

The second is that Luke, the narrator, when not controlled by his Markan and logia sources, *lets his implied reader (and readers) understand that Jesus is the Lord right from the start.* Thus Luke in his Gospel presents us with both a preresurrection understanding of Jesus, which stems from his sources, and a postresurrection understanding of Jesus, which is a product of the church's confessions and his own experience.

In Acts, however, the title "Lord" has a prominent place in both the speeches and the narrative of the activities of the early church. As mentioned earlier, it is not always easy to determine when the term refers specifically to Jesus. In such phrases as "the fear of the Lord" (9:31), "the grace of the Lord" (15:40), "the way of the Lord" (18:25), "the word of the Lord" (11:16; 13:48, 49; 19:10), "the hand of the Lord" (11:21; 13:11), and "the will of the Lord" (21:14), for example, only the context is able to provide clues to whether the referent is God or Jesus. And often these clues are not very evident. Many of the other fifty-three uses of the title "Lord" in Acts, however, clearly refer to "the Lord Jesus" (e.g., 1:21; 4:33; 7:59; 8:16; 11:20; 15:11; 16:31; 19:5, 13, 17; 20:24, 35; 21:13). Furthermore, the threefold expression "the Lord Jesus Christ" appears four times in Luke's second volume (11:17; 15:26; 20:21; 28:31), and "Jesus Christ" is explicitly proclaimed to be "Lord of all" (10:36).

Throughout Luke's two volumes, therefore, Jesus is predominantly portrayed as being both Christ and Lord—the first directly and uniformly throughout his writings; the second in two forms in the Gospel (portraying the consciousness of his characters and reflecting his own perspective as the narrator of the story) but with one voice in Acts. The evangelist, in writing his two volumes, can thus be viewed as shaped by, and attempting to support, the early Christian confessions that "Jesus is the Messiah (Christ)" and "Jesus is Lord."

New Relationships Established
through the Work of Christ

Of all the Gospel writers, Luke is the most obviously concerned to relate how the gospel affects the poor, the oppressed, the marginalized, and women. It is Luke, in fact, who supports more strongly than the other evangelists the early Christian confession "new relationships have been established because of Christ's work."

A prominent theme that runs throughout Luke's Gospel is the attention Jesus pays to the poor, the oppressed, and the marginalized in society. In the Nazareth pericope of 4:16–30, which is often seen as programmatic for Luke's understanding of Jesus' mission in the Gospel and the church's mission in Acts, Jesus declares his messianic task in words taken from Isa 61:1–2a (cf. also 58:6):

> The Spirit of the Lord is on me;
>> therefore he has anointed me
>> to preach good news to the poor.
> He has sent me to proclaim freedom for the prisoners
>> and recovery of sight for the blind;
> to release the oppressed,
>> to proclaim the year of the Lord's favor. (4:18–19)

The phrase "to preach good news to the poor," in Luke's usage, seems to function as the caption for the ministries of both Jesus and the church. The origin of the concept "preaching good news" (εὐαγγελίζομαι) may be debated. But certainly Luke had in mind the positive message of joyful tidings that signals a new era of salvation brought about by the ministry of Jesus and the extension of that ministry through the church.

In Luke's Gospel there are five lists of people that include a reference to "the poor" (οἱ πτωχοί):

4:18–19   poor . . . prisoners . . . blind . . . oppressed

6:20–22   poor . . . hungry . . . mournful . . . persecuted

7:22   blind . . . lame . . . lepers . . . deaf . . . dead . . . poor

14:13   poor . . . crippled . . . lame . . . blind

14:21   poor . . . crippled . . . blind . . . lame

To some extent, the other categories of people in these lists serve, by association, to interpret or amplify Luke's understanding of "the poor." Accordingly, "the poor" connotes, for Luke, people who are primarily defined by their social status as dishonorable outsiders, and not necessarily just by their economic status.

Furthermore, though Jesus announced that his mission was to "the poor," Luke does not portray Jesus' words or actions as directed simply to the economically impoverished. Rather, he presents Jesus as continually reaching out to, and associating with, those on the fringes of society: the demon-possessed (4:33–37, 41; 6:18; 8:2, 26–39; 9:37–43), the sick (4:40; 5:17, 31; 6:18–19; 7:1–10), the blind (18:35–43), the paralyzed and disabled (5:18–26; 6:6–10), slaves (7:1–10), lepers (5:12–16; 17:11–19), prostitutes (7:36–50), tax collectors (5:27–32; 19:1–10; cf. 18:9–14), Samaritans (17:16, 18; cf. 10:25–37), Gentiles (7:1–10), children (18:15–17), widows (7:11–17; cf. 18:1–8; 21:1–4), and women in general (7:36–50; 8:2–3, 40–56). Defying the rich of this world, who care not for the plight of the poor, Jesus overturned the standards of status that had been determined by such factors as gender, family heritage, financial position, and religious purity. Jesus' message, as announced in the Nazareth pericope by his quotation of Isa 61:1–21a, was that in the kingdom of God such status markers no longer apply, for all can now receive freely the grace of God.

Two accounts in Luke's portrayals of Jesus' ministry illustrate particularly well this Lukan picture of Jesus' mission. The first is the story of the call of Levi in 5:27–32, which was evidently drawn from Mark (it is a triple-tradition pericope). The second is the story of the quest of Zacchaeus in 19:1–10, which material is unique to Luke's Gospel (perhaps used by Luke to form a balance with 5:27–32). These stories are roughly parallel, for both relate Jesus' encounter with a tax collector (5:27; 19:2), reveal the marginal status of these tax collectors as "sinners" (5:30; 19:7), and highlight the proper behavior of one who chooses to repent and follow Jesus—Levi by leaving everything and preparing a great banquet for Jesus (5:28–29); Zacchaeus by giving half of his possessions to the poor and making fourfold restitution to those whom he had defrauded (19:8). More importantly, both end with a pronouncement by Jesus clarifying the contours of his mission: "I have not come to call the righteous but sinners to repentance" (5:32) and "For the Son of Man came to seek and to save the lost" (19:10).

These stories depict a Savior who reaches out to "sinners"— that is, to social outcasts—with a call to salvation and discipleship. The fact that Jesus eats with such sinners, which is a common theme in Luke (cf. 5:29–32; 7:34; 15:1–2; 19:1–10), demonstrates his acceptance of them, which results in their repentance and salvation. Thus both Levi and Zacchaeus, though previously excluded from the community of Israel, are restored to the status of those who experience God's salvation. And it is in this sense, it seems, that Jesus is to be understood in Luke's Gospel as proclaiming good news to the poor.

The theme of salvation as a reversal of status, which figures prominently in the narratives about Levi and Zacchaeus, runs throughout Luke's Gospel. It was evident in the Lukan infancy narrative, particularly in Mary's Magnificat: "He has scattered those who are proud in their inmost thoughts. He has brought down rulers from their thrones but has lifted up the humble. He has filled the hungry with good things but has sent the rich away empty" (1:51b–53). It also appears frequently in Luke's portrayals of Jesus' ministry, in such passages as the stories about Simon the Pharisee and the sinful woman (7:36–50), the rich man and Lazarus (16:19–31), and the Pharisee and the tax collector (18:9–14). In each case it is the lowly outcast who receives forgiveness, salvation, and peace (7:47–50), whereas those who have "the good things" of this life (16:25) receive a reversal of fortune: their final lot is one of no forgiveness (7:47–48), no mercy (16:24), and no justification (18:14). Often, though not always, "rich and poor" language is found in association with this theme of reversal.

Also to be included in any discussion of Jesus' mission to the marginalized is Luke's emphasis on the gospel vis-à-vis women, which appears very early in the Gospel and continues to the end. In his infancy narrative, for example, Elizabeth's barrenness, which was a disgraceful condition in antiquity, is divinely addressed; and after becoming pregnant, she exults, "The Lord has done this for me. He has shown his favor and taken away my disgrace among the people" (1:25). Similarly, Mary is depicted as "highly favored" (1:28). Many interpreters, in fact, have found in Luke's portrayal of Mary the supreme model of Christian discipleship, for, though initially troubled and questioning, she submits to the will of God ("I am the Lord's servant. May it be to me as you have said," 1:38; cf. 1:45), ponders what she does not understand (2:19, 51), and perseveres through the sorrow of Jesus' death (2:34–35) to become a member of the post-Easter community (Acts 1:14).

Luke's concern for the status and role of women can be seen, as well, throughout his portrayals of Jesus' ministry. In particular, it comes to expression in material unique to his Gospel: the mention of women who supported Jesus and his inner circle of twelve disciples in their travels (8:1–3), the story of Mary and Martha (10:38–42), and the account of Jesus' healing of a woman on the Sabbath (13:10–17). And in his passion and resurrection accounts, Luke alone recounts stories of the women who wept for Jesus on his way to Golgotha (23:27–31) and of the women who, though unbelieved, first told the eleven disciples gathered in Jerusalem of Jesus' resurrection (24:10–11).

A number of scholars have noted a particularly Lukan technique of "pairing parables" and "pairing narratives" in which men and women are featured in parallel fashion. One set of Luke's pairing parables, which can also be found in Matt 13:31–33, are the parables that compare the kingdom of God first to a mustard seed a man plants in his garden (13:18–19; cf. also Mark 4:30–32 for this first parable) and then to yeast a woman mixes into flour (13:20–21). Another set can be seen in the accounts of the healing of a demoniac (4:33–37) and the healing of Simon's mother-in-law (4:38–39), which were evidently drawn from Mark 1:23–31 (cf. also Matt 8:14–15 for the second account). A number of examples of this pairing technique, however, are unique to Luke: the annunciations to Zechariah (1:5–25) and Mary (1:26–38), the prophecies of Simeon (2:25–35) and Anna (2:36–38), the references to "a widow in Zarephath" (4:26) and "Naaman the Syrian" (4:27), the Sabbath healings of a woman (13:10–17) and a man (14:1–6), the parables about a man who lost a sheep (15:4–7) and a woman who lost a coin (15:8–10), and the sayings about two men in a bed (17:34) and two women at a mill (17:35). Luke even balances his listing of Jesus' male followers (6:12–16) with a list of Jesus' female followers (8:1–3).

Luke's interest in the status and role of women continues in his second volume, Acts, which depicts women functioning in various ways in the early church. Women, including Mary the mother of Jesus, are portrayed as being with the small group of Jesus' male disciples in prayer in the upper room (1:12–14). And although the bulk of the narrative of Acts concerns the ministries of Peter and Paul, some of the accounts also include references to specific women: Dorcas (9:36–43), Rhoda (12:13–15), Timothy's mother (16:1), Lydia (16:14–15, 40), Damaris (17:34), Priscilla (18:1–4, 18–19, 26), and Philip's four daughters who had the gift of prophecy (21:9). In addition, Luke seems to take pains in Acts to show that women generally were part of the overall activity in the advance of the gospel (cf. 8:3, 12; 9:2; 13:50; 16:13; 17:4, 12; 21:5; 22:4).

Some modern interpreters have criticized Luke for not saying more about the liberation of the poor, the oppressed, and the marginalized, and for leaving women in their expected roles in the patriarchal structures of the first century rather than depicting more clearly their equal leadership roles with men. Like many involved in the early stages of a renewal movement, however, Luke, as Joel Green reminds us, "faced the necessity of working *within* the constraints of one's historical particularity while at the same time calling those constraints into question."[14]

Luke's highlighting of the inauguration of new social relationships because of Christ's work and the prominence that he gives to women because of Christians' oneness in Christ, therefore, must be seen as remarkable testimonies to the nature and impact of the gospel of Christ. In so doing, Luke was informed by, and lent his support to, what the early Christians confessed when they spoke of "new relationships established through the work of Christ."

The Passion Narrative (22:1–23:56) and Resurrection Account (24:1–53), with Attendant Themes in Acts

Christ's Redemptive Death on a Cross

Jesus' passion and the cross in Luke's Gospel are not depicted in terms of vicarious suffering, human redemption, or the expiation of sins as much as they are in Mark or Matthew. Rather, they primarily exemplify Jesus' unconditional obedience to God and become patterns of service for his followers to emulate. Luke hinted at such an understanding in 9:23 by adding the adverbial expression "daily" (καθ' ἡμέραν) to Jesus' words from Mark 8:34: "Those who would come after me must deny themselves and take up their cross *daily* and follow me." And he also suggested such an understanding when he included Q material in 14:27: "Those who do not carry their cross and follow me cannot be my disciples."

This is not to say that suffering, sacrifice, and salvation are absent in Luke's portrayal of Jesus' passion. The evangelist spoke in 9:31 about Jesus' going to Jerusalem in order to fulfill his "departure"—or, more literally, his "exodus" (τὴν ἔξοδον αὐτοῦ), a term that would certainly have evoked ideas about the redemptive significance of Jesus' passion to anyone familiar with the OT. More than any of the other evangelists, in fact, Luke emphasizes the necessity of Jesus' suffering and death (cf. 9:22; 16:33; 17:25; 22:37; 24:7, 26–27, 44, 46–47). Thus the cross, in Luke's Gospel, must be seen as part of God's plan of salvation. Indeed, in the passion narrative of Luke, the evangelist explicitly refers to the Last Supper as a Passover meal (22:7, 8, 11, 13, 15) and repeats Jesus' words of institution at that meal: "This is my body given for you. . . . This cup is the new covenant in my blood, which is poured out for you" (22:19–20).

Yet by omitting in 22:24–30 the Markan saying "to give his life a ransom for many" (Mark 10:45b; cf. Matt 20:28b), Luke indicates that what he wanted his readers to think most about when they thought of Jesus' passion was not just a soteriological theory but Jesus' life of service for others and their service for God. And throughout Luke's passion narrative the theme of Jesus' passion and cross as exemplary for Christian living and service is to the fore.

Probably the best way to understand the enigma of the meaning of Jesus' death in Luke's Gospel is to appreciate that the evangelist views human redemption as based on the whole Christ event, with Jesus' death being the essential aspect of that event that culminates his entire ministry of service. In

Luke's Gospel the whole Christ event brings salvation—Jesus' birth (2:11, 30), his life of service (19:9–10; 22:27), and his suffering and death, which is "for you" (22:19–20). And in Acts the exemplary nature of Christ's death sets the paradigm for Stephen's death, for both Christ and Stephen refer to the Son of Man at the right hand of God (Luke 22:69; Acts 7:56), both ask God to forgive their oppressors (Luke 23:34; Acts 7:60), and both, with their dying breaths, commit their spirits to another (to God the "Father" in Luke 23:46; to the "Lord Jesus" in Acts 7:59).

Jesus as the Obedient Son of God

The portrayal of Jesus' prayer in Gethsemane (Luke 22:39–46) shows how Luke understood Jesus as the obedient Son of God. For, as in the other Synoptic Gospels, Jesus' willingness to accept the cup of suffering and death demonstrates his faithfulness and obedience to the will of God, his Father (cf. Mark 14:36, 39; Matt 26:39, 42, 44). What is distinctive about Luke's account, however, is that (1) this agonizing period of prayer was the climax of Jesus' entire life of prayer, (2) it reflects Jesus' own piety, and (3) it highlights the special relation that Jesus had with God.

Luke presents Jesus as praying at or before many of the major events in his life and ministry: at his baptism (3:21), before choosing the twelve disciples (6:12), in the context of Peter's confession (9:18–20), at his transfiguration (9:28), and before giving to his disciples the Lord's Prayer (11:1)—all of which culminates in his Gethsemane prayer on the Mount of Olives: "Father, if you are willing, take this cup from me; yet not my will, but yours be done" (22:42). He even prays while on the cross, asking his Father to forgive his tormentors: "Father, forgive them, for they do not know what they are doing" (23:34).[15]

Also of significance in Luke's version of Jesus' Gethsemane prayer is the evangelist's emphasis on Jesus' piety. For Luke lays stress on the fact that Jesus' going to the Mount of Olives, apparently to pray, "was his custom" (cf. 22:39), and he suggests that there Jesus came to "the place" where he customarily prayed (cf. 22:40). Likewise, Luke highlights the special relationship that

Jesus had with God his Father, not only in Jesus' words "not my will, but yours be done" (22:42) but also in the statement that "there appeared to him an angel from heaven [i.e., from God], who strengthened him" (22:43).[16] With such deft touches, Luke elaborates on the church's confession of Jesus as God's obedient Son, seeking not only to be informed by this confession but also to support it in a manner that goes somewhat beyond what he found in his Markan source.

Christ's Resurrection/Exaltation to New Life

More than the other synoptic evangelists, Luke goes into great detail regarding Jesus' resurrection (24:1–12), his post-resurrection appearances (24:13–49), his ascension (24:50–51), and the varied reactions of his followers to these events (ch. 24, including vv. 41, 52–53). Ultimately, these events gave the disciples "great joy," which resulted in their worship of Jesus and their praise of God (24:52–53). And it was from the perspective of his resurrection that they viewed anew and reinterpreted all that had transpired in Jesus' ministry and death—reaching back even to the circumstances of his birth and moving forward in their thoughts to the implications of such events for a believer's life, thought, and actions.

Luke begins his Acts narrative about the church's ministry with this resurrection/exaltation theme, reminding his readers of Jesus' ascension (1:2), resurrection (1:3a), and teachings (1:3b–5). He focuses the ministry of the early church on the proclamation of Jesus' resurrection by recounting the rationale of the earliest apostles in choosing someone to replace Judas:

> It is necessary to choose one of the men who have been with us the whole time the Lord Jesus went in and out among us, beginning from John's baptism to the time when Jesus was taken up from us. For one of these must become a witness with us of his resurrection. (1:21–22)

Furthermore, he portrays Peter's Pentecost sermon as having for its central theme the vindication of Jesus by God in raising him from the dead (2:24–32). And in almost all of the sermons he records, he presents the resurrection of Jesus as the crucial topic and focal point of what was proclaimed (cf., e.g., 4:2, 33; 5:30–32; 10:40–41; 13:30–31; 17:3, 18, 31–32; 23:6–8; 24:15, 21).

Thus, it may concluded that Luke's writings were inspired and informed by the church's confession regarding Christ's resurrection/exaltation to new life. But they support this confession as well, a point that has not always been fully appreciated.

CHAPTER FIVE

The Fourth Gospel and the Johannine Apocalypse

t would be difficult to argue that either the Fourth Gospel or the Johannine Apocalypse was written simply "to produce an account" of the Christian movement or that the author's principal motivation was to demonstrate how the early Christian confessions were supported by the story of Jesus and/or by events in the early church. Nonetheless, both John's Gospel and the Johannine Apocalypse were inspired and shaped by the central confessions of the earliest believers in Jesus. Likewise, they were written "out of faith and for faith"—whether to evoke faith, to strengthen it, or both—in order to support the church's life, worship, and ministry.

Both the Fourth Gospel and the Johannine Apocalypse reach back—each in its own distinctive fashion—into the storeroom of the early Christian confessions and evidence something of how these confessional materials were developed in certain Christian quarters during the late first century. In so doing, they reflect a further stage in the contextualization of these confessions as this process of contextualization is represented in the NT—a process that (1) began with the basically functional portrayals of Paul's earliest letters and Mark's kerygmatic Gospel, (2) was developed in some of the later NT letters and the more didactic Gospels of Matthew and Luke, and (3) came to fuller expression in the more interpretive and expansive portrayals of John's Gospel and the Johannine Apocalypse.

▓ 1. THE FOURTH GOSPEL

The Fourth Gospel and the Synoptic Gospels, while alike in their focus on Jesus, are decidedly different in their presentations and perspectives. Certain differences are immediately obvious. The locale of the story of Jesus, for example, is set in John's Gospel almost entirely in Judea (only in 2:1–12, 4:43–54, and 6:1–71 is Jesus presented as being in Galilee, while in 4:1–42 he is in Samaria), whereas Jesus' ministry, before his final journey to Jerusalem, takes places in the Synoptics mostly in Galilee. Likewise, the Jewish feasts of Passover (Pesach), Tabernacles (Booths), and Hanukkah (Dedication) figure prominently in the accounts about Jesus in the Fourth Gospel, which mentions at least three different Passovers (2:13; 6:4; 11:55; 12:1; 13:1; 18:28; and 19:14; perhaps also 5:1)—implying that Jesus' ministry lasted for at least two years, perhaps for three or even four. In the synoptic accounts, by contrast, Jesus' ministry could be understood to have occurred during less than one year. Furthermore, in the Fourth Gospel, Jesus' teaching is presented in the form of extended discourses, and no sayings or parables are included; on the other hand, individual sayings, collections of sayings, and parables of Jesus abound in the Synoptic Gospels, where the only discourse is the Olivet discourse (Mark 13:1–37; Matt 24:1–25:46; Luke 21:5–36).

More particularly, there is in John's Gospel a broader sweep in the portrayal of divine redemption, a greater clarity of theological perspective, and a more intense focus on the person of Jesus than in the Synoptic Gospels. The prologue of the Fourth Gospel, in fact, interprets the story of Jesus even before it is told—providing the reader with a theological interpretation that seems far more suitable for the opening of a NT letter (e.g., Romans, Ephesians, Hebrews, 1 Peter, and 1 John) than the beginning of a Gospel. "In John," as George Beasley-Murray points out, "the lifting up of the Son of Man on his cross reaches to the throne of heaven; and as the shadow of the cross marks the entire story of Jesus, so the glory of the Resurrection event suffuses every hour of his ministry, and even reaches back to the morning of creation."[1]

This is not to say that John's own Christology was "higher" than that of Mark, Matthew, or Luke, as has often been claimed. Rather, it is simply that the fourth evangelist has taken pains to spell out the conclusion to which the other three evangelists, each in his own way, were pointing: that the glory for which all of creation was made and the redemption that God inaugurated have been brought to actuality in the work and words of Jesus. In effect, though without any necessary literary connection between them, John's Gospel has translated the kerygmatic (proclamation) presentation of Mark's Gospel and the didactic (teaching) presentations of Matthew and Luke into other structures, forms, and expressions in order to highlight the significance of what was held, preached, and taught by the earliest Christians. Or to change the metaphor somewhat, John's Gospel has transposed early Christian preaching and teaching into a different key so that the resonances and nuances inherent in the Christian message might be better appreciated, both in their range and in their meaning.

It is this difference of theological range and perspective that prompted many early church fathers to call John's Gospel "the Spiritual Gospel," thereby highlighting its more "spiritual" interpretive qualities—as distinguished from the other three Gospels, which were first called "the Corporeal Gospels" (particularly among Alexandrian allegorists) and then "the Synoptic Gospels." Thus, throughout the history of the Christian church, many have assumed that the Synoptic Gospels are historical depictions of Jesus and that John's Gospel is a strictly theological portrait.

But such a distinction can no longer be held. For it is today recognized that all four Gospels weave together both history and theology, with each evangelist presenting the story of Jesus in terms of his own interests and the perceived needs of his addressees. As Beasley-Murray notes, "The process of interpretation and clarification of the kerygma which Mark began in relation to his own church's situation [has been] carried to its logical conclusion in the Fourth Gospel." As a result, "what we find in the Fourth Gospel is a development of earlier lines of understanding which seem to be demanded by the traditions themselves."[2]

Although translation and transposition are abundantly evident in John's Gospel, the basic confessions of the earliest believers in Jesus still reverberate throughout the evangelist's writing. Five such confessions provide the foundation and superstructure for all that he presents: (1) "God is the initiator, sustainer, and ultimate agent of redemption," (2) "Jesus is Israel's Messiah (the Christ)," (3) "Jesus is God's Son," (4) "Jesus is humanity's redemptive Lord," and (5) "Christ has accomplished redemption on a cross." Other motifs can also be found in the Fourth Gospel—for example, the unveiling of Christ's glory through "miraculous signs," the lifting up and glorification of the Son by the Father, the realized nature of eschatology because of Jesus' presence, the divine revelatory voice from the cross, and the explicit call for people to believe. But these five basic confessions serve as the warp and woof of the Gospel, holding everything else together.

God as the Initiator, Sustainer, and Ultimate Agent of Redemption

Through the use of such theological categories as "life," "light," "glory," "grace," and "truth," the prologue of the Fourth Gospel (1:1–18) highlights God's role as the initiator, sustainer, and ultimate agent of redemption. It is in Jesus that these qualities are incarnated. As "the Word" and "the Son," Jesus is presented as having been "with God" (vv. 1–2), "come from the Father" (v. 14), and "made God known" (v. 18). God's action of sending the Son (cf. 4:34; 5:24; 17:3; 20:21), therefore, means that divine redemption has been effected.

The prologue further highlights God's saving activity when it speaks of John the Baptist: "There came a man who was sent from God; his name was John. He came as a witness to testify concerning that light. . . . He himself was not the light; he came only as a witness to the light" (1:6–8). The plan of redemption, therefore, is presented in the following manner: God sent John to bear witness to Jesus, God's unique agent, who, in his own person and ministry, bore witness to God's character of life, light, glory, grace, and truth. And these divine qualities, manifested in Jesus, God's Son—though rejected by those to whom he was sent

(vv. 10–11)—are available to all those who believe in Jesus and receive him (vv. 12–13).

Jesus as Israel's Messiah (the Christ)

The portrayals of Jesus as Israel's Messiah (the Christ) in the Synoptic Gospels are not abandoned in John's Gospel. On the contrary, questions regarding messiahship and the depictions of Jesus as the focus of Israel's messianic hope appear more frequently in the Fourth Gospel than in the Synoptic Gospels. For example, John the Baptist insists that he is not the Christ but only the one sent ahead of him to prepare his way (1:19–27; 3:28–30). Likewise, Andrew tells his brother Simon, "We have found the Messiah" (1:41); and Philip tells Nathaniel, "We have found the one Moses wrote about in the Law, and about whom the prophets also wrote" (1:45). Furthermore, the Samaritan woman and her neighbors come to believe in Jesus as the Messiah (4:25–26, 28–30, 39–42); the crowds (7:25–31, 40–43; 12:34) and the religious authorities (7:52; 9:29; 10:24–25) discuss whether Jesus is the Christ, questioning his origin and debating about his miracles as qualifications for messiahship; and Simon Peter confesses that Jesus is "the Holy One of God," which is probably a messianic title (6:69). The title "Christ" (Χριστός), in fact, appears seventeen times in John's Gospel, and the compound name "Jesus Christ" (Ἰησοῦς Χριστός) appears two times. In addition, the Greek term Μεσσίας, a transliteration of the Hebrew *Mashiah* or Aramaic *Meshiha*, is used twice in John's Gospel (in 1:41 and 4:25; only in John), followed by an explanation that this term means "the Christ."

Although the evangelist of the Fourth Gospel agrees with the synoptic evangelists concerning the central importance of the confession "Jesus is the Christ," he also treats this confession in a slightly different manner. For example, there is no "messianic secret" in John's depiction of Jesus, though it appears prominently in Mark and is carried on, to an extent, in Matthew and Luke. True, John's Gospel contains an "unveiling" motif—which some have equated with the "messianic secret" motif—particularly in the so-called Book of Signs (chs. 2–12). And coupled with this "unveiling" motif is the theme of Jesus' messiahship being hidden from those who are unbelieving (cf. 1:10–11; 10:24–26; 12:39–41). But the emphasis in the "unveiling" motif of John's Gospel is on the revelation of Jesus' nature and character to those who will believe in him (cf. 1:12–14; 2:11, 23; 3:15–21, 36; 4:39–42; passim), not on its hiddenness.

John's Gospel includes no demand by Jesus to remain silent about his messiahship. Nor is there any tension between a preresurrection silence and a postresurrection confession of Jesus as Israel's Messiah. Rather, the messiahship of Jesus is openly announced at the beginning of the Gospel (esp. 1:19–34, 41, 45, 49). Furthermore, the tension that John's Gospel presents in the acclamation of Jesus as the Christ is not that of time—that is, between a preresurrection experience and a postresurrection perspective—but of presently believing or presently not believing in Jesus, and this tension is predicted to continue into the future (14:22–24).

Another difference between John and the synoptic evangelists is that in the Fourth Gospel there is a rather sharp juxtaposition between the then current Jewish messianic expectations, which were largely nationalistic and political in nature, and the Christian interpretation of Jesus as Israel's Messiah. The polemic in John's Gospel is between "the Jews," seen collectively, who do not know enough about either their own traditions or the character of Jesus to recognize that he really does fulfill their ancestral expectations, and believing Christians, who rightly confess Jesus as the Christ. This juxtaposition is set out early in the prologue by the contrast between those who "did not recognize him" and "did not receive him," on the one hand, and those who "received him" and "believed in his name," on the other (1:10–13). It also appears in the formulaic statement "The law was given through Moses; grace and truth came through Jesus Christ" (1:17). And it comes to expression in many of the Gospel's conflict dialogues—particularly where the acknowledgment of Jesus as Israel's Messiah was considered by Jewish officials to be an offense punishable by excommunication from the synagogue (9:22; 16:2), which may very well also reflect controversies between the Johannine community and Jewish authorities during the later decades of the first century.

A third difference is that messiahship and kingship are more directly associated in John's Gospel than in the Synoptic Gospels. John does not use the title "son of David," which appears in the Synoptic Gospels on the lips of the people to indicate the messiahship of Jesus. But he does include several references to Jesus as Israel's messianic king. In the prologue, Nathanael declares Jesus' kingship when he exclaims, "You are the Son of God; you are the King of Israel" (1:49), even though he may not have known the full implications of what he was confessing. After the miracle of the feeding of the five thousand, Jesus rejects an attempt by the people to force him to become king (6:15). But this does not mean that Jesus rejected all notions of a royal messianic office. For in the account of his "triumphal" entrance into Jerusalem, the crowd hails him as "King of Israel" (12:13)—and the fourth evangelist interprets this event in the light of Zech 9:9, which speaks of Zion seeing its king coming, seated on a donkey's colt (12:14–15). However superficial the crowd's acclamation might have been, John seems to have intended his readers to see in Jesus the true king of Israel.

The precise nature of Jesus' kingship becomes finally apparent in his trial before Pilate and its aftermath. In the extended dialogue between Pilate and Jesus, the reader learns that Jesus is indeed a king, although his kingdom is "not of this world" but "from another place" (18:33–39). The answer to Pilate's question "Are you the king of the Jews?" is, then, that Jesus' kingdom is of a divine, not a human, order. And following this dialogue, eight more references to Jesus as a king appear in chapter 19: one by mocking soldiers (v. 3); one by "the Jews" who tell Pilate, "Anyone who claims to be a king opposes Caesar" (v. 12); two by Pilate when presenting Jesus to "the Jews" (vv. 14, 15); three by the chief priests, who at one point make the astounding declaration "We have no king but Caesar" (vv. 15, 21 [twice]); and one recording the wording of the sign placed on Jesus' cross, "Jesus of Nazareth, the King of the Jews" (v. 19). Thus, although the Jewish and Roman opponents of Jesus are portrayed as ignorant of the ironic truth of their mockeries and accusations, by the end of his Gospel the evangelist leads his readers to understand the full impact of Nathanael's early confession: "You are the King of Israel!"

Jesus as God's Son

John's Gospel refers nine times to Jesus as "the Son of God" (1:34, 49; 3:18; 5:25; 10:36; 11:4, 27; 19:7; 20:31) and an additional nineteen times to Jesus as "the Son." The designation "the Son" is an abbreviation of the title "Son of God," for it always appears in the context of God's action in sending the Son (3:16, 17) or in Father-Son language where "the Father" means God (1:18; 3:35–36; 5:19–26; 6:40; 8:36–38; 14:13; 17:1). The divine sonship of Jesus is also attested in the Fourth Gospel by the fact that Jesus over fifty times refers to God as his "Father."

Two particular linguistic features in this regard are significant in the Fourth Gospel, for they highlight the distinctive nature of John's portrayal of Jesus as God's Son. First, only John among the evangelists uses the term μονογενής to refer to Jesus (1:14, 18; 3:16, 18; cf. 1 John 4:9). While μονογενής was used in the Greek world to mean "sole descendant" or "the only child of one's parents," it was also widely used in both classical and Koine Greek to signal ideas more of quality than of derivation or descent—"peerless," "matchless," "unique," "of singular importance," or "the only one of its kind." Luke's Gospel uses the term in the sense of "sole descendant" or "the only child of one's parents" when speaking about a widow's son who was dead (7:12), Jairus's daughter who was dying (8:42), and a man's son who was convulsed by an evil spirit (9:38). In John's christological usage, however, it means "one and only" or "unique"—as it does also in Heb 11:17 with reference to Isaac as Abraham's "favored," "chosen," or "unique" son (cf. Gen 22:2, 12, 16; *Jubilees* 18:2, 11, 15; possibly also Josephus, *Antiquities* 1.222). The KJV translation of μονογενής as "only begotten" stems from Jerome's use of *unigenitus* in the Latin Vulgate to translate this Greek term and came about in response to the Arian assertion that Jesus was "made" and not "begotten."

A second linguistic feature to note in John's portrayal of Jesus as God's Son is that while the Synoptic Gospels (particularly Matthew) frequently refer to Jesus as "the Son of God" (e.g., Matt 14:33; 16:16; 28:19; cf. Mark 1:1; Luke 1:32, 35) and to Christians as "sons of God" (e.g., Matt 5:45; Luke 6:35)—as do also the letters of the NT (e.g., "Son of God" in Rom 1:3, 4, 9; 5:10; 8:3, 29, 32, etc.; Heb 1:2, 8; 4:14; 5:8, etc.; "sons of God" in Rom 8:14, 19; 9:26; 2 Cor 6:18; Gal 3:26; 4:6–7)—the pattern is different in John's Gospel. For in John, "Son of God" refers to Jesus with greater frequency than in the Synoptic Gospels (e.g., John 1:49; 3:16–18, 35–36; 5:19–26; 6:40; 8:35–36, etc.; see also 1 John 1:3, 7; 2:22–24; 2 John 3, 9), but those who are Jesus' followers are never called "sons of God." Rather, they are called "children of God" (τέκνα θεοῦ; 1:12; 11:52; cf. 1 John 3:1, 2, 10; 5:20). The designation "Son of God" is reserved for Jesus alone.

Like the Synoptic Gospels, the Fourth Gospel presents Jesus, God's Son, as perfectly obedient to the Father's will (4:34; 5:30; 8:29). But the theme of sonship is also transposed in John's Gospel into a higher key in order to highlight a number of other important—often transcendental—features that the evangelist sees as inherent to Jesus' sonship. One such feature is the Son's *intimacy* with the Father: the Father loves the Son (5:20; cf. 3:35; 10:17; 17:23), the Son can do nothing by himself (5:19), and the Son "has seen" and "knows" the Father (6:45–46; 8:54–55; 10:15; 15:15). The Son, therefore, has special access to the Father (14:6, 13–17) and shares all things with the Father (16:15). Another feature is the Son's *authority*, which stems from his intimate relationship with the Father: the Son shares in the work of the Father (5:19; 9:4; 10:37), particularly in giving life to those who believe (5:21, 24, 26, 28–29; 6:40; 10:10, 14–18) and in enacting judgment (5:22; cf. 5:27, 30; 8:16).

There is, in fact, such a personal, transcendental, and metaphysical relationship between Jesus "the Son" and God "the Father" in John's Gospel that the two can be portrayed as sharing both a moral likeness and an essential identity. For not only do they share common creative and redemptive work (5:17–23), they are one in purpose and moral character (10:30–39). Furthermore, they possess a common identity, since to see and know the Son is to see and know the Father (14:9–11). As C. K. Barrett points out, "The charge that Jesus, by claiming to be the Son of God and to work continuously with him, makes himself equal to God, is never rebutted. John does not mean to rebut it."[3]

All of this goes beyond, and is expressed quite differently than in, the Synoptic Gospels. It is a transposition of the Son of God theme into a higher key. Nonetheless, John's portrayal of Jesus as God's Son can be seen rooted in the early Christian confession that "Jesus is the obedient Son of God," and so should be understood as a contextualization and outworking of the nuances inherent in that confession.

Jesus as Humanity's Redemptive Lord

The term "Lord" is applied to Jesus forty-three times in the Fourth Gospel, either as a title ("the Lord") or as a vocative address ("Lord"). As in the Synoptic Gospels, however, it is not always clear whether the fourth evangelist uses the term as a form of polite address ("sir") or as worshipful acclamation. He often seems to use it simply as a courteous address. Even when the disciples or followers such as Mary, Martha, and Mary of Magdala address Jesus as "Lord," it is not always possible to determine whether the term connotes simple respect or transcendent worth. Yet six times within John's Gospel the evangelist, acting as the narrator, refers in honorific fashion to Jesus as "the Lord" (6:23; 11:2; 20:18, 20, 25; 21:12). This is similar, as we have seen, to Luke's practice as the narrator in his Gospel. And in these places, at least, it may be concluded that the christological sense of the title "Lord" has been incorporated into the narrative, thereby reflecting the early Christian confession that "Jesus is humanity's redemptive Lord."

In addition, John's Gospel sometimes depicts the followers of Jesus, in their use of the vocative "Lord," as at least approaching a christological affirmation, if not actually voicing their worshipful acclamation. Thus Peter says, "Lord, to whom shall we go? You have the words of eternal life. We know and believe that you are the Holy One of God!" (6:68–69). And the blind man whom Jesus healed, when asked, "Do you believe in the Son of Man?" (9:35), first responds, "Who is he, Lord [Sir]?"; but when told, "You have now seen him; in fact, he is the one speaking with you," he declares: "Lord, I believe!"—and the evangelist adds that he then worshiped Jesus (9:35–38). Furthermore, Martha is presented as coupling the vocative "Lord" with a full-blown christological confession when, in answer to Jesus' question, "Do you believe this?" she replies, "Yes, Lord, I believe that you are the Christ, the Son of God, who was to come into the world" (11:27). In these instances, at least, the evangelist seems to have intended his readers to understand that more than a respectful form of address was involved in the vocative use of "Lord."

Two postresurrection occurrences of "Lord" in John's Gospel clearly reflect a transcendent connotation. The first is in 20:28, where Thomas, who had earlier doubted Jesus' resurrection, cries out on seeing the risen Jesus, "My Lord and my God!" The second is in 21:7, where the beloved disciple, after catching so many fish in response to Jesus' command, exclaims, "It is the Lord!" It is sometimes argued from these occurrences that Jesus was truly known and confessed to be Lord only as a result of the disciples' encounter with the risen Lord. But such a judgment, while probably true historically, overstates the case when dealing with the literary phenomena of not only Matthew and Luke (though not Mark) but also John. For just as the Fourth Gospel represents the disciples as recognizing Jesus as Messiah and Son of God before Easter, so too, the fourth evangelist imports later Christian reflection regarding Jesus as Lord into his narrative and onto the lips of Jesus' followers before the resurrection—as did Luke in his editorial comments and Matthew with reference to Jesus' disciples.

Christ Has Accomplished Redemption on a Cross

Like Mark's Gospel, the Fourth Gospel foreshadows the cross from the first chapter onward. The first indication of Jesus' death appears in the proem of 1:1–18, which was probably penned after the body of the Gospel was written and so admirably sums up much of Johannine Christology: "The Word became flesh and lived for a while among us [lit. tented among us], and we have seen his glory" (1:14). Here John signals two important concepts that are developed throughout the rest of his Gospel. First, Jesus sojourned on earth for a limited time, at the end of which he died and rose again. As the fourth evangelist seems to have understood it, Jesus' life was a journey, for he comes from his preexistent state with God in heaven, dwells among humanity, and then returns to heaven (cf. 3:31; 6:38; 8:23; 13:1–3). Second, the way back to the Father in heaven was, for Jesus, through death on a cross—an event described, paradoxically, as a glorification and an exaltation.

As Jesus approaches his passion, he knows that the time has come for him to leave this world and return to the Father (13:1). He knows his betrayer and even encourages him to act (6:70–71; 13:2–3, 21, 26–27). More than that, he speaks about his impending death as a "glorification" of himself (using his favorite self-designation, "the Son of Man") and a "glorification" of God (13:31–32; 17:1, 4–5). During his earthly ministry Jesus repeatedly referred to "being lifted up" (3:14; 8:28; 12:32), which for the evangelist points to both Jesus' crucifixion and his exaltation. Thus, when the prologue states, "We have seen his glory," it is not only the glory exhibited in Jesus' earthly ministry (e.g., 2:11; 11:40; 12:41) but also—and preeminently—the glory revealed in Jesus' crucifixion and exaltation.

John's Gospel portrays a sovereign Jesus who announces defiantly, "No one takes [my life] from me, but I lay it down of my own accord. I have authority to lay it down and authority to take it up again" (10:18). Jesus heads toward his death on a cross not praying for deliverance from the approaching time of trial, as in the Synoptic Gospels, but in complete self-assurance, for this is "the hour" when the whole purpose of his life is to be fulfilled (12:27–28). He knows his betrayer long beforehand (6:70; 13:11), and he even sets in motion his betrayer's act of betrayal (13:27).

The passion narrative of the Fourth Gospel (18:1–19:42) presents Jesus fully in charge of the proceedings. Of those who have come to arrest him, he asks whom they are seeking; and they fall back powerless when he reveals himself as the "I am" (Ἐγώ εἰμι)—which is the LXX translation of God's self-identification to Moses at the burning bush and God's declarations of transcendence and matchlessness in Isaiah 41–48. Furthermore, he negotiates the release of his disciples, and he expresses supreme confidence in his Father's will: "Shall I not drink the cup the Father has given me?" (18:1–11).

When conversing with Annas and Pilate, Jesus in John's Gospel speaks more like a judge than the accused (18:19–23,

33–38; 19:8–12). Pilate is afraid before the one who claims to be the Son of God and who declares, "You have no power over me that was not given to you from above" (19:8–11). And Pilate seeks, though in vain, to find a way to set him free (19:12–16). Indeed, Jesus is declared to be a king—derisively by the Roman soldiers, accusingly by the Jewish leaders, and declaratively by an inscription written in three languages that Pilate prepares and fastens to the cross. And Jesus accepts this acclamation, though he qualifies it by saying that his kingdom is not of this world (cf. 18:36).

Needing no assistance, Jesus "bears his own cross" to Golgotha (19:17). His serenity and control are likewise evident as he hangs on the cross, for he arranges for the care of his mother (19:25–27) and gives up his life of his own accord (19:28–30). Even his burial is not unprepared for, as in the other Gospels; rather, his body is wrapped in seventy-five pounds of spices as befits a king (19:38–42).

Despite, however, all these portrayals of majesty, power, and control, John's Gospel also presents the death of Jesus as a redemptive sacrifice that gives life to the world. This theme appears initially in 1:29, 36, where John the Baptist points out Jesus as "the Lamb of God, who takes away the sin of the world." Though the title "Lamb of God" can carry a number of nuances,[4] it probably should be seen as a sacrificial lamb, a Passover lamb, or both, in the Fourth Gospel. This is suggested by the Baptist's statement "who takes away the sin of the world" and by the evangelist's portrayal of Jesus' death as a Passover sacrifice (cf. esp. 18:28; 19:14, 31).

Several symbolic details may be noted in the evangelist's portrayal of Jesus' death as a Passover sacrifice. First, Jesus is sentenced to death at noon on the day of Preparation (19:14), the very time when the priests begin to slaughter the paschal lambs in the temple precincts in preparation for the Passover. Furthermore, the presence of hyssop and a basin at the cross (19:29) recalls for perceptive readers the first Passover, when hyssop, a fernlike plant, was used to sprinkle the blood of the paschal lamb on the door frames of Israelite houses (Exod 12:7, 22). Likewise, the evangelist's emphasis on seeing the blood flow from the side of Jesus (19:34–35) may recall the words of God to Moses at the first Passover: "When I see the blood, I will pass over you" (Exod 12:13). Finally, the soldiers do not break the legs of the crucified Jesus, as they did those of the two criminals crucified with him (19:31–37); this seems to be yet another allusion to Jesus as the paschal lamb, for a sacrificial animal's legs were not to be broken (Exod 12:46). All of these images, then, support the early Christian confession of Jesus' redemptive work on a cross.

In addition to these specifically related passion texts, there are also other passages in John's Gospel that allude to Jesus' death on a cross as a redemptive act. In the discourse on the Bread of Life of 6:25–59, Jesus declares, "Unless you eat the flesh of the Son of Man and drink his blood, you have no life in you. Whoever eats my flesh and drinks my blood has eternal life" (6:53–54). These two parallel sayings, expressed in sacramental terms, refer to the necessity of participation in Jesus' death as the means of receiving eternal life. It is thus implied that Jesus' death was "for others." Similarly, the preposition ὑπέρ ("on behalf of") is used in the Fourth Gospel to underscore the redemptive nature of the cross in 6:51; 10:11, 15; 11:50–52; and 18:14. Finally, it needs to be noted that Jesus' washing of his disciples' feet at his final meal with them was understood by John not only as exemplary behavior but also as a symbol of Jesus' saving death (13:8–11).

■ 2. THE JOHANNINE APOCALYPSE

The Apocalypse of John has traditionally been seen as written during the reign of the Roman emperor Domitian (81–96 CE), the son of Vespasian (69–79 CE) and brother of Titus (79–81 CE). It was rumored that Domitian murdered Titus to take his place. And ancient historians claimed that, at various times during his reign, Domitian persecuted Jews and other people of his empire, including, during his later years, Christians.

Eusebius of Caesarea, the fourth-century bishop and church historian, explicitly associates the writing of the Johannine Apocalypse and Domitian's persecution of Christians, even identifying Domitian as a second Nero:

Domitian, indeed, having exercised his cruelty against many, and unjustly slain no small number of noble and illustrious men at Rome, and having, without cause, punished vast numbers of honorable men with exile and the confiscation of their property, at length established himself as the successor of Nero, in his hatred and hostility to God. He was the second that raised a persecution against us, although his father Vespasian had attempted nothing to our prejudice. (*Ecclesiastical History* 3.17; cf. 3.18–20; 4.26.5–11)

This view of the Johannine Apocalypse vis-à-vis Domitian's persecution was held by many early church fathers—for example, Irenaeus (*Against Heresies* 5.30.3, written sometime during 182–188 CE) and Tertullian (*Apology* 5, ca. 193–216 CE). It was common among the church fathers of the third and fourth centuries and has continued to dominate to the present day.

Lately, however, it has been argued that much of Domitian's negative reputation was undeserved and that he instigated no persecution against Christians, either officially or unofficially.[5] Thus, it is often proposed today that the Johannine Apocalypse is responding either (1) to a perceived persecution that did not actually exist at the time, but which the writer viewed as imminent, or (2) to some local opposition against Christians, such as broke out sporadically at various places in the Roman Empire and that the author of the Apocalypse viewed as paradigmatic of Roman persecution generally.

In any event, John had been deported to Patmos, an island in the South Aegean Sea just off the coast of Asia Minor and west of Miletus and Ephesus. There he was imprisoned "because of the word of God and the testimony of Jesus" (1:9). In addition, Antipas, who is the only Christian martyr mentioned in the Apocalypse of John, had been killed in the city of Pergamum because of his "faithful witness" (2:13). Together these events could well have triggered the perception of an imminent, widespread, and officially sanctioned persecution.

The first word of the Johannine Apocalypse has provided scholars with the term "apocalypse" (ἀποκάλυψις) as the designation for a distinctive genre of Jewish and Jewish Christian writings: "The apocalypse [revelation] of Jesus Christ, which God gave him to show his servants what must soon take place" (1:1). In this verse, "apocalypse" is used to describe the content of what was given by God to Jesus Christ, who then "made it known by sending his angel to his servant John," who, as 1:2–3 goes on to say, testified to it by writing it down for his readers. The term in its original context, therefore, does not refer to a literary genre ("apocalypse") or a type of material ("apocalyptic") but to the message itself.

The church fathers, however, picked up on the term to describe various noncanonical, supposedly revelatory writings—the *Apocalypse of Adam*, the *Apocalypse of Sedrach*, and other "apocalyptic" writings that claimed to have been written by such pseudonymous figures as Shem, Enoch, Peter, etc. When numerous additional works of this nature began to come to the fore in the nineteenth century, the terms "apocalypse" and "apocalyptic" were used to describe their literary genre.

The Apocalypse of John is the only full-blown apocalypse in the NT. The Olivet Discourse probably circulated separately among the early Christians before being finally incorporated (and redacted) by the synoptic evangelists, and is now found in Mark 13, Matthew 24–25, and Luke 21. Other extended apocalyptic portions in the NT include Luke 17:22–37, Rom 8:19–22, 1 Cor 15:51–57, Phil 3:20–21, 1 Thess 4:13–5:11, 2 Thess 2:1–12, and 2 Pet 3:3–13. And underlying many statements in the NT are all sorts of apocalyptic themes and motifs, such as in Phil 4:5, Heb 9:28, Jas 5:8, and 1 Pet 4:7. But the Apocalypse of John stands alone as to genre as the only NT writing cast entirely (or at least almost entirely) in an apocalyptic mold.

In response to some situation of intense hostility—whether Domitian's persecution or some other more localized circumstance; whether a persecution then being experienced or a future persecution anticipated—the author of the Johannine Apocalypse portrays Rome and its emperors as the willing accomplices of Satan who try in vain to destroy the people of God. The three series of eschatological plagues—the seven seals in 6:1–8:1, the seven bowls in 8:2–11:19, the seven trumpets in 15:1–16:21—are divine punishments directed against those responsible for the persecution of God's people (cf. 6:12–17; 16:5–6; 18:4–8). The persecutors become the persecuted. And when the enemies of God and of God's people are finally conquered in the decisive eschatological battles (19:11–21; 20:7–10), the Last Judgment takes place (20:11–14), followed by the triumphal appearance of the new Jerusalem on a transformed earth (21:1–22:6).

The form of an apocalypse is quite different from that of a Gospel or a letter. In an apocalypse the kerygma (proclamation) is transmitted through symbolic portrayals of the present and highly stylized visions of the future. Likewise, the circumstances for the writing of an apocalypse are very different from those for a Gospel or a letter. An apocalypse is primarily concerned with meeting the onslaughts of pagan persecution and giving hope to believers for the future, whereas Gospels and letters are concerned with evangelizing nonbelievers, instructing believers in doctrine and ethics, rebuking apostasy, and polemicizing against heresy.

Such differences of form and circumstance between the Johannine Apocalypse, on the one hand, and the Synoptic Gospels, the Fourth Gospel, the Pauline Letters, and the other epistolary writings of the NT, on the other, mean that the confessional materials used and contextualized in these Gospels and letters may be expected to come to expression in somewhat different fashion in John's Apocalypse. In particular, they may be rather more hidden and allusive in the Apocalypse—as is, in fact, the case. Nonetheless, even if we take into account such differences, five early Christian confessions make their presence felt in the Apocalypse of John: "Jesus is the Messiah," "Jesus is God's Son," "Jesus is humanity's redemptive Lord," "Jesus died redemptively on a cross," and "Jesus is resurrected/exalted to new life."

Jesus as the Messiah (Christ)

The title "Christ" (Χριστός) occurs seven times in the Apocalypse of John. Three times it appears as part of the name "Jesus Christ" in the opening prologue (1:1–3) and salutation (1:4–5), that is, in 1:1, 2, 5. Twice it appears in announcements by heavenly voices in conjunction with references to God: "The kingdom of the world has become the kingdom of our Lord and of his Christ [τοῦ Χριστοῦ αὐτοῦ]" (11:15); "Now have come the salvation and the power and the kingdom of our God, and the authority of his Christ [τοῦ Χριστοῦ αὐτοῦ]" (12:10). The phraseology of these announcements echoes Ps 2:2: "The kings of the earth take their stand and the rulers gather together against the Lord and against his Anointed One [κατὰ τοῦ κυρίου καὶ κατὰ τοῦ Χριστοῦ αὐτοῦ]." That this passage was used by early Christians as a christological testimonium is evident from the quotation of Ps 2:1–2 in Acts 4:25–26. Here in John's Apocalypse, however, the announcements by the heavenly voices celebrate proleptically the divine conquest of the world and the establishment of God's promised kingdom. In addition, the title "Christ" is twice used when reference is made to the martyrs of the tribulation period who come to life to reign with "the Christ" for a thousand years (20:4, 6).

A messianic portrayal of Jesus also comes to the fore in references to David, to the eschatological king, and to the supreme ruler. There are three references to Jesus in relation to David. In 5:5 one of the twenty-four elders gathered around the throne of God speaks of the victorious Lamb as "the Lion of the tribe of Judah, the Root of David [ῥίζα Δαυίδ]"; and in 22:16 Jesus is portrayed as saying of himself: "I am the Root and Offspring of David [ἡ ῥίζα καὶ γένος Δαυίδ]." These references to Jesus as "the Root of David" depend on Isa 11:1 and 10, which were interpreted messianically in both Second Temple Judaism and early Christianity (cf. *Testament of Judah* 24:5; Rom 15:12). And in 3:7 Jesus is described as the one "who has the key of David, who opens and no one can shut and who shuts and no one can open." This text points back to the concluding statement of the glorified Son of Man in 1:18 ("I hold the keys of death and Hades"), which echoes the words of Isa 22:22.

The expression "the key of David" also, it seems, has in John's Apocalypse a messianic significance, suggesting that to Christ belongs complete authority over admission into, or exclusion from, the city of David, the new Jerusalem. Furthermore, in 17:14 and 19:16 Jesus is described as "King of kings and Lord of lords" (in either order), and in 1:5 he is called "the ruler [ὁ ἄρχων] of the kings of the earth."

Jesus as God's Son

The Johannine Apocalypse does not make much of Jesus' status as God's Son. And where it does bring in this confessional motif, it emphasizes not so much the functional nature of sonship (that is, being in loving, obedient relation to the Father) as the more ontological nuances of intimacy and identity with God the Father—as in Hebrews and the Fourth Gospel. Thus in 2:18 the angel of the church in Thyatira speaks of the glorified figure "whose eyes are like blazing fire and whose feet are like burnished brass" (cf. 1:13–16) as "the Son of God." Conversely, in three of the messages to the seven churches this glorified figure is portrayed as referring to God as "my Father" (2:27; 3:5, 21), and twice John the Seer, as narrator, refers to God as "his [Jesus'] Father" (1:6; 14:1).

Perhaps also it should be noted that in the vision of the dragon and the woman in chapter 12, the Seer sees the woman give birth to a son who is "snatched up to God and to his throne." This son, who is also said to be the one "who will rule the nations with a rod of iron," is likely a representation of Jesus and so—bringing together the motifs of messiahship and sonship in an allusive manner—is both the son of true Israel and the true Son of God.

Jesus as Humanity's Redemptive Lord

The title "Lord" with reference to Jesus appears six times in the Apocalypse of John. Twice it occurs in the expression "King of kings and Lord of lords" (17:14 and 19:16, in either order), and twice in the final words of the Apocalypse, which represent the Seer's response: "Come, Lord Jesus" (22:20) and "The grace of the Lord Jesus be with all [God's people]" (22:21). In 11:8 the author describes Jerusalem as the city "where their Lord was crucified." Here the reference is to the two witnesses, Moses and Elijah *redivivus*, who are killed by the beast (the antichrist) in Jerusalem. Their deaths elicit a comparison to the death of "their Lord"— that is, to the death of Jesus, which also occurred in Jerusalem. Finally, "Lord" appears in 14:13 where it is said of the martyrs, "Blessed are the dead who die in the Lord from now on." The phrase "the dead who die in the Lord" is reminiscent of similar phrases in Paul's letters: "those who have fallen asleep in Christ" (1 Cor 15:18) and "the dead in Christ" (1 Thess 4:16).

Jesus Has Died Redemptively on a Cross

The noun "cross" (σταυρός) does not appear at all in the Apocalypse. And the verb "crucify" (σταυρόω) occurs only once, in 11:8—though with reference to Jesus' crucifixion in Jerusalem. Nonetheless, despite such a paucity of traditional terms for crucifixion, the redemptive death of Jesus is depicted frequently by means of the imagery of "the Lamb [τὸ ἀρνίον] who was slain [τὸ ἐσφαγμένον]" or who appears "as slain [ὡς ἐσφαγμένον]."

Twenty-seven times in eleven chapters throughout John's Apocalypse the term "Lamb" designates Jesus the crucified Messiah (starting at 5:6, 8, 12, 13, and concluding with 22:1, 3). The Greek word in every case is ἀρνίον, which is peculiar to the Apocalypse; elsewhere in the NT ἀμνός is used (John 1:29, 36; Acts 8:32; 1 Pet 1:19). Acts 8:32 is a quotation of Isa 53:7b: "He was led like a sheep to the slaughter, and as a lamb [ὡς ἀμνός] before the shearer is silent, so he did not open his mouth." Acts 8:34–35 goes on to say that Philip (and presumably the early Christians) interpreted this passage as referring to Jesus. The Seer's reference to the exalted Jesus as "a Lamb looking as if it had been slain" in 5:6 (the first reference to the Lamb in the Apocalypse) must be seen as highly significant, for it is also clearly derived from Isa 53:7, even though ἀρνίον is used rather than ἀμνός.

In addition, in the Johannine Apocalypse the verb "slay" (σφάζω), which occurs four times in connection with Jesus the Lamb, connotes a sacrificial slaughter (5:6, 9, 12; 13:8). And the phrase "looking as if it had been slain" of 5:6 suggests that those death wounds are to be taken as readily visible on the body of Jesus—though, of course, he is not dead but alive (cf. 1:18; 2:8).

This depiction of Jesus as the Lamb includes two distinct ideas. The first is that of a lamb as a *sacrificial victim*. This idea, already described above, portrays the sacrificial and redemptive work of Jesus. In six verses in his Apocalypse the Seer speaks of Jesus as the Lamb in connection with either "blood" (5:9; 7:14; 12:11) or being "slain" (5:6, 9, 12; 13:8). Thus the redemptive death of Jesus is envisioned as part of the eternal plan of God, for Jesus is spoken of as "the Lamb slain from the foundation of the world" (13:8; cf. 1 Pet 1:19–20). And the sacrificial blood of the

Lamb is understood to be the price paid to purchase humanity for God (5:9).

The second idea included in the Lamb metaphor is that of a *victorious leader*—whether a spiritual leader, as in 7:17; 14:1, 4, or a military leader, as in 5:6 (where the Lamb "has seven horns and seven eyes") and 17:14 (where the Lamb overcomes ten kings who make war against him). The figure of a military leader with horns probably comes from various Jewish apocalyptic writings. *First Enoch* 89, for example, refers to Samuel, David, and Solomon as lambs, but Judas Maccabaeus, the military leader, is pictured as a lamb "with a great horn" (90:9, 12). And in *1 Enoch* 90.38 the Messiah is also symbolized as a horned lamb (cf. *Testament of Joseph* 19:8). What is interesting, however, is that these two ideas of sacrificial victim and victorious leader are merged in the Johannine Apocalypse, for in 5:6 Jesus the Lamb is both the suffering Messiah, whose blood has redeemed people to God, and the triumphant Messiah, who leads his people to victory. It is, in symbolic language, the same message as appears throughout the rest of the NT: Jesus is the triumphant conqueror at the eschatological end because he was the Lamb who was sacrificed on the cross.

Thus, the portrayal of Jesus as a sacrificial Lamb in John's Apocalypse witnesses to the early Christian confession that Jesus died redemptively, and the one brief reference to Jesus' crucifixion in 11:8 ties this redemptive death to the cross on which he died. This concept is announced in the opening doxology of 1:5b–6: "To him who loves us and has freed us from our sins by his blood, and has made us to be a kingdom and priests to serve his God and Father—to him be glory and power for ever and ever! Amen."

Jesus as Resurrected/Exalted to New Life

The early Christian confession that Jesus is resurrected/exalted to new life receives veiled support in three texts of John's Apocalypse. The first is in the salutation at 1:5a, which refers to Jesus Christ as "the faithful witness, the firstborn from the dead [ὁ πρωτότοκος τῶν νεκρῶν], and the ruler [ὁ ἄρχων] of the kings of the earth." Two of the terms here also appear (at least in cognate form) in the confessional material of Col 1:18: "He is the be-

ginning [ἀρχή], the firstborn from among the dead [πρωτότοκος
ἐκ τῶν νεκρῶν]"—which suggests a possible correspondence between this early confessional portion and the statement by John
the Seer. The second text is 1:18a, where the glorified Son of
Man declares, "I am the Living One; I was dead, and behold I am
alive for ever and ever!" And the third is 2:8, which presents the
opening words of the glorified Son of Man to the church in
Smyrna: "These are the words of him who is the First and the
Last, who died and came to life again." In this manner the Seer of
the Apocalypse has contextualized the early Christian conviction
regarding Jesus' resurrection/exaltation to new life, using it to
highlight the authority of the words of the living Christ to his redeemed people.

PART 3

The Contextualization of the Confessions Today

hristians have always been involved in contextualizing the gospel. For if the message of the kingdom of God as focused in Jesus is to be communicated effectively, it must always be proclaimed and worked out in ways that are relevant to the worldview and culture of those being addressed. Or to express matters in the imagery used by Jesus himself, "New wine *must* be poured into fresh wineskins" (Luke 5:38)—for to pour new wine into old wineskins is to "spill" the wine and "destroy" the skins, but when new wine is poured into fresh wineskins, "both are preserved" (Matt 9:17; cf. Mark 2:22; Luke 5:37-38).

The most important catalyst for "thinking contextually" as Christians has always been, and is today, the missionary enterprise of the church. It is at the frontiers of the Christian mission that the church directly encounters other religions, other worldviews, and other cultural values, and so it is at the frontiers of the Christian mission that the most intensive study of contextualization takes place. And since every discipline of study requires something of its own vocabulary, it is among missiologists that certain terms either have been coined or have taken on a distinctive nuance—such as "dialogue," "adaptation," "accommodation," "analogy," "indigenization," "inculturation," "localization," and even the term "contextualization" itself.

Before the 1950s, most Western Christians, church leaders, and theologians seem to have taken it for granted that the Christianity of Europe and North America was supraterritorial, supra-ideological, and supracultural, and so directly accessible to all the people of the world, whatever their backgrounds, worldviews, or cultures. Such a view appears to have been based on assumptions regarding (1) the givenness of Western Christianity's understanding of the gospel, (2) the superiority of Western Christendom's cultural traditions, and (3) the homogeneity of all people, whatever their various outlooks and cultures. Thus the church, it was thought, did not need to adapt its message to the cultures and societies it addressed; rather, those evangelized needed to adopt the Christian religion as it was known and practiced by Western Christendom.

A number of factors, however, have brought about a rather dramatic shift in the church's understanding of its mission and the need to contextualize its message. Probably most significant in the development of a modern theory of Christian mission have been (1) the deliberations of the World Missionary Conference held in Edinburgh in 1910, which was preceded by similar events in London in 1888 and New York in 1900, (2) the work of the International Missionary Council, which was formed in 1921 to continue the work of the 1910 World Missionary Conference, and (3) the activities and writings of such missionary statesmen as Stephen Neill and Lesslie Newbigin.[1] On a practical level, the largely indigenous growth of Christianity in Asia, Africa, and South America, which has come to the Western world's attention only during the last half of the twentieth century, has brought about a growing realization that Western ways of contextualizing the gospel do not always fit the understanding and circumstances of non-Western people.

Furthermore, people during the past few decades have become painfully aware that differing cultures are often openly in conflict with one another, that diverse ideologies often pit themselves against one another, and that regional nationalisms often strive for their own distinctiveness and independence. The utopian dream of "One World for One People," with all its different parts and diverse personalities eventually coming together, has been shattered. And with that shattering, an idealistic view of Christianity as only able to be properly expressed in Western garb has come to an end.

Almost everyone today, in whatever field, faces challenges of communicating and understanding cross-culturally. The mass migration of people to the West, bringing with them differing ideologies and lifestyles, has brought many diverse cultural issues home to us who live in Europe and North America. Likewise, the modern media and worldwide travel have alerted us, as never before, to the complexity of multiculturalism throughout the world. And with the resultant continuing redefinition and readjustment of values, we in the West have come to appreciate that issues of differing ideological stances and cultural values have not just been foisted on us from the outside but are also indigenous within our own societies.

The question, therefore, that faces the Christian church today—and that it has always, more or less, had to face throughout its history—is simply this: How can we communicate the good news of Jesus Christ most responsibly and most effectively *and* at the same time stay both faithful to the gospel message itself and sensitive to the circumstances of those being addressed? Many answers have been given by Western Christians, and each of these responses has been influenced, whether overtly or unconsciously, by the theological and cultural perspectives of its advocates. Of even greater significance is the fact that with the maturing of Christian churches in the mission fields of the past, much of the most creative thinking today regarding the contextualization of the gospel stems from so-called third-world theologians.

Our own response to the question of contextualizing the gospel—which, it must be admitted, is also theologically and culturally conditioned—is in the form of a three-part proposal: First, we must begin by giving attention to the early Christian confessions incorporated within the writings of the NT, for these materials express the heart of the gospel and so should serve as the basis for all of our attempts to contextualize the gospel (Part 1, above). Second, we need to observe how the NT writers themselves contextualized these early Christian confessions in addressing the particular mind-sets, problems, and circumstances of their day, for from their endeavors we gain not only a historical perspective but also sensitivity and insight into how the essential features of the gospel can be contextualized in the varying situations of our day (Part 2, above). And third, we are called by God to work out both a philosophy of and a program for contextualizing these same Christian confessions for people today who live with different worldviews and in differing cultures, subcultures, and circumstances, whether in our own country or other regions of the world (Part 3). Thus, while Christian theology must always be rooted in its revelational base, it must also always attempt to be relevant by working out an appropriate missiological philosophy and program for communicating the gospel—allowing its theories in these areas to guide the formulation of its statements and the actualization of its practices.

In any study of contextualization, issues of theory and practice are inextricably intertwined. For purposes of analysis, however, they can be separated. In what follows, therefore, we will deal first with a philosophy of contextualization, setting out various models of understanding and proposing a path to be followed (ch. 6). Then we will raise issues regarding the practice of contextualization, offering some proposals that may help in implementing an incarnational and contextualized theology today (ch. 7).

CHAPTER SIX

Models for an Understanding of Contextualization

Models are merely mental constructs of existing realities. They are not the realities themselves. They attempt to explain in abstract fashion how something can be viewed and put into practice. Yet though they are only abstractions, they are still useful, for they often present in a particularly cogent manner the major thrust of a position or stance. They may not explain or illuminate everything about the position in question. Nor can they be treated in any exclusivist fashion, as though there are no areas of overlap between positions. Nonetheless, since models for understanding can take us into the heart of a person's thought or a system's practice, they provide important starting points for evaluating competing philosophical approaches and for presenting one's own view vis-à-vis all the others that claim a hearing.

The process of contextualizing the Christian gospel can be understood along the lines of one or the other of the following models: (1) a transferal model, (2) a translation model, (3) an anthropological model, (4) an ethnological model, (5) a transcendental model, (6) a semiotic model, or (7) a synergistic-developmental model. The first two (the transferal and translation models) begin with Scripture, the gospel, and tradition and then seek either to apply (as in the case of the first) or to adapt (as in the case of the second) this message to a receptor people and culture. The next two (the anthropological and ethnological models) begin with a people and its culture, first analyzing the people's experiences and circumstances and then attempting to show how the Christian gospel speaks to the perceived needs of that people and culture.

The fifth (the transcendental model) begins with individual persons as cultural and religious subjects and asserts that there exists in each person an *a priori* basis of knowledge, which is distinct in some fashion from Scripture, tradition, or culture. It then attempts to gain insight for authentic and meaningful living from all that has affected the particular person externally—from Scripture, tradition, and culture, but not necessarily taking any of these as being normative or authoritative. The sixth (the semiotic model) begins by attempting to discover the essential symbols of a particular culture and its people, on the one hand, and of Scripture and Christian tradition, on the other, believing that by means of a sustained dialogue between these two sets of symbols a valid contextual theology will develop. The seventh (the synergistic-developmental model) proposes that, based on a developmental understanding of the message of Scripture and a developmental understanding of a particular culture and its people, a synergistic interaction between the central core of the Christian gospel—which, as we are arguing, is found in the early Christian confessions of the NT—and the noblest features of the culture in question will produce a truly valid Christian theology, whatever particular expressions, forms, rites, and practices may ensue.

By spelling out more fully each of these models, it is hoped that this chapter will help clarify and explicate a philosophy and practice for today.

1. THE TRANSFERAL MODEL

The transferal model of contextualization lays almost exclusive emphasis on the content of the Christian message, with some consideration also given, more or less, to how this content has been explicated down through the centuries. It stresses the Christian Scriptures, but it gives little or no attention to the ideological, ethnological, sociological, or cultural diversities in the various receptor situations or localities. Like a design or pattern that is transferred from one surface to another, with thought given only to how the design should be positioned on the receptor surface, the gospel message is seen as being transferred from early times to the present, with attention directed mainly to what the gospel displaces in a particular culture and how it should be positioned amidst the various ideas and practices current in the culture. Much of Western mass evangelism follows the transferal model; most TV evangelists and all practitioners of so-called power evangelism are extreme examples of this approach.

The strength of the transferal model is the seriousness with which it takes the Christian gospel. At times it is also strong in its understanding of certain features in the history of the gospel's transmission. Its weaknesses, however, stem from its reticence to understand the people or the society being evangelized. In the main, this model only uses certain superficial features that it finds in the culture encountered—usually only to make contact with the people it addresses.

A number of mitigating factors serve to alleviate some of the weaknesses of this approach. First, some ideological perspectives and some cultural expressions seem to be common to all people—though, admittedly, it is always difficult to identify these matters with precision. Such perspectives and features provide a minimal base for the reception of the gospel on a transferal model. Second, not only has mass communication tended to homogenize much of Western culture, it has also profoundly effected the ideologies and cultures of the East and people's thinking throughout the third world. A transferal model of contextualization will, therefore, often experience some success—though the number of people it alienates, simply because it pays little attention to differing philosophical stances and the needs of people in different societies, will probably continue to be high compared with those that it affects in a positive manner.

A third important mitigating factor, particularly from a Christian theistic perspective, is that there is no circumstance or cultural situation where God is not present and where God cannot work out his redemptive purposes. God is sovereign. God can do the unexpected as he wills. One might bray like Balaam's donkey in preaching, confuse matters terribly in teaching, and be entirely inept in ministry, yet somehow God is able to take an earnest Christian's poor endeavors and use them for his glory and the benefit of others, whatever their varied situations and cultures. A holy serendipity, of course, is always to be welcomed. Yet it cannot justify one's laziness or stubbornness in espousing only a transferal model for the contextualization of the gospel.

▪ 2. THE TRANSLATION MODEL

The translation model of contextualization starts with the Christian message, as that message has been understood in the church's history of interpretation, and then endeavors to adapt the essential principles of this Christian proclamation to new situations and cultures. It follows a two-step procedure: (1) the deculturalization of the revelatory data of the Christian message, which allows for the principles of the gospel to stand freely apart from the specific circumstances or cultural conditioning in which they were originally given; (2) the reculturalization of these data into a new situation or culture, which allows for these principles to be expressed in a fashion indigenous to the receptor people and culture. The imagery often used in a translation model is that of a kernel of grain in its husk: the kernel represents what is translated into a new situation or culture, and the husk represents the context in which it was previously incarnated—or, when reculturalized, the receptor situation or culture into which it becomes newly planted.

The watchword of the translation model is "functional equivalence" or "dynamic equivalence." This means, as in modern Bible translation, the distilling of biblical words and images into their essential conceptual forms and then the translating of those concepts into the language, imagery, and ethos relevant to a particular situation and culture. The translation model is probably the oldest and most common model for contextualizing the gospel. It is the one that people almost instinctively associate with the missionary enterprise of the church. Two of its prominent advocates today are the translation theorist Eugene A. Nida and the missionary anthropologist Charles H. Kraft.

The strengths of the translation model are many. Chief among them are that (1) it attempts to be true to the biblical data, seeking to discern its essential principles, (2) it attempts to be true to the history of interpretation regarding this data, allowing variations of understanding and application down through history and in various localities to aid in separating the essential principles from their situational and cultural wrappings, and (3) it attempts to be true to the receptor situation and culture, seeking how best to express these essential principles for people in a different situation and culture.

It also, however, has weaknesses. First, this model often finds it difficult to discern between the essential principles and the situational-cultural wrappings of the biblical message. Second, in its biblical interpretation it often treats Scripture in a rather static fashion, without giving due credence to developments between the testaments or to differences within the testaments. Third, it all-too-often assumes the ability of outside experts to understand and decode the perspectives, customs, and cultures of the recipients, and so it can make rather superficial judgments about the meaning of certain images and the interrelationship of certain ideas of the receptor people.

Translation models of contextualization, as Robert Schreiter points out, "are generally the first kind of model to be used in pastoral settings."[2] The reason is simply that when faced with another situation and another culture, the pastor or missioner experiences the immediate need to adapt his or her message to local circumstances—whether translating the Christian gospel into imagery that will be understandable to a particular people; translating the language, imagery, and ethos of the Bible into another language; translating the teachings of Scripture into concepts able to be appreciated by local thinkers; translating the ethics of Scripture into meaningful Christian living in a different culture; or translating the rituals associated with the Bible and Christendom into rites conducive to the furtherance of the gospel in another environment.

But the adaptation of the Christian message to another situation or another culture takes a great deal of time. More important, it often requires more than just equivalent forms of expression.

Many times it requires a combination of what could be called (1) a *developmental* method of treatment, both in understanding the biblical message and in understanding a particular culture and worldview, and (2) a *synergistic* method of treatment in working out relations between the gospel and human culture—as will be suggested in the seventh model, below.

▦ 3. THE ANTHROPOLOGICAL MODEL

The anthropological model roots revelation not in Scripture or in any other traditional formulations but in humanity generally and in the spiritual experiences of a given people in particular. It views human nature as basically good and essentially oriented toward God, and it finds this goodness and orientation most often in the lives of ordinary people. Human cultures, therefore, are generally to be understood, appreciated, and affirmed, for, unless they have become despotic by the imposition of other forces, they most often express in communal fashion the basic goodness and God-ward orientation of ordinary people. Thus, one cannot speak of bringing Christ to a people or proclaiming the gospel to other cultures, since human experience is itself holy and human cultures compose the matrix where God's message is to be found.

The anthropological model does not see its task to apply, adapt, or accommodate the Christian gospel to a particular people or culture. Though perhaps somewhat hidden, the essence of the gospel, it is claimed, has been a part of every culture all along, for people—who are already God's own by creation and because of his presence among them—are the basic units of society. Revelation, in fact, is to be found in all of the human cultures of the world. Therefore, people and their spiritual experiences form the basis and criteria for all theological truth; the movement is from a people's indigenous spirituality to the expression of religious faith in terms of that people's own experiences and culture.

This has been the approach of classical liberalism, which continues in many forms today. The imagery used in this model is not that of pouring the "new wine" of Christian proclamation into "fresh wineskins," but of developing a newer and truer wine. This newer and truer wine (though, of course, inspired by the "new wine" of Jesus) has been distilled from the God-consciousness of people themselves, and so readily resonates with their inherent spirituality.

A primary concern of Christians who follow this model is the expression of their self-identity. Should they view themselves as Filipino Christians, as African Christians, as Asian Christians, or whatever (with the noun "Christian" signaling their essential identity and the cultural adjective referring to a particular group within this larger body)? Or should they think of themselves as "christianized" Filipinos, "christianized" Africans, "christianized" Asians, or whatever (with their cultural heritage signaling their essential identity and the adjective indicating a particular feature that is important in their thinking)?

There is much in the anthropological model that is attractive and that provides a basis for helpful dialogue. It certainly upholds the essential dignity and worth of every individual, which is an important biblical and Christian truth. And it often helps people see Christianity in terms of their particular culture in a new and fresh way. On the other hand, it minimizes the presence of evil in every person and every society, trivializes the Christian proclamation of redemption in Christ, and turns theology into philosophy and Christian ethics into situational moralism. It can also easily become prey to a cultural romanticism that opposes all forms of change—whether religious, cultural, or social; whether personal or corporate—thereby fossilizing the supposed situations of "the happy native" and "pristine, primitive cultures" (*à la* Jean Jacques Rousseau, the eighteenth-century philosopher).

■ 4. THE ETHNOLOGICAL MODEL

The ethnological model for contextualizing the gospel focuses on Christian identity within a culture and highlights the features of social change taking place within that culture. It understands revelation as God's ongoing activity in history—activity manifested in particular situations and concrete events. Theology consists, it argues, in this: to discern, through analysis, where God is acting, and then to attempt, through Scripture, tradition, and reflective action, to act in these situations as God's partner. This

way of understanding contextualization, therefore, begins with
an analysis of human conditions within a particular culture, then
turns to Scripture and Christian tradition for data to inform a
Christian's moral conscience, and then, most important, attempts to work out solutions to the identifiable problems in the
crucible of political and social action. In effect, it sees the interaction between the analysis of a human problem, a Christian moral
conscience, and resultant political and social action as a sort of di-
alectical upward spiral, where thought and action are always in
process toward accomplishing the greater good for people in
their particular situations.

One particularly important feature of this approach is its
emphasis on human cultures as exceedingly complex. Cultures
are not viewed simply in terms of their language patterns, modes
of behavior, or social customs. Rather, the emphasis in most ethnological models today is on the political and economic systems
that dominate various cultures. Another important feature of this
approach is its stress on theology not done in ivory towers or expressed in academic books but shaped by, and accomplished
through, action. Thus, most theologians today who use this
model are primarily interested in the liberation of people from
some type of oppression, whether political, economic, or social—
or, more commonly, some combination of all three.

The role of the theologian, therefore, is understood as like
that of a midwife, enabling others to become empowered instead
of being subjugated. Using such an approach, one begins with (1)
an analysis of the political, economic, and/or social realities that
confront people in their everyday experiences and (2) an analysis
of Scripture and Christian tradition, usually using what has been
called a "hermeneutic of suspicion" regarding most past interpretations. On the basis of such theologizing, one then engages in
such actions as seem appropriate to rectify the particular situation,
incorporating into one's activities the moral imperatives that were
highlighted in one's analyses and reflection. After this, one moves
forward to reflect on those actions vis-à-vis the situation confronted, and so the process continues, over and over again.

Liberation theology—whether the liberation theology of
Latin America, black liberation, women's liberation, or whatever—

is a vital movement on the world scene today. Its great strengths lie in (1) highlighting the dynamic relationship that must always exist between knowledge and practice in Christianity, or between orthodoxy ("right thinking") and orthopraxis ("right doing"), and (2) challenging in the name of Christ certain ingrained, *status quo* features in society, whether these traditionally accepted stances be political, economic, or social. Its weaknesses, however, are that (1) it is better at analyzing the political, economic, and/or social situations faced than listening to the gospel, often making the latter fit the former, and (2) it can easily become tyrannical itself, merely exchanging one form of oppression for another, for liberated people are to be free and not enslaved to anyone's dogma, however noble.

■ 5. THE TRANSCENDENTAL MODEL

The transcendental model of contextualization stems from the "transcendental method" of Immanuel Kant, which has been developed philosophically by Joseph Maréchal and theologically by Karl Rahner and Bernard J. F. Lonergan. It postulates a transcendental, *a priori* knowledge that resides inherently in every person—even, particularly for those more theologically inclined, a supernatural and mystical knowledge. Thus, it begins not with Scripture, tradition, or culture but with one's own experience as a cultural and religious subject. It shifts attention from the external world of that which can be objectified—whether the teachings of Scripture and ecclesial tradition, on the one hand, or the values of a particular culture and its worldview, on the other—to the interior world of the person. It focuses on one's self-experience both as a Christian and as a subject within a unique culture. And it proceeds by asking questions such as: How well do I know myself? How genuine is my own religious experience, which I am trying to interpret? How free am I of bias? How comfortable do I feel with the particular expression of my own religious experience? Do I really understand what I am saying?

Two tenets figure prominently in a transcendental approach to contextualization: (1) the working of the human mind is transcultural, and so there is a universal way of coming to truth; and (2) revelation is found only in one's own personal experience, which can be stimulated by Scripture, Christian tradition, or one's culture, even though such external realities are not to be seen as containing within them an objective deposit of revelation. By attending to the exigencies of one's own mind—which has been formed by one's own experiences, understandings, judgments, and decisions—one comes to truth about one's self, about God, and about all that exists. Admittedly, what one experiences, how one comes to understanding, the criteria for judgment, and the results of a decision will vary from culture to culture, as well as from one historical period to another. But transcendental thinkers are convinced that the basic operations remain the same.

The imagery of contextualization for a transcendental model is that of a pair of scissors, with one blade representing the subject's culture and the other blade the subject's religious experience. Theology happens when the two blades are brought together. Little concern is expressed for the rightness or wrongness of the theology that is thereby contextualized. For it is not right or wrong content that is important but the authentic or inauthentic subjectivity of the person doing theology.

The transcendental model points to a new way of doing theology. It argues that theology is not principally concerned with a set of right answers that may be "out there" somewhere but, rather, with the presence of God's love in one's life in a way that is always and everywhere culturally conditioned. Thus it highlights what it claims to be a universally valid process for doing theology.

The weaknesses of a transcendental model, however, seem all too evident. For the questions must be asked: (1) Is there really a transcendental body of knowledge that is universal among all people, or is this just another imagined feature imposed by Western thinkers? (2) Do all people really understand in basically the same fashion, or is the thought process of people also culturally conditioned? (3) Is subjective authenticity really the only criterion for an authentic theology, or in denying the necessity for objective truth has this approach merely retreated into a questionable abstraction?

▓ 6. THE SEMIOTIC MODEL

Robert J. Schreiter of Chicago's Catholic Theological Union recently developed the semiotic model of contextualization. A manuscript version of his position circulated widely in 1977 for purposes of discussion and interaction, and his monograph *Constructing Local Theologies* was published in 1985. His model builds generally on the work of Roland Barthes in France and a number of eastern European scholars. But it develops most particularly the work of Clifford Geertz, for whom cultures are "systems of significant symbols." Schreiter calls his proposal "local theology," or simply a "contextual model." It has, however, been dubbed by others "the semiotic model," and this label is probably the most accurate.

At the heart of Schreiter's position is his call for a contextualization of the gospel that "listens to culture" by means of a semiological analysis—that is, by giving attention to the essential signs and symbols of a culture (the term "semiotic" stems from the Greek word σημεῖον, "sign" or "symbol"). He believes that by a sensitive semiotic listening, one can discover the basic symbols of a culture and thus identify the primary features around which a contextual theology can develop. Just as intently, however, one must also listen to the message and spirit of the gospel proclamation and to the entire tradition of the whole people of God. Thus, Schreiter understands revelation as something discovered within a specific cultural context itself, although it is also that which adheres, in some practical manner, to the Christian Scriptures and ecclesial tradition. Furthermore, it is by a semiotic reading of a people's culture, on the one hand, and of Scripture and tradition, on the other, that correspondences can be made. For the symbols of Scripture and the church's tradition change a people's understanding of its culture; conversely, the symbols of a people's culture change traditional understandings of Scripture.

The procedure of a semiotic model, as proposed by Schreiter, is complex. One begins by analyzing the symbols of a culture, looking not just at its expressions and patterns but primarily at their contexts and meanings in these contexts. But one must also attend to the Scriptures and ecclesial tradition in the same manner.

Only as one correlates the primary symbols of culture and Scripture-tradition, understood as two parallel columns, that can one begin to build a local theology. And it is this construct of a local theology that has a transforming impact on a local culture.

Schreiter's model has won high praise in many quarters, for it takes both culture and Scripture-tradition seriously and recognizes that Christianity in any culture must be homegrown and not transplanted. Furthermore, it utilizes methods drawn from semiotic linguistics and symbolic anthropology, which many believe to be the most appropriate ways to analyze a culture. One of its main difficulties, however, is that because of its complexity the model leaves many with a sense of bewilderment. Another difficulty is that, in its view, Scripture does not possess any intrinsic revelational authority but is revelation ordained by God only because it has stood the test of time by containing "successful local theologies."

▓ 7. THE SYNERGISTIC-DEVELOPMENTAL MODEL

The synergistic-developmental model, as I have coined and use this expression, seeks to be true to the apostolic faith and witness of the NT and to the circumstances, culture, and ideological perspectives of those being addressed. It profits from observing how the gospel has been contextualized in the past (by studying contextualizations in the apostolic period and throughout church history) and how it is being contextualized in various countries and regions of the world today (by being alert to modern linguistic, sociological, and anthropological studies and to reports of missionary activities worldwide). But it considers all past and present attempts at contextualizing the gospel to be only temporal and local expressions of the one normative Christian message. And it judges all past and present attempts to contextualize the Christian gospel on the basis of how accurately they embody the essentials of the earliest Christian convictions and how well they communicate these convictions to the peoples and cultures they address.

Basic to a synergistic-developmental model are two fundamental realizations: (1) that an understanding of Scripture and an understanding of a particular culture can not come about simply from a static view of the phenomena but, rather, must be constructed with an appreciation that development has taken place in both sets of data; and (2) that relations between the gospel and any culture are synergistic—that is, they are meant by God to work together in order to produce a truly contextualized theology and lifestyle. The first realization highlights the need to study Scripture and its resultant traditions, on the one hand, and particular peoples and their cultures, on the other, in terms of their central concerns and their cultural variations. Such a developmental understanding must note both the features that reflect an essential unity within the data and the features that evidence patterns of expressional diversity. To state matters somewhat differently, it must note both what can be identified as the coherent center within a system of thought and various contingent ways of giving form to this coherent center. For not everything is equally valid, of the same importance, or necessarily transcultural, either in Scripture or in a particular society.

The second realization asserts the need to find areas of correspondence between the gospel and a particular culture. Admittedly, one cannot be so naive as to think that everything in a culture has, or can be seen to have, some correspondence to the gospel. Sin and evil are rampant in every culture, for cultures reflect the conditions of sinful people. Nonetheless, there are numerous features of nobility, love, and greatness in all cultures, even though variously expressed. And it is the task of a contextual theology to identify these nobler features and to relate the essence of the gospel to them, with each side interacting with the other in a synergistic fashion.

A synergistic-developmental model may be compared to what happens when two seeds from one nursery plant are planted in different soils and climates. Both mature, though with minor differences. For although both seeds are identical, they will differ in appearance under different circumstances. Their fruit, however, will remain essentially the same. Yet as the new plants cross-pollinate with native plants they will produce a hybrid—which hybrid will produce fruit somewhat different, but still very much like the fruit of the original seed. The referent of this imagery is the planting of the seeds of the Christian gospel into various ideological contexts and diverse cultural situations, where the seeds come to maturity and cross-pollinate in the context of their respective receptor peoples and cultures—with those new flowerings of Christianity faithful both to the apostolic faith of the NT and to the cultures and perspectives of those addressed.

The watchwords of a syncretistic-developmental model are *adaptation*, "to become suitable to a new or special use or situation," and *analogy*, "correspondence in some respects, especially in function or position, between things otherwise dissimilar." The term *imagination* is also appropriate in its secondary sense, "the ability to deal creatively with reality" (but not, as is usually understood, "the formation of a mental image or concept of that which is not real or present").[3]

Like the translation model, a syncretistic-developmental model recognizes the need, first of all, to adapt the gospel to the understanding of a receptor people and to the sensibilities of a receptor culture. That is, there is the need, at least at the beginning, to work in terms of a "dynamic equivalence" of language, imagery, and ethos. But as the contextualizing of the gospel continues, there arises more and more the need to find areas of correspondence between the gospel and the particular culture so as to allow the gospel to grow in an indigenous fashion and permit it to have a direct impact on the culture. In this process the method of analogy comes into play, for it is only through analogy that apparent dissimilarities between the gospel and a culture can be overcome and valid correspondences drawn.

The obvious strengths of a synergistic-developmental model are that it seeks to (1) uphold the integrity of the apostolic tradition, (2) understand both the apostolic tradition and those being addressed in terms of a coherent set of foundational convictions and various contingent ways of expressing these central convictions, and (3) respect the perspectives and cultures of those being addressed. In particular (spelling out our own thesis), it highlights, on the one hand, the importance of the early Christian confessional materials in the NT, finding in them the basic norms for all Christian thought and practice, and, on the other, attempts to contextualize these confessions in a manner appropriate to the people, circumstances, and culture being addressed. In so doing, it seeks to engage in a pattern of contextualization that can be seen in the NT itself, though not always evident in the annals of church history or in some contemporary missionary practices.

The weaknesses of a developmental model, however, are also apparent. One weakness is that the synergistic-developmental model presents an ideal that is always skewed by the human factors of finitude and sin, both in our endeavors to identify the central features of the Christian gospel and in our attempts to contextualize these features in a particular circumstance or setting. A further weakness is that such an approach can be somewhat naïve about the purity of a receptor situation, not always appreciating that there is no such thing as a pristine culture or environment. For competing factors are always present in every situation, whether intrinsic to the situation or brought in from the outside.

The experiences of Christians in mainland China, particularly those living in the country regions, may come the closest to the ideal of an indigenous Christianity that is developing in its own fashion today. People in many regions of China have been, it seems, rather brutally cut off from their past philosophic traditions and from all outside Christian influence. Yet reports filtering out of China suggest the existence of a thriving and vital Christianity that has no contact with Western Christendom—and that, indeed, desires not to be contaminated by Western Christianity's influence. Still, even in many of the isolated regions, memories of the past continue—memories of past Confucian teachings, past Christian teachings, and past Communist teachings, along with their respective practices. Undoubtedly there is something of a hybridization of Christian faith going on throughout mainland China, and this probably reflects not only a unity amidst diversity but also great diversity within an essential unity. With the country largely closed to Western eyes, the situation of the church and the state of Christian theology in China are difficult to determine. But from what is known, it seems that a number of contextualized versions of Christian thought and practice are taking place in various regions of China today.

Despite the problems of implementing a synergistic-developmental model of contextualization, it is an eminently biblical model. Indeed, it finds its ultimate paradigm in God, who has set the pattern for Christian ministry in his own redemptive activity. For God (1) has revealed himself and his redemptive purposes to humanity in an incarnational and developmental manner and (2) has contextualized his love and redemption in a synergistic fashion in the midst of diverse situations and cultures. Incarnational and contextualized theology is, therefore, at the very heart of the biblical message. Furthermore, the writers of the NT, in their development of the gospel message and their adaptations of its principles to audiences and situations, have presented a number of paradigms for carrying out similar synergistic-developmental contextualizations today.

As argued earlier, Jesus' use of the imagery of "new wine into fresh wineskins" (Mark 2:22, par.) rather clearly indicates that his followers are to be involved in just such a developing and synergistic contextualization. Likewise, his concluding words to his parables of the kingdom in Matthew's Gospel also suggest such an enterprise. For at the conclusion to his parables of Matthew 13 Jesus asked his disciples, "Have you understood all these things?" (v. 51). When they answered "Yes," he gave them another parable: "Every teacher of the law who has been instructed about the kingdom of heaven is like the owner of a house who brings out of his storeroom new treasures as well as old" (v. 52).

Many features of this brief concluding parable are fairly easy to understand. The "kingdom of heaven" is certainly the reign of God in people's lives, as proclaimed by, effected by, and focused in Jesus. Likewise, the "teacher of the law who has been instructed about the kingdom" is one who is committed to and instructed by Jesus—that is, a Christian teacher, not some Jewish scribe trained in the traditions of the Pharisees. It is also obvious that the parable has something to do with how Christians are to interpret divine revelation and apply its message to their day, for it comes at the end of a group of seven parables that do just that for the disciples.

Furthermore, the parable in its context suggests that Jesus is, in some manner, the paradigm for Christian teachers. Just as

Jesus' pattern of ministry is the paradigm for Christian discipleship ("It is enough for the student to be like his teacher, and the
servant like his master" [Matt 10:25]), so Jesus' manner of interpretation is to have some bearing on how Christians interpret
and apply Scripture. Thus, just as Jesus is portrayed in Matthew's
Gospel as the new Moses (esp. chs 5–7)—a new and better inter-
preter of the Torah—so here his disciples are exhorted to be new
and better scribes of the kingdom.

The most difficult feature of the parable, however, is Jesus'
comparison of Christian teachers to a householder "who brings
out of his storeroom new treasures as well as old." What did Jesus
mean by "new" and by "old"? As his followers today, seeking to
interpret and proclaim the Christian message, what are we to understand by the phrase "new treasures as well as old," and how
are we to relate the new and the old?

Most commentators have concluded that by "old" and
"new" here is meant what we would call the religion of Israel and
the message of the NT—that is, to use some other favored expressions, "the Old Dispensation of Judaism," "the Mosaic law,"
and/or "the Old Testament promises," on the one hand, and "the
New Dispensation that has come with Christ," "the fulfillment of
the Mosaic law in Jesus' ministry," and/or "Jesus' own teaching,"
on the other. Some take "old" and "new" to refer more broadly to
such concepts as "the Holy Scriptures and the disciples' own in-
ward experience of what true religion is" or even "the Old
Evangel of the Bible and the new insights of recent scholarship."
Others have despaired of ever being able to determine what the
words might have meant, either to Jesus or to the evangelist
Matthew.

Recently, however, there has been a tendency to view the
old and new of Matt 13:52 in terms of, respectively, (1) the gospel
proclamation, which has as its focus the teaching and work of
Jesus, and (2) fuller understandings and new applications of this
proclamation for various new situations and circumstances faced
by Christian prophets and teachers—including Matthew's own
shaping of the Jesus tradition in his Gospel for his own community and audience. In agreement with this, I propose that here
Jesus speaks of the Christian teacher as one who (1) is rooted in

the gospel proclamation—its foundation being the salvation history of the OT, its focus being the redemptive work of Christ, and its central convictions first coming to expression in the early Christian confessions—*and* (2) makes the gospel relevant to current times and circumstances by understanding more fully and applying more adequately the proclamation to his or her own situation.

Relevancy entails contextualization. Thus, what is needed today is a synergistic-developmental model for the contextualization of the gospel—in particular, the contextualization of the early Christian confessions. The following chapter will develop this approach, offering some suggestions on how to implement an incarnational and contextualized theology.

CHAPTER SEVEN

Toward an Incarnational
and Contextualized Theology

Second Corinthians 5:19a captures the heart of the gospel in its early Christian confession: "God was in Christ reconciling the world to himself, not counting people's sins against them." The statement incorporates two vital motifs. The first is explicit: the incarnation. In the OT, God is portrayed as "dwelling" in the tabernacle, in the Jerusalem temple, in the city of Jerusalem itself, and, preeminently, among his people Israel in a way in which he did not dwell in any other sanctuary, city, or nation. Among the early Christians, however, the foundational conviction was that God was present in the ministry and person of Jesus of Nazareth in a manner unparalleled in human history—that is, that God was more intensively and personally incarnate in Jesus than in any of his earlier relationships with his people; that in Jesus the divine nature and will were focused in a historical person who was both fully human and fully divine.

The second motif of 2 Cor 5:19a, though implied, still deserves to be taken seriously: the contextualization motif. The statement suggests (1) that what God accomplished in and through Jesus was brought about in ways that could be understood and appreciated—though also, of course, misunderstood and perverted—by people of that day and (2) that what God accomplished redemptively in and through Jesus is to be worked out and applied by the church, under the guidance and enablement of God's Spirit, to all people in their various circumstances and different cultures in ways that can be understood and appreciated by them. Thus, at the heart of the Christian gospel is this dual recognition: (1) that as God was present, active, and understood in the life of the nation Israel, so he was present, active, and understood—though in a much more intensive and personalized fashion—in the work and person of Jesus of Nazareth; and (2) that as God's Spirit worked through the prophets and apostles to contextualize God's purposes for people of their times, so the church, under the guidance of this same Spirit, is engaged in contextualizing God's redemption through Christ for people today.

In response to what God did in and through Jesus, the earliest believers in Jesus, as we have seen, both confessed their faith in a christocentric fashion and attempted to contextualize what they confessed—applying the message of those confessions to the exigencies of their own lives and the lives of others and seeking to make it relevant in the contexts of differing situations and somewhat different cultures. The early Christians seem to have known intuitively that a gospel that was incarnational in its origin and contextualized in its proclamation to them must also be contextualized in its outreach to others if, indeed, other people were to experience the fullness of a true incarnational theology.

The challenge for Christians today is not only to affirm the same gospel that the early Christians confessed in their hymns, *homologiai*, confessional sayings, and single-statement affirmations, but also to carry on their work of contextualizing this same gospel. The early Christians began the work of contextualization, but they hardly can be said to have completed it. Rather, what they began must be carried on in our day.

In some respects, the task of contextualizing the gospel is more daunting today than it was for the writers of the NT. They were able to use what seems to have been fairly well known materials—widely accepted confessions, hymns, prayers, narrative materials, sayings sources, catechetical collections, an eschatological discourse, and the like—in attempting to contextualize the gospel for the needs of their congregations and addressees. And they worked within cultures that were fairly homogenized in ways of thinking (because of the influence of Greek thought) and civic practice (because of Roman law). Today, however, in our attempts at contextualizing, we are frequently called on to deal with a greater variety of situations and outlooks, all of which have been affected, to some extent, by greater differences of time, ideological perspective, and culture. Furthermore, we are required to take into consideration all of the church's previous efforts at contextualization (or miscontextualization) and to make value judgments regarding their respective merits (or demerits). The task, therefore, has grown larger with the passing of time and our own increased awareness of diversity among cultures.

Nonetheless, the writers of the NT—and the writers of the OT, though in analogous fashion—have presented paradigms for contextualizing the gospel. They have shown how what Christians confess can be contextualized for purposes of worship, proclamation, doctrinal formulation, and ethical living. Some suggestions drawn from these paradigms will be put forward here as we attempt to explicate a synergistic-developmental model of contextualization (as proposed in ch. 6, above), seeking to understand how the message of the Christian gospel can be extended to other people, new situations, and different cultures.

■ 1. THE CONTEXTUALIZATION OF WORSHIP

Worship is undoubtedly the appropriate place to begin a discussion of contextualization, for it was in the context of worship that the earliest Christian confessions first came to expression. Furthermore, forms of worship often become rather rigidly fixed. Being basically traditional in temperament, most people tend to prefer the emotional stability of familiar liturgies, lections, prayers, hymns, and styles of preaching and to feel threatened by changes or variations. Sadly, often a preference for the familiar focuses on such mundane matters as the length of a minister's preaching (whether a five-minute "homily," a fifteen-to-twenty-minute "sermon," or a thirty-to-forty-minute "exposition"), the length of the pastoral prayers, or the number of verses sung in a hymn. And just as often, the contextualization of worship is viewed only in terms of adjusting these matters to a particular congregation's taste.

The Bible, however, is replete with examples of contextualization in worship that go far beyond such superficial matters. Discoveries at Ras Shamra (Ugarit), for example, have shown that many of the canonical Psalms—the hymns of worship in the religion of Israel, whether first associated with the temple or composed by individual prophets or kings—evidence rhythmical patterns, literary styles, and idiomatic expressions typical of Canaanite poems found at Ras Shamra. Thus, while the Hebrews were opposed to polytheism and the gross religious practices of the Canaanites, their worship of Yahweh during the late Amarna period probably often paralleled Canaanite worship of Baal and his cohorts in its styling and expressions.

At times, it seems, the Israelites not only shared common religious language with the Canaanites but also borrowed key Canaanite terms and imagery for their own use. An example of such borrowing appears in Ps 68:5 (LXX 68:4), which refers to God as "the Rider of the Clouds." This particular epithet, as the Ugaritic texts have shown, was used by the Canaanites to honor Baal. Evidently, however, it was reused by the Israelite psalmist in praise of Yahweh. This is not meant to imply that the psalmist was careless in his use of existing religious language or had capitulated to the religion of Baal. Like all the writers of the OT, the psalmist was fervently opposed to the Baal cult and its repugnant practices. Yet he seems to have found no problem in lauding God with the religious imagery then current, however an expression may have been used in a neighboring religion.

Such synergistic borrowing was probably done quite frequently when terms and expressions were considered to be more or less neutral in significance. But even when particular images or motifs carried adverse connotations because of their close association with the Baal cult, they seem to have been simply "disinfected" and "rebaptized" for use in Israel's worship if they were thought to be useful for greater purposes.

Most startling, perhaps, is Solomon's building of the Jerusalem temple (1 Kings 5–8; 1 Chronicles 17, 21–22, 28–29; and 2 Chronicles 2–7). Although David delivered to Solomon the plans for the temple, which he received by God's Spirit and wrote out for his son (1 Chron 28:11–19), the layout of the finished product turned out to be similar, in many respects, to temples that archaeologists have unearthed in Phoenicia. And although Solomon conscripted many of his own people as laborers and used predominantly native materials in building the temple (1 Kgs 5:13–18; 2 Chron 2:2, 17–18), he employed artisans from Phoenicia and imported from Lebanon the fine woods for the building (1 Kgs 5:1–12; 2 Chron 2:3–16).

What Solomon built was—if not exactly in form, at least in appearance and decor—something that looked remarkably like a Phoenician temple. Who would have expected, for instance, that the walls of the temple would be carved, both inside and out, with scroll-like flower patterns, palm trees, and cherubim? Or that the two large bronze pillars in front of the temple portico would have capitals in the shape of lilies with intricate designs of interwoven chains and pomegranates? Or that the great basin for ritual washings in front of the temple would be supported by twelve large oxen sculptured in cast metal? This is not to suggest that Solomon simply capitulated to the worship of the Phoenician gods. Rather, in building a temple for the worship of Yahweh, he felt free to use in synergistic fashion the architectural forms and artistic motifs of the day to express this worship, even though he might well have known how such forms and motifs were used in other religious contexts.

What is true of the contextualization of worship in the OT is also true in the NT. For example, in the earliest days of the Jerusalem church, believers in Jesus probably celebrated two kinds of communal meals: (1) a sacred paschal meal in their corporate gatherings, which commemorated the death of Jesus and followed the pattern of the Jewish Passover and Jesus' Last Supper with his disciples (cf. Acts 2:42), and (2) a joyful fellowship meal in their homes, which commemorated Jesus' resurrection and continued presence with his disciples and followed the pattern of the Jewish *Haburah* ("fellowship") meals and Jesus' eating with his disciples during his earthly ministry (cf. Acts 2:46b–47a). These two meals, it seems, became combined into one communal feast when the gospel penetrated Gentile regions and when Jewish influence upon Christian worship diminished. But even though the tradition of one meal became rooted among Gentile Christians, Paul at

Corinth felt free to change matters and to disengage the Lord's Supper and the more expressly fellowship-oriented communal meals when disunity and abuse occurred (cf. 1 Cor 11:17–34). Evidently, in order to preserve the principles of the gospel in the Lord's Supper, he was willing to alter an established practice rather than have that practice, when misused, pervert these principles.

Likewise, in an entirely Jewish Christian setting of prayer, when selection of a replacement for Judas among the twelve disciples was necessary, Acts 1:20–26 reports that two men were considered to have the proper qualifications, but only Matthias was chosen on the basis of prayer and the old Jewish practice of casting lots. In Acts 13:1–3, however, with a mixed group of Jewish and Gentile believers present in the congregation at Antioch of Syria, the will of God about Barnabas and Saul was determined through fasting and prayer, with no mention of casting lots.

Illustrative as well are the various ways in which the canonical evangelists adapted the story of Jesus to suit the understanding and appreciation of their readers, and so to engender worship on their part. A number of such redactional features in the evangelists' portrayals of the Jesus story have already been highlighted above (chs. 4 and 5). Three other adaptations can be cited here, for they easily illustrate the point and have a bearing on worship.

One significant adaptation appears in the way the Lord's Prayer is presented in Matt 6:9–13 and Luke 11:2–4. If anything were to be kept in exactly the form in which it was given, we would think that it would be a prayer Jesus taught his disciples. Yet Luke's version is shorter and simpler:

> Father, hallowed be your name. Your kingdom come. Give us each day our daily bread. Forgive us our sins, for we also forgive everyone who sins against us. And lead us not into temptation. (11:2–4)

Matthew's version, however, is a bit different and certainly more expansive (as the italicized words indicate):

> *Our* Father *in heaven*, hallowed be your name. Your kingdom come, *your will be done, on earth as it is in heaven*. Give us today our daily bread. Forgive us our *debts*, as we also have forgiven *our debtors*. And lead us not into temptation, *but deliver us from the evil one*. (6:9–13)

And from the fifth century on, some manuscripts (e.g., W and L) added to Matthew's version the conclusion "For yours is the kingdom and the power and the glory forever, Amen!"—the form many Protestant churches use today.

Two somewhat more incidental adaptations in the Gospels may also be cited. One is the difference of imagery between Jesus' conclusion in the Sermon on the Mount (Matt 7:24–27) and that in the Sermon on the Plain (Luke 6:47–49). Matthew uses the imagery of Palestine, with rocky terrain, severe winds from the west bringing heavy rains, dry river beds turned by these spring rains into torrential rivers, and sand all around. But Luke's imagery is that of a plateau area with extensive topsoil, probably outside Palestine. Thus, in Matt 7:24 the one who hears and puts into practice Jesus' words, "is like a wise man who built his house on a rock," whereas in Luke 6:48 this person "is like a man building a house, who dug down deep and laid the foundation on rock"; and in Matt 7:26 the one who hears and does not put into practice Jesus' words "is like a foolish man who built his house on sand," whereas in Luke 6:49 this person "is like a man who built a house on the ground without a foundation."

The other adaptation concerns Jesus' position of prayer in Gethsemane in Mark 14:32–36 and the parallel texts in Matthew and Luke, as well as—following Luke's emphasis on example in his passion narrative—the Christian's position in prayer. Whereas Mark 14:35 says that Jesus "fell on the ground and prayed" and Matt 26:39 that Jesus "fell on his face and prayed," Luke 22:41 reports that he "knelt down and prayed."

Comparing Matthew and Luke's version of the Lord's Prayer, most scholars today argue that Luke's should probably be considered the original version, with Matthew filling it out to what Jesus taught in a more expansive manner. Joachim Jeremias's axiom that "in the early period, before wordings were fixed, liturgical texts were elaborated, expanded, and enriched"[1] has often been understood to mean that the shorter liturgical portions in the NT are the original versions of longer redactional renderings of the same materials found elsewhere in the NT (although the history of the transmission of Jewish liturgical materials does not always move from shorter and simpler to longer and more complex). In the other two adaptations cited above, however, it appears that Matthew's version should probably be viewed as the original words of Jesus, simply because of the Palestinian imagery and the portrayal of a Semitic posture in prayer. But whichever version was original in each case, an adaptation of the story of Jesus—even concerning prayer and worship, matters most susceptible to traditional treatments—has occurred, with analogous circumstances synergistically drawn into the account.

The annals of church history are also replete with accounts of adaptation and contextualization in worship—which often became, as time went by, themselves rather traditional and, for some, sacrosanct. The Methodist revivalist movement of the mid–eighteenth century in England and North America, for example, is a case in point. Although John Wesley, guided by scruples of "decency and order," at first disapproved of preaching to rough and disorderly miners in the open fields around Bristol and environs, he soon came to realize God's guidance in the matter and found himself (together with his brother Charles and George Whitefield) preaching to crowds numbering up to forty thousand at a time. And although he initially opposed lay preachers (instead of those ordained under apostolic succession), extemporary prayers (instead of those of the Anglican prayer book), and dissent from the established church (the Church of England), he eventually came, through various circumstances, to believe in, encourage, and practice all of these things. He even founded a body of lay preachers, organized his converts into dissenting local societies, which became the structural backbone of the Methodist movement, and finally acknowledged in theory as well as in practice his own status as a dissenter from the established church. Similarly, when the Wesleys and Whitefield could not teach the miners of Kingswood and the towns around Bristol to chant, they fitted Christian theology to attractive tunes of the day—many sung in distinctly nonreligious contexts and with different words by the miners themselves—and so conveyed Christian teaching in a manner that was easy to learn but difficult to forget.

The early Methodist experience is but one example of a contextualization of worship that took place in a particular period in the history of the Christian church. Every denomination, as it scans its own history, is able to report parallel phenomena. In large measure, differing contextualizations of worship have been the reason for the founding and continuance of different denominations, with both good and bad results. Later generations, however, all too frequently forget that such earlier contextualizations incorporated features of adaptation, analogous thinking, synergistic correlation, and creative imagination as their leaders attempted to deal with this question: How should we most fittingly and strategically worship God in the circumstances of our day?

It is almost always the circumstances of the day that force Christians, at any time and in any region, to reconsider the nature and forms of their worship, and so to begin to think more analogically, synergistically, and creatively. Most people are rather traditional in their outlooks and would prefer not to think about changing unless they have to. In the last half of the twentieth century, however, the sensitivities of Christians in the Western world regarding worship have been stirred and sharpened. This has largely taken place because of (1) the reports and creative thinking of missiologists, who are constantly faced with such issues, and (2) religious pluralism, which challenges the church to think seriously about such matters. Thus, difficult as the question might be, Christians today must also ask themselves, How do we contextualize Christian worship most appropriately, both in our own society at home and in the church's missionary enterprise among other cultures abroad?

It is no easy task to adapt, to think analogically, to identify synergistic correlations, or to exercise our imaginative powers creatively. There are no handbooks to tell us how to contextualize our worship of God in ways that are understandable, meaningful, and theologically proper. Nor can an owner's manual be produced on the subject. It is often difficult even to identify features in our own culture that are noble, or that are neutral, or that are depraved, so that we can distinguish between features that can be used in the worship of God and features that carry too much contrary freight. And this nagging difficulty is exacerbated when we try to make such distinctions for a culture other than our own.

Nonetheless, as Christians individually and the church corporately, we are called on by both God's Spirit and the needs of people to contextualize Christian worship in our day, our locality, and our world—that is, to direct our prayers and praise to God in ways that are relevant and meaningful to people living at a particular time and in a particular culture. The task is of the nature of a science, for it requires knowledge about the patterns of contextualization in the Scriptures, the experiences of the church in various situations throughout history and the world, and contemporary anthropological, sociological, and cultural studies of people and their societies. It is also something of an art, for it calls on us to engage in analogical thinking, synergistic correlations, and creative imagination. Ultimately, however, the task is a spiritual discipline, for it depends on the direction and enablement of God's Holy Spirit.

▓ 2. THE CONTEXTUALIZATION OF PROCLAMATION

Since the Christian confessions of God and of Jesus Christ were and are rooted in worship, we began this chapter with a discussion of the contextualization of worship. But because true worship always leads to proclamation, it is necessary to speak about the contextualization of the early confessions in Christian preaching.

The classical rhetoricians analyzed addresses, whether oral or written, in terms of three major criteria: *logos*, or content and argument; *ethos*, or the personal character of the speaker or writer; and *pathos*, or the power to stir the emotions. These three criteria have been seen to be valid by rhetoricians throughout the course of history, and so have been carried over into our day in every synchronic rhetorical analysis of an address or writing. But proclaimers of the Christian gospel must also take into account issues of contextualization. For those who hear must be able to understand and respond in a valid manner, and not be deceived by some other message that they thought they heard because of the preacher's garbled delivery.

With regard to content *(logos)*, Christian proclamation has as its focus God's redemptive activity in the ministry and person of Jesus as set out in the NT. Each of the early Christian confessions, whether in the form of poetry or prose, narrates a portion of the story about Jesus as God's redemptive agent. And each, whether separately or together, is meant to trigger a recall of this story so that people may live in response to what "God in Christ" has done.

Those who proclaim the gospel need continually to be reminded of this first axiom of Christian preaching, for we all are tempted, at various times, to turn our sermons into quasi-philosophical discourses on goodness, love, or justice—or, worse yet, into "pop psychology" treatments of interpersonal relations, marital harmony, or healthy self-affirmation. Sometimes, indeed, so-called Christian preaching renders itself inane by its pseudo-political diatribes, with attention most often directed to matters of economic decline, moral morass, or cultural disintegration. That our preaching needs to deal in a relevant manner with issues of a philosophic, psychological, moral, cultural, economic, and/or political nature is true beyond debate. But the question must always be asked: What is the focus of our preaching? Preaching, to be truly Christian, must always focus on the story of God's saving and reconciling activity, which has Jesus Christ as its main character.

Furthermore, Christian preaching, to be true to its confessional base, needs to be dominantly functional in its proclamation concerning both God and Jesus Christ. It must always emphasize what "God in Christ" has done redemptively for humanity and how a person should appropriately respond. The earlier confessional materials of the NT give priority to such functional features; the more ontological and speculative matters came into the picture only somewhat later. And Christian preaching today, rather than trying to solve all of the doctrinal issues discussed in our contemporary volumes of theology, should concentrate on setting forth the drama of divine redemption as focused in the work of Christ, allowing most of the ontological issues and speculative implications inherent within this proclamation to be spelled out as converts grow in maturity.

In addition to content, however, Christian proclamation must also convey both the personal character of the speaker or writer *(ethos)* and the power of that message to stir the emotions of the hearers or readers *(pathos)*—reflecting this *ethos* and *pathos* in the act of preaching itself. For matters of character, disposition, attitude, emotion, and response are just as important as reason and argument in the proclamation of the Christian message. Thus, we must not only present the drama of divine redemption, which focuses on the story of Jesus, we must also recognize that preaching such a message is part and parcel of Christian devotion and worship. Conversely, where preaching is divorced from devotion and worship, no proclamation, in the Christian sense, has occurred.

But as important as the factors of content, character, and emotion are, Christian proclamation cannot stop there. It must also give attention to contextualization—that is, to the adaptation of the gospel message to the understanding and appreciation of its hearers, using analogies, synergistic correlations, and creative imagination to clarify what is meant and what is called for in response. The confessional materials of the NT, as we have noted, use the language and metaphors of their day in speaking about the work of Christ and its redemptive significance. At times they even contain expressions and metaphors that are so related to a specific past time and culture that they are difficult to comprehend today. But these confessions spoke successfully to those whom they addressed. And we need to unpack the meaning of their words, develop the significance of what they said, and adapt the fullness of their message in the language and metaphors of those we address.

Likewise, the writers of the NT contextualized the early confessional materials for people of their day, using the forms of expression that were at hand in their day—certainly in their services of corporate worship, in their preaching, and in their teaching, but also by means of pastoral letters, narrative accounts of Jesus and the early church, and the Johannine Apocalypse. It is our task also to contextualize these early Christian confessions for people of our day, using the forms of expression that lie at hand in our culture or other cultures and that can legitimately be used for such a purpose. In some cases, particular forms and modes of expression (e.g., songs, dramas, paintings, and dramatic readings) may be either sufficiently positive or sufficiently neutral to be readily used for the conveyance of the gospel. In other cases, they may need first to be "disinfected" of extraneous nuances and "rebaptized" for the purposes of the gospel.

Missiologists report on the difficulties that people in other lands often have with some of the biblical images that we as Western Christians take for granted. For example, in parts of Africa where tending animals is a task assigned to those who are mentally defective, people have trouble thinking of Jesus as the Good Shepherd (John 10; cf. Psalm 23). Or in parts of Indonesia where pigs are viewed as the only proper animals for sacrificial purposes, people have difficulty appreciating the biblical references to Jesus as the sacrificial Lamb of God (John 1:29, 36; Rev 5:6, 8, 12–13). Likewise, the Chinese, who regard dragons positively, often fail to catch any ominous nuance in the depiction of Satan as a dragon (Rev 12:2–13:1). And in tropical lands, where it never snows, portrayals of the glorified Christ with clothing or hair as white as snow (Mark 9:3; Matt 28:3; Rev 1:14) and statements about sins becoming white as snow (Isa 1:18) are largely without meaning.

More significantly, Christians of other cultures often read the Bible in ways different from those of Western Christians. For example, those with animist backgrounds focus more on the accounts of Jesus' conquest over evil spirits than on references to his death and resurrection. Those with Confucian backgrounds often read and appreciate more the OT book of Proverbs than Paul's letters. And in the Western world—where sin has become largely passé and the major problems of life are seen to be the lack of meaning in life, dysfunctional relationships between people, warfare, and death—most people seem more interested in a gospel that speaks about meaning for people's lives, the mending of broken relationships, peace among warring parties, and the allaying of fears about the future than in a gospel that enjoins us to embrace forgiveness, justification, redemption, and holiness.

The contextualization of Christian proclamation assuredly entails being true to the *logos, ethos,* and *pathos* of the gospel message. But it also calls on us to be sensitive to how people at any given time and in any given locality hear this message and how the message can be proclaimed so that it will be better understood and more appreciated by those to whom it is directed. What is needed, as Charles Kraft says of his own attempts in this regard, is "to be orthodox with respect to the truth but venturesome in its application."[2] To be "venturesome in its application" means to be alive to issues of "dynamic equivalence." But it also means to be seeking out further ways of authentic adaptation by means of analogical thought, synergistic correlations, and creative imagination.

■ 3. THE CONTEXTUALIZATION OF DOCTRINAL FORMULATION

The story of Christian doctrine incorporates four highly significant factors: (1) progressive revelation, (2) development in understanding, (3) synergistic formulation, and (4) relevant contextualization. All of these factors have worked together throughout the course of history to produce what we today identify as Christian theology. Indeed, it may be confidently declared that there can be no valid theology, in the Christian sense, where one or more of these factors is ignored.

God revealed himself and his will progressively in Israel's history. This progressive revelation was related to personal relations with his people (e.g., through the covenants) and his redemptive activity on their behalf (e.g., in the Exodus). And it was understood by God's people in a developmental manner, formulated in a synergistic fashion by the use of language and concepts that were then current, and contextualized in ways that were meaningful to the nation's life at that time. Furthermore, this conjunction of progressive revelation, developmental understanding, synergistic formulation, and relevant contextualization—while important and applicable for each phase of Israel's history— pointed toward future, fuller revelations of God, further developmental understandings, continued synergistic formulations, and more significant contextualizations, all of which would culminate in the coming of God's Anointed One, the Messiah (cf., e.g., Gen 3:15; Deut 18:15, 18; Jer 31:31–34; Mal 3:1).

Thus, in the OT, the Latter Prophets reinterpreted the Former Prophets, and the Writings reapplied Mosaic law. In each case, later revelation did not oppose earlier revelation, but expressed its significance more fully and applied its message to new situations. One obvious example of this is Daniel 9, where Jeremiah's prophecy of "seventy years" (cf. Jer 25:11–14) is reinterpreted to mean "seventy heptads" and to have eschatological significance beyond what was initially thought (cf. esp. Dan 9:1–3, 20–27). Another is Psalm 110, where the Canaanite chieftain Melchizedek of Gen 14:18–20 is brought into the lineage of Israel as one of the nation's ancient worthies (cf. Ps 110:4).

In the NT there is a similar conjunction of these four features. The earliest preaching of the apostles, for example, was cast almost entirely in personal terms and functional categories, as the opening of Peter's Pentecost sermon illustrates:

> Men of Israel, listen to this: Jesus of Nazareth was a man accredited by God to you by miracles, wonders, and signs, which God did among you through him, as you yourselves know. This man was handed over to you by God's set purpose and foreknowledge; and you, with the help of wicked men, put him to death by nailing him to the cross. But God raised him from the dead, freeing him from the agony of death, because it was impossible for death to keep its hold on him. (Acts 2:22–24)

It is a message that stressed God's intervention in human history in the person of Jesus of Nazareth and focused on God's redemption of humanity through what Jesus, as God's accredited Messiah, did in his ministry, death, and resurrection. Presupposed in the message were many theological nuances, which came to be more clearly understood, more ably expressed, and more suitably applied later by the writers of the NT. At first, however, full-blown ontological formulations and developed theological stances were largely confined to the substratum of the apostles' earliest preaching and resonated only in the overtones of their message.

As Jews, the apostles and early believers in Jesus possessed a basic theology regarding God's person and divine redemption. As Christians, however, their distinctive theological affirmations were derived from God's self-revelation and redemptive activity in Jesus. They worked from functional categories of thought (what God did in and through Jesus) to more theological, ontological, and speculative categories (how this should be understood; who Jesus is; why it all came about; and what it means for everyday living). Thus, in the NT we have a record of how these early Christians began to work out the nuances of their basically functional understanding of Jesus and his redemptive activity—under the guidance of God's Spirit—to a rudimentary system of Christian doctrine. And so the NT, paralleling the OT, contains a record of God's progressive self-revelation and God's unfolding redemption on behalf of humanity, coupled with accounts of his people's developing endeavors to work out the theological ramifications of this revelation and redemption.

Jesus' promise of the Spirit, as recorded in John 14–16, includes the expectation that in the future his disciples would have fuller understandings of his teachings and ministry—fuller understandings not divorced from God the Father and Jesus, but rooted in all that Jesus said and did:

> I have much more to say to you, more than you can now bear. But when he, the Spirit of truth, comes, he will guide you into all truth. He will not speak on his own; he will speak only what he hears, and he will tell you what is yet to come. He will bring glory to me by taking from what is mine and making it known to you. All that belongs to the Father is mine. That is why I said the Spirit will take from what is mine and make it known to you. (John 16:12–15)

At two places in John's Gospel, in fact, there are explicit statements that the disciples became more perceptive in their understanding of Jesus' ministry vis-à-vis Scripture after Jesus' resurrection—the implication being that because of the Spirit's ministry there would be advances in their theology. In John 2 the evangelist reports that only after Jesus' resurrection did his disciples understand Ps 69:9 as relevant to Jesus' ministry: "His disciples remembered that it is written: 'Zeal for your house will consume me.' . . . After he was raised from the dead, his disciples recalled what he had said. Then they believed the Scripture and the words that Jesus had spoken" (John 2:17, 22). And in John 12, regarding Jesus' entry into Jerusalem and John's quoting of Ps 118:25–26 and Zech 9:9, we are told, "At first his disciples did not understand all this. Only after Jesus was glorified did they realize that these things had been written about him and that they had done these things to him" (John 12:16).

Synergistic developments in the understanding, expression, application, and contextualization of the basically functional affirmations of the earliest believers in Jesus, as found in their confessional materials, abound in Paul's letters and the other epistolary writings of the NT(see ch. 3, above). Likewise, such synergistic developments are abundantly evident in the Gospels, the Acts, and the Apocalypse (see chs. 4 and 5, above). All of these data on the contextualization of the early Christian confessions in the NT are significant and interesting in their own right. They are also, however, particularly important for our contextualizing of the gospel today, for they set out paradigms for both our theory and our practice.

Admittedly, concepts of development, synergism, analogy, and creative thinking are relatively modern. Jewish theologians saw their activities in terms of conservation, distillation, and application, but not as any advance in their understanding of God's revelation, nor as any contextualization of this revelation in a synergistic fashion, and certainly not as a creative enterprise. Jesus ben Sirach, for example, the author of the second-century Wisdom writing called Sirach (or Ecclesiasticus, "the church's book," as Jerome called it), thought of himself as "one who gleans after the grape gatherers [i.e., the Sages]" and whose work was to distill for posterity the essence of the Sages' wisdom (cf. *Sirach* 33:16–18). So, too, the Pharisees, the various apocalyptic writers, the Dead Sea covenanters, the Tannaitic and Amoraic rabbis of the Talmud, the Geonim, and the Rishonim (e.g., Rashi and Maimonides)—to name only a few prominent schools of Jewish interpretation—saw their task mainly (if not exclusively) in terms of conservation, distillation, and application.

Likewise, the church fathers, the medieval exegetes, and even the Protestant Reformers (Luther, Calvin, etc.) viewed their interpretations of Scripture and their theological statements not as developments in exegesis or doctrine but as summaries *(compendia)* and distillations of biblical truth. They might have looked on their writings as creative in the sense of being a better subjective understanding and contemporary application of the gospel. But they would not have considered them developments in the content of Christian theology. Nor did they have any awareness of developments of understanding, synergistic expression, or contextualization within Scripture itself.

Yet virtually all modern historians of theology agree that, despite their claims to the contrary, almost all of the Jewish and Christian interpreters mentioned above have, in fact, produced materials that go beyond mere "compendia with contemporary applications." In a real sense, each writer, in his own way, has been creative and has treated both Scripture and tradition in a fashion that can be called developmental, synergistic, and contextual.

Indeed, Christian theology must always be a conservative enterprise, for it is rooted in God's redemptive activity in Jesus Christ, which has been preeminently attested in the early Christian confessions of the NT. It must always seek to be true to its revelational base. But Christian theology must also always be a creative enterprise, both in its process and in its product. Because of better understandings of its revelational base, changing challenges to its central affirmations, differing cultural contexts in which it is required to be expressed, and diverse ideological perspectives to which it is called to speak, it is always in a state of development. Christian theology must, therefore, be constantly rewritten both for each new generation and for all the differing cultures, and its theologians must be always sensitive to issues concerning developments in understanding, synergistic correlations, analogical thinking, and creative imagination.

4. THE CONTEXTUALIZATION OF ETHICS

Just as the NT is no textbook on theology but, rather, as we have argued, contains a record of God's progressive self-revelation and God's unfolding redemption on behalf of humanity, coupled with accounts of his people's developing endeavors to work out the theological ramifications of this revelation and redemption, so too the NT is no compendium of ethical theory or practice. Rather, in the area of ethics, we have in the NT (1) a declaration of the gospel and of the ethical principles that derive from the gospel, as principally contained in the early Christian confessions, and (2) a description of how this proclamation and its principles were put into practice in various situations during the apostolic period. Its proclamation and principles, because they are rooted in the early Christian confessions, are to be taken as normative.

The ways that this proclamation and its principles were put into practice in the first century, however, should be understood as signposts at the beginning of a journey, which serve to point out the path to be followed in living out the gospel both personally and socially.

In matters of personal morality, Jesus' commands to his disciples reiterate the central, binding commands of the OT: "Love the Lord your God with all your heart, and with all your soul, and with all your mind, and with all your strength" (Mark 12:30, par.; cf. Deut 6:5); "Love your neighbor as yourself" (Mark 12:31, par.; cf. Lev 19:18); and "Honor your father and mother" (Mark 10:19, par.; cf. Exod 20:12; Deut 5:16). "Love" and "Honor." These commands require no further advance in divine revelation or human understanding, particularly when they are internalized and allowed to develop new attitudes within a person. They can, of course, be restrictively applied in a casuistic fashion, and so perverted (as with honoring one's parents in Mark 7:6–13 // Matt 15:3–9 or loving one's neighbors in Matt 5:43–48 // Luke 6:27–36). But they are meant to be expansively applied, reflecting God's "perfection" and "mercy" (cf. Matt 5:48; Luke 6:36).

In matters of social morality, however, it will not do simply to ask, "Does the NT say anything explicit about this or that social issue?" with the intention of repeating this answer if it does and of remaining silent if it does not. Such an approach assumes the NT to be a static codification of ethical maxims. Rather, we need to ask, "What principles derived from the gospel proclamation does the NT declare to be important for social morality?" and, "What practices in the application of these principles does the NT describe as setting a paradigm for our reapplication of these same principles today?" In answering such questions, we need to be both as expert as possible in historical-cultural-grammatical exegesis and as open as possible to the Spirit's guidance so that we can (1) distinguish between declared principles and described practices in the NT and (2) contextualize these principles and paradigmatic practices in the differing situations of our day in a manner that lays stress on development, synergism, analogy, and creativity.

The writers of the NT did not settle every ethical issue. They were not omniscient, and so could not see every situation in advance. Nor did God, by his Spirit, so illuminate them that they could. What they did, however, was highly significant, both for their day and for ours: they proclaimed the message of new life in Christ, and they began to work out the implications of this gospel for the situations they encountered—not always, admittedly, as fully or as adequately as we might wish from our later perspectives, but appropriately for their day and pointing the way to a fuller understanding and a more adequate application in later times. We should not try to make them out to be all-knowing or all-wise in every area of social concern. Conversely, we should not disparage them because they were not. Instead, as Christians, we ought to (1) attempt to recapture the principles of the gospel, as incorporated in their confessions and their declarations, that have ramifications for social morality and (2) endeavor to follow the path they marked out for the application of these gospel principles, seeking to carry out their work in fuller and more significant ways.[3] In so doing, we will be involved in a process of developmental explication, synergistic correlation, analogical relationships, and creative thinking as we attempt to explicate the principles of the early Christian confessions for the ethical circumstances and needs of our day.

Epilogue

Three enigmatic, though startling, statements of Jesus have particular relevance for any discussion of contextualizing the Christian gospel. The first is the parabolic statement of Mark 2:22, Matt 9:17, and Luke 5:37–38, which speaks about the necessity of pouring "new wine" into "fresh wineskins." It suggests that one can "spill" the wine or "destroy" the wineskins when attention is not given to the newness of both the wine and the skins, but that when both the new wine and the fresh wineskins are honored by allowing them to interact synergistically with one another in a proper fermenting process, "both are preserved."

The second appears as the conclusion to Jesus' seven parables of the kingdom in Matthew's Gospel:

> Every teacher of the law who has been instructed about the kingdom of heaven is like the owner of a house who brings out of his storeroom new treasures as well as old. (Matt 13:52)

Here Jesus, we have argued, is speaking of the Christian teacher as one who is (1) rooted in the gospel proclamation—its foundation being the salvation history of the OT, its focus being the redemptive work of Christ, and its central convictions first coming to expression in the early Christian confessions—*and* (2) relevant to current times and circumstances by understanding more fully and applying more adequately the proclamation to his or her own situation. In Matt 13:52, therefore, we should understand Jesus as giving his immediate disciples—and those who follow them as teachers in the Christian church—the mandate for a synergistic-developmental model of contextualizing the early Christian confessions: to bring out of their storerooms new treasures as well as old!

The third statement is found close to the beginning of Jesus' long farewell speech to his disciples in John 14–16:

> I tell you the truth, all who have faith in me will do what I have been doing; and they will do even greater things than these, because I am going to the Father. (John 14:12)

Throughout most of the history of the Christian church, this promise has usually been viewed as something of a hyperbole—that is, an exaggeration or extravagant statement used as a figure of speech—which may, as hyperboles go, possess great motivational qualities, but in practice is simply unimaginable and unfulfillable. Modern travel and the modern media have enabled many missionaries and preachers to speak to more people than Jesus ever did during his ministry, and some evangelists have used that fact to support their claim that this verse has been fulfilled in their ministries. Various "healers" have also claimed this verse as validation for their ministries. I propose, however, that Jesus' words in John 14:12 should be taken as having principally in mind the recontextualization of the Christian gospel, a recontextualization that would come about in different cultures and at later times.

Perhaps some in the early church saw such a contextualization taking place in the Gentile ministry of Paul, whose missionary maxim was:

> I have become all things to all people so that by all possible means I might save some. I do all this for the sake of the gospel, that I may share in its blessings. (1 Cor 9:22–23)

But the words of Mark 2:22, par. ("new wine into fresh wineskins"), Matt 13:52 ("new treasures as well as old"), and John 14:12 ("greater things than these") comprise also a mandate for Christians today. For we, too, are to (1) be rooted in the gospel that was first articulated in the early Christian confessions, (2) contextualize this gospel in our worship, proclamation, doctrinal

formulation, and ethics, and (3) work out these contextualizations in terms of a developmental understanding of, and synergistic correlations between, the Scriptures, Christian tradition,
and the various receptor peoples and cultures, using analogical
and creative thinking prominently throughout.

Without any disparagement of Christ's earliest followers
and apostles, we, as believers in Jesus Christ and guided by God's
Spirit, are called on today to have a more significant Christian
theology and a truer Christian ethic than even the earliest believers in Jesus. Such a mandate—that is, to be true to both the "new
wine" of the gospel and the "fresh wineskins" of the day—presents
us with both exhilarating opportunities and a humbling challenge.

Endnotes

▣ INTRODUCTION

1. Martin Dibelius, *From Tradition to Gospel* (trans. B. L. Woolf; New York: Scribner's, 1934). Originally published as *Die Formgeschichte des Evangeliums*. Tübingen: Mohr, 1919.

2. Rudolf Bultmann, *The History of the Synoptic Tradition* (3d ed.; trans. J. Marsh; Oxford: Blackwell,1963). Originally published as *Die Geschichte der synoptischen Tradition*. Göttingen: Vanderhoeck & Ruprecht, 1921.

3. C. H. Dodd, *The Apostolic Preaching and Its Developments* (London: Hodder & Stoughton, 1936).

4. Cf. Theological Education Fund, *Ministry in Context: The Third Mandate Programme of the Theological Education Fund, 1970–77* (Bromley, England: New Life, 1972), 29.

5. Robert J. Schreiter, *Constructing Local Theologies* (Maryknoll: Orbis, 1985), 1.

6. Cf. J. Christiaan Beker, *Paul the Apostle: The Triumph of God in Life and Thought* (Philadelphia: Fortress, 1980), 11–19, passim.

▣ CHAPTER 1

1. Johannes Weiss, "Beiträge zum paulinischer Rhetorik," in *Theologische Studien (Festschrift B. Weiss; ed. C. R. Gregory et al.;* Göttingen: Vandenhoeck & Ruprecht, 1897), 165–247.

2. Eduard Norden, *Die antike Kunstprosa vom VI. Jahrhundert vor Christus bis in die Zeit der Renaissance* (2 vols.; Leipzig: Teubner, 1898; repr., Stuttgart: Teubner, 1983).

3. Ibid., 2:841–70.

4. Eduard von der Goltz, *Das Gebet in der ältesten Christenheit* (Leipzig: Hinrichs, 1901).

5. Alfred Seeberg, *Der Katechismus der Urchristenheit* (Leipzig: Deichertschen, 1903; repr., Munich: Kaiser, 1966).

6. Norden, *Die antike Kunstprosa*, esp. 2:810–29.

7. Eduard Norden, *Agnostos Theos: Untersuchungen zur Formengeschichte religiöser Rede* (Leipzig: Tuebner, 1913; repr., Leipzig: Teubner, 1956), 240–308.

8. Full bibliographic data for works in this list appear in the bibliography.

9. 2 vols.; Göttingen: Vandenhoeck & Ruprecht, 1928 and 1930.

10. Reinhard Deichgräber, *Gotteshymnus und Christushymnus in der frühen Christenheit: Untersuchungen zu Form, Sprache, und Stil der frühchristlichen Hymnen* (Göttingen: Vandenhoeck & Ruprecht, 1967).

11. London: Nicholson and Watson, 1940; rev. ed.; London: SCM, 1961.

12. Stuttgart: Kohlhammer, 1941; ET *New Testament Theology* (trans. J. Marsh; London: SCM, 1955).

13. Paris: Presses Universitaires de France, 1943; ET *The Earliest Christian Confessions* (trans. J. K. S. Reid; London: Lutterworth, 1949).

14. Grand Rapids: Eerdmans, 1963.

15. Deichgräber, *Gotteshymnus und Christushymnus*, 107–12.

16. Klaus Wengst, *Christologische Formeln und Lieder des Urchristentums* (Gütersloh: Mohn, 1972); William H. Gloer, "Homologies and Hymns in the New Testament: Form, Content, and Criteria for Identification," *Perspectives in Religious Studies* 11 (1984): 115–32.

17. Göttingen: Vandenhoeck & Ruprecht, 1913.

18. Ernst Lohmeyer, *Kyrios Jesus: Eine Untersuchung zu Phil. 2, 5–11* (Heidelberg: Winter, 1928); Ernst von Dobschütz, "Kurios Iesous," *Zeitschrift für die neutestamentliche Wissenschaft* 30 (1931): 97–123.

19. Full bibliographic data for works in this list appear in the bibliography.

20. Stauffer, *New Testament Theology*, 237.

21. Jack T. Sanders, *The New Testament Christological Hymns: Their Historical Religious Background* (Cambridge: Cambridge University Press, 1971).

22. Wengst, *Christologische Formeln und Lieder des Urchristentums*, 1972.

23. Deichgräber, *Gotteshymnus und Christushymnus*, 132.

24. Stauffer, *New Testament Theology*, Appendix III; Cullmann, *Earliest Christian Confessions*, passim.

25. James H. Charlesworth, "A Prolegomenon to a New Study of the Jewish Background of the Hymns and Prayers in the New Testament," *Journal of Jewish Studies* 33 (1982): 277–78.

26. Martin Hengel, *The Son of God: The Origin of Christology and the History of Jewish-Hellenistic Religion* (Philadelphia: Fortress, 1976), 2.

▓ CHAPTER 2

1. Eduard Schweizer, "Zum religionsgeschichtlichen Hintergrund der 'Sendungsformel' Gal 4:4f., Rm 8:3 f., John 3:16f., I Joh 4:9," *Zeitschrift für die neutestamentliche Wissenschaft* 57 (1966): 199–210; *idem, Jesus.* Trans. D. E. Green. Richmond: John Knox, 1971, pages 81ff.; *idem,* "υἱός." *Theological Dictionary of the New Testamentd.* Ed. G. Kittel and G. Frederich. 8:354–57 and 363–92.

2. Oscar Cullmann, *The Christology of the New Testament* (trans. S. C. Guthrie and C. A. M. Hall; London: SCM, 1959), 223.

3. Cf. Morna D. Hooker, "Interchange in Christ," *Journal of Theological Studies* 22 (1971): 349–61; *idem,* "Interchange and Atonement," *Bulletin of the John Rylands Library* 60 (1976): 462–81; *idem,* Interchange and Suffering," in *Suffering and Martyrdom in the New Testament,* ed. W. Horbury and B. McNeil (Cambridge: Cambridge University Press, 1981), 70–83; *idem,* "Interchange in Christ and Ethics," *Journal for the Study of the New Testament* 25 (1985): 3–17. Also note Klaus Berger's use of the expression *ein Tauschgeschäft* in "Abraham in der paulinischen Hauptbriefen," *Munchener Theologische Zeitschrift* 17 (1966): 52.

4. For explications of these matters, see Richard N. Longenecker, *New Testament Social Ethics for Today* (Grand Rapids: Eerdmans, 1984; repr., Vancouver: Regent College Bookstore, 1993), 29–97.

▓ CHAPTER 3

1. Hans Dieter Betz, *Galatians: A Commentary on Paul's Letter to the Churches in Galatia* (Philadelphia: Fortress, 1979), 149–51.

2. Hans J. Schoeps, "The Sacrifice of Isaac in Paul's Theology," *Journal of Biblical Literature* 65 (1946): 385–92; *idem, Paul: The Theology of the Apostle in the Light of Jewish Religious History,* trans. H. Knight (Philadelphia: Westminster, 1961), 141–49; Nils A. Dahl, "The Atonement— An Adequate Reward for the Akedah? (Rom. 8.32)," in *Neotestamentica et Semitica* (*Festschrift* M. Black), ed. E. E. Ellis and M. Wilcox (Edinburgh: T. & T. Clark, 1969), 23–24; *idem, Studies in Paul: Theology for the Early Christian Mission* (Minneapolis: Augsburg, 1977), 133–34; Geza Vermes, *Scripture and Tradition in Judaism* (Leiden: Brill, 1961), 193–227.

3. Richard B. Hays, *The Faith of Jesus Christ: An Investigation of the Narrative Substructure of Galatians 3:1–4:11* (Chico: Scholars, 1983), esp. 89–90, 112–21.

4. For explications of these matters, see Richard N. Longenecker, *Galatians* (Dallas: Word, 1990), 7–9 and 121–23.

5. Cf. ibid., 150–52.

6. Cf. ibid., 155–58 and 166–72.

7. They probably looked to the Jerusalem church and a Jewish Christian tradition, as I will argue in a forthcoming NIGTC commentary on Romans (Grand Rapids: Eerdmans).

8. Cf. Joachim Jeremias, "Isolated Sayings of the Lord," in *New Testament Apocrypha*, 2 vols., ed. E. Hennecke, W. Schneemelcher, and R. McL. Wilson (London: Lutterworth, 1963), 1:87–88; *idem, Unknown Sayings of Jesus*, trans. R. H. Fuller (London: SPCK, 1964), 80–3. See also Richard N. Longenecker, "The Nature of Paul's Early Eschatology," *New Testament Studies* 31 (1985): 89–91.

▇ CHAPTER 4

1. Werner Kümmel, *Introduction to the New Testament* (rev. ed.; trans. H. C. Kee; Nashville: Abingdon, 1975), 37.

2. Arnaldo Momigliano, *Alien Wisdom: The Limits of Hellenization* (Cambridge: Cambridge University Press, 1976), 92.

3. Ibid., 92–93.

4. C. F. D. Moule, "The Intention of the Evangelists," in *New Testament Essays: Studies in Memory of T. W. Manson* (ed. A. J. B. Higgins; Manchester: Manchester University Press, 1959), 172; repr. in *The Phenomenon of the New Testament* (London: SCM, 1967), 109.

5. Ibid., *New Testament Essays*, 176; *Phenomenon of the New Testament*, 113.

6. Ibid., *New Testament Essays*, 170–71; *Phenomenon*, 107–8.

7. Ibid., *New Testament Essays*, 167, 169; *Phenomenon*, 102, 105.

8. Ibid., *New Testament Essays*, 173; *Phenomenon*, 110.

9. On God's judgmental fishing, see Jer 16:16; Ezek 29:4; 32:3–4; 38:4; Amos 4:2, and Hab 1:14–17. On fishing as an eschatological event with positive, soteriological features, see, e.g., the consciousness of the Qumran Teacher of Righteousness in 1QH 5.7–8: "Thou hast caused me to dwell with the many fishers who spread a net upon the face of the waters, and with the hunters of the children of iniquity; Thou hast established me there for justice." Cf. Wilhelm H. Wuellner, *The Meaning of "Fishers of Men"* (Philadelphia: Westminster, 1967).

10. Graham N. Stanton, "The Origin and Purpose of Matthew's Gospel: Matthean Scholarship from 1945 to 1980," in *Aufsteig und Niedergang der römischen Welt II*, ed. H. Temporini and W. Haases (Berlin: de Gruyter, 1984), 25.3: 1906.

11. Cf. particularly Dale C. Allison Jr., *The New Moses: A Matthean Typology* (Minneapolis: Fortress, 1993), 137–270.

12. Günther Bornkamm, G. Barth, and H. J. Held, *Tradition and Interpretation in Matthew* (trans. P. Scott; London: SCM, 1963), 41.

13. On Luke's fulfillment use of Scripture, cf. Martin Rese, *Alttestamentliche Motive in der Christologie des Lukas* (Gütersloh: Mohn,

1969); Darrell Bock, *Proclamation from Prophecy and Pattern: Lucan Old Testament Christology* (Sheffield: JSOT, 1987).

14. Joel B. Green, *New Testament Theology: The Theology of the Gospel of Luke* (Cambridge: Cambridge University Press, 1995), 143–44.

15. This verse is omitted by such external witnesses as the third-century Bodmer Papyrus, the fourth-century Codex Vaticanus, and the fifth- to sixth-century Codex Bezae; perhaps also by a recension of the fourth-century Codex Alexandrinus.

16. Both Mark and Matthew include the words of 22:42. The statement of 22:43, however, is unique to Luke's Gospel, though this verse is omitted by the Bodmer Papyrus, the Codex Vaticanus, and the Codex Sinaiticus (first corrector).

■ CHAPTER 5

1. George R. Beasley-Murray, *John* (Waco: Word, 1987), xxxiv.

2. Ibid., xxxiii–xxxiv.

3. C. K. Barrett, *The Gospel according to St. John* (London: SPCK, 1956), 60.

4. E.g., a sacrificial lamb (ἀμνός), which was offered twice daily to atone for sin (Exod 29:38–46); a Passover lamb, which was not strictly a sacrifice for sin but a symbol of deliverance from evil (Exod 12:3–11; Num 9:11–12); a lamb to which the Suffering Servant is likened (Isa 53:7); or a victorious horned lamb or ram (ἀρνίον or ἀρήν), as the Messiah is portrayed in several Jewish and Jewish Christian apocalyptic writings (cf. *1 Enoch* 90:38; *Testament of Joseph* 19:8–11; *Testament of Benjamin* 3:8; Rev 5:6, 8, 12–13; 6:1, 16; 7:9–10, 14, 17; and passim).

5. Cf., e.g., T. D. Barnes, "Legislation against the Christians," *Journal of Roman Studies* 58 (1968): 32–50; L. F. Janssen, "'Superstitio' and the Persecution of Christians," *Vigiliae Christianae* 33 (1979): 131–59; P. Keresztes, "The Imperial Roman Government and the Christian Church," *Aufstieg und Niedergang der römischen Welt* II.23.2 (1980): 247–315; R. MacMullen, *Christianizing the Roman Empire* (New Haven: Yale University Press, 1984); B. W. Jones, *The Emperor Domitian* (London: Routledge, 1993).

■ CHAPTER 6

1. Cf. esp. Stephen Neill, *Christian Partnership* (London: SCM, 1952); *idem, Call to Mission* (Philadelphia: Fortress, 1970); Lesslie Newbigin, *A Word in Season: Perspectives on Christian World Missions* (Grand Rapids: Eerdmans, 1974); *idem, The Open Secret: Sketches for a Missionary Theology* (Grand Rapids: Eerdmans, 1978).

2. Robert J. Schreiter, *Constructing Local Theologies*, 7.

3. *American Heritage Dictionary*. (Boston–New York: Houghton Mifflin, 1969), pages 14, 47 and 657.

■ CHAPTER 7

1. Joachim Jeremias, *The Prayers of Jesus* (trans. C. Burchard and J. Reumann; Philadelphia: Fortress, 1978), 90.

2. Charles H. Kraft, *Christianity in Culture: A Study in Dynamic Biblical Theologizing in Cross-Cultural Perspective* (Maryknoll: Orbis, 1979), 38.

3. Cf. Richard N. Longenecker, *New Testament Social Ethics for Today*.

Select Bibliography

■ PART 1—In the Beginning Was the Confession

Barth, Markus. *Ephesians: Introduction, Translation, and Commentary on Chapters 1–3.* Garden City: Doubleday, 1974.

_____. "Traditions in Ephesians." *New Testament Studies* 30 (1984): 3–25.

Best, Ernest, "The Use of Credal and Liturgical Material in Ephesians." Pages 53–69 in *Worship, Theology, and Ministry in the Early Church: Essays in Honor of Ralph Martin.* Ed. M. J. Wilkins and T. Paige. Sheffield: Sheffield Academic Press, 1992. Reprinted as pages 51–68 in *Essays on Ephesians.* Edinburgh: T. & T. Clark, 1997.

Bornkamm, Günther. "Das Bekenntnis im Hebräerbrief." *Theologische Blätter* 21 (1942): 56–66.

_____. "Der Lobpreis Gottes: Röm 11,33–36." *Aufbau und Besinnung* 5 (1951): 70–75

_____. "Zum Verständnis des Christus-Hymnus Phil 2,5–11." Pages 177–87 in his *Studien zu Antike und Urchristentum.* Munich: Kaiser, 1963.

_____. "Lobpreis, Bekenntnis, und Opfer." Pages 46–63 in *Apophoreta: Festschrift für Ernst Haenchen.* Ed. W. Eltester. Berlin: Töpelmann, 1964.

Bultmann, Rudolf. *The History of the Synoptic Tradition.* 3d ed. Trans. J. Marsh. Oxford: Blackwell, 1963. Originally published as *Die Geschichte der synoptischen Tradition.* Göttingen: Vandenhoeck & Ruprecht, 1921.

Cerfaux, Lucien. "Hymnes au Christ des lettres de Saint Paul." *Revue diocésaine de Tournai* 2 (1947): 3–11.

Charlesworth, James H. "A Prolegomenon to a New Study of the Jewish Background of the Hymns and Prayers in the New Testament." *Journal of Jewish Studies* 33 (1982): 265–85.

_____. "Jewish Hymns, Odes, and Prayers (ca. 167 B.C.E.–35 C.E.)." Pages 411–36 in *Early Judaism and Its Modern Interpreters*. Ed. R. A. Kraft and G. W. E. Nickelsburg. Philadelphia: Fortress, 1986.

Cullmann, Oscar. *The Earliest Christian Confessions*. Trans. J. K. S. Reid. London: Lutterworth, 1949. Originally published as *Les premières confessions de foi chrétiennes*. Paris: Presses Universitaires de France, 1943.

_____. *The Christology of the New Testament*. Trans. S. C. Guthrie and C. A. M. Hall. London: SCM, 1959. Originally published as *Die Christologie des Neuen Testaments*. Tübingen: Mohr, 1957.

Daniélou, Jean. *The Theology of Jewish Christianity*. Trans. J. A. Baker. Chicago: Regnery, 1964. The translation is an extensively revised version of *La théologie du judéo-christianisme*. Paris: Deselee, 1958.

Deichgräber, Reinhard. *Gotteshymnus und Christushymnus in der frühen Christenheit: Untersuchungen zur Form, Sprache, und Stil der frühchristlichen Hymnen*. Göttingen: Vandenhoeck & Ruprecht, 1967.

Dibelius, Martin. *From Tradition to Gospel*. Trans. B. L. Woolf. New York: Scribner's, 1936.

Dodd, C. H. *The Apostolic Preaching and Its Developments*. London: Hodder & Stoughton, 1936.

Fitzmyer, Joseph A. "The Aramaic Background of Philippians 2:6–11." *Catholic Biblical Quarterly* 50 (1988): 470–83.

Fowl, Stephen E. *The Story of Christ in the Ethics of Paul: An Analysis of the Function of the Hymnic Material in the Pauline Corpus*. Sheffield: JSOT, 1990.

Fuller, Reginald H. *The Foundations of New Testament Christology*. New York: Scribner's, 1965.

Georgi, Dieter. "Der vorpaulinische Hymnus Phil 2,6–11." Pages 263–93 in *Zeit und Geschichte. Festschrift* R. Bultmann. Ed. E. Dinkler. Tübingen: Mohr, 1964.

Gloer, William H. "Homologies and Hymns in the New Testament: Form, Content, and Criteria for Identification." *Perspectives in Religious Studies* 11 (1984): 115–32.

Gundry, Robert H. "The Form, Meaning, and Background of the Hymn Quoted in 1 Timothy 3:16." Pages 203–22 in *Apostolic History and the Gospel: Biblical and Historical Essays Presented to F. F. Bruce on His 60th. Birthday*. Ed. W. W. Gasque and R. P. Martin. Grand Rapids: Eerdmans, 1970.

Hahn, Ferdinand. *The Titles of Jesus in Christology: Their History in Early Christianity*. Trans. H. Knight and G. Ogg. London: Lutterworth, 1969. Originally published as *Christologische Hoheitstitel: Ihre Geschichte im frühen Christentum*. Göttingen: Vanderhoeck & Ruprecht, 1963.

Hengel, Martin. *The Son of God: The Origin of Christology and the History of Jewish-Hellenistic Religion.* Philadelphia: Fortress, 1976.

_____. "Hymns and Christology." Pages 173–97. *Papers on Paul and Other New Testament Authors.* Vol. 3 of *Studia Biblica 1978.* Ed. E. A. Livingstone. Sheffield: JSOT, 1980. Reprinted as pages 78–96, 188–90 of *Between Jesus and Paul: Studies in the Earliest History of Christianity.* Philadelphia: Fortress, 1983.

_____. *Studies in Early Christology.* Edinburgh: T. & T. Clark, 1995.

Hofius, Otfried. *Der Christushymnus Philipper 2, 6–11.* Tübingen: Mohr-Siebeck, 1976.

Hooker, Morna D. "Philippians 2:6–11." Pages 151–64 in *Jesus und Paulus: Festschrift für Werner Georg Kümmel zum 70. Geburtstag.* Ed. E. E. Ellis and E. Grässer. Göttingen: Vandenhoeck & Ruprecht, 1975.

Hunter, A. M. *Paul and His Predecessors.* London: Nicholson & Watson, 1940. Rev. ed., London: SCM, 1961.

Hurtado, Larry W. *One God, One Lord: Early Christian Devotion and Ancient Jewish Monotheism.* Philadelphia: Fortress, 1988.

Karris, Robert J. *A Symphony of New Testament Hymns: Commentary on Philippians 2:5–11, Colossians 1:15–20, Ephesians 2:14–16, 1 Timothy 3:16, Titus 3:4–7, 1 Peter 3:18–22, and 2 Timothy 2:11–13.* Collegeville: Liturgical, 1966.

Käsemann, Ernst. "Kritische Analyse von Phil. 2.5–11." *Zeitschrift für Theologie und Kirche* 47 (1950): 313–60.

_____. "A Primitive Christian Baptismal Liturgy." Pages 149–68 in *Essays on New Testament Themes.* Trans. W. J. Montague. London: SCM, 1964.

Kehl, N. *Der Christushymnus im Kolosserbrief.* Stuttgart: Katholisches Bibelwerk, 1967.

Kramer, Werner. *Christ, Lord, Son of God.* Trans. B. Hardy. London: SCM, 1966. Originally published as *Christos, Kyrios, Gottessohn.* Zurich: Zwingli, 1963.

Kroll, Josef. *Die christliche Hymnodik bis zu Klemens von Alexandreia.* Darmstadt: Wissenschaftliche, 1921.

_____. "Die Hymnendichtung des frühren Christentums." *Antike* 2 (1926): 258–81.

Lohmeyer, Ernst. *Kyrios Jesu: Eine Untersuchung zu Phil. 2,5–11. Sitzungsberichte der Heidelberger Akademie der Wissenschaften* 18, 1927–1928. Repr., Heidelberg: Winter, 1928.

_____. *Die Briefe an die Philipper, an die Kolosser, und an Philemon.* 2 vols. Göttingen: Vandenhoeck & Ruprecht, 1928, 1930.

Longenecker, Richard N. *The Christology of Early Jewish Christianity.* London: SCM, 1970. Repr., Grand Rapids: Baker, 1981.

Lohse, Eduard. *Die Einheit des Neuen Testaments.* Stuttgart: Kohlhammer, 1972, pages 276–84.

Lyonnet, Stanislas. "L'hymne christologuique de l'Épitre aux Colossiens et la fête juive du Nouvel An." *Recherches de science religieuse* 48 (1960): 93–100.

Marshall, I. Howard. "The Christ Hymn in Philippians 2:5–11." *Tyndale Bulletin* 19 (1968): 104–27.

Martin, Ralph P. *An Early Christian Confession: Philippians II. 5–11 in Recent Interpretation.* London: Tyndale, 1960.

_____. *Carmen Christi: Philippians 2.5–11 in Recent Interpretation and in the Setting of Early Christian Worship.* Cambridge: Cambridge University Press, 1967. Rev. ed. Grand Rapids: Eerdmans, 1983.

_____. *Worship in the Early Church.* Rev. ed. Grand Rapids: Eerdmans, 1974.

_____. "Some Reflections on New Testament Hymns." Pages 37–49 in *Christ the Lord: Studies in Christology Presented to Donald Guthrie.* Ed. H. H. Rowdon. Leicester: InterVarsity, 1982.

Metzger, Witmar. *Der Christushymnus 1 Tim. 3.16.* Stuttgart: Calwer, 1979.

Neufeld, Vernon H. *The Earliest Christian Confessions.* Grand Rapids: Eerdmans, 1963.

Norden, Eduard. *Die antike Kunstprosa vom VI. Jahrhunderts vor Christus bis in die Zeit der Renaissance.* 2 vols. Leipzig: Teubner, 1898.

_____. *Agnostos Theos: Untersuchungen zur Formengeschichte religiöser Rede.* Leipzig: Teubner, 1913.

Robinson, James M. "A Formal Analysis of Col 1:15–20." *Journal of Biblical Literature* 76 (1957): 270–87.

_____. "Die Hodayot-Formel in Gebet und Hymnus des Frühchristentums." Pages 194–235 in *Apophoreta: Festschrift für Ernst Haenchen.* Ed. W. Eltester. Berlin: 1964.

Sanders, Jack T. *The New Testament Christological Hymns: Their Historical Religious Background.* Cambridge: Cambridge University Press, 1971.

Schattenmann, J. *Studien zum neutestamentlichen Prosahymnus.* Munich: Beck, 1965.

Schille, Gottfried. *Frühchristliche Hymnen.* Berlin: Evangelische, 1962.

Schüssler Fiorenza, Elisabeth. "Wisdom Mythology and the Christological Hymns of the New Testament." Pages 17–41 in *Aspects of Wisdom in Judaism and Early Christianity.* Ed. R. L. Wilken. Notre Dame: University of Notre Dame Press, 1975.

Seeberg, Alfred. *Der Katechismus der Urchristenheit.* Leipzig: Deichertschen, 1903. Repr., München: Kaiser, 1966.

Segert, Stanislav. "Semitic Poetic Structures in the New Testament." *Aufstieg und Niedergang der römischen Welt II.* 25.2:1432–62. Ed. H. Temporini and W. Haase. Berlin: de Gruyter, 1984.

Stauffer, Ethelbert. *New Testament Theology.* Trans. J. Marsh. London: SCM, 1955, esp. Appendix III, "Twelve Criteria of Creedal Formulae in the New Testament" (from *Die Theologie des Neuen Testaments*, 1941).

Stenger, Werner. *Introduction to New Testament Exegesis*. Grand Rapids: Eerdmans, 1993, esp. pages 118–22 and 129–32.

Strecker, Georg. "Redaktion und Tradition im Christushymnus Phil. 2,6–11." *Zeitschrift für die neutestamentliche Wissenschaft* 55 (1964): 63–78.

Wengst, Klaus. *Christologische Formeln und Lieder des Urchristentums*. Gütersloh: Mohn, 1972.

■ PART 2—The Contextualization of the Confessions in the New Testament

Chapter 3. The Pauline Corpus and the Other Letters

Attridge, Harold W. *The Epistle to the Hebrews*. Philadelphia: Fortress, 1989.

Barrett, C. K. *A Commentary on the Epistle to the Romans*. BNTC 6. Peabody: Hendrickson, 1987.

_____. *The Pastoral Epistles*. London: Oxford University Press, 1963.

_____. *A Commentary on the First Epistle to the Corinthians*. BNTC 7. Peabody: Hendrickson, 1968.

Barth, Markus. *Ephesians*. 2 vols. Garden City: Doubleday, 1974.

Beare, Francis W. *A Commentary on the Epistle to the Philippians*. London: Black, 1959.

Beker, J. Christiaan. *Paul the Apostle: The Triumph of God in Life and Thought*. Philadelphia: Fortress, 1980.

Best, Ernest. *1 Peter*. London: Oliphants, 1971.

_____. *A Commentary on the First and Second Epistles to the Thessalonians*. BNTC 13. Peabody: Hendrickson, 1972.

Betz, Hans D. *Galatians*. Philadelphia: Fortress, 1979.

Bruce, F. F. *The Epistle of Paul to the Romans*. London: Tyndale, 1963.

_____. *The Epistle to the Hebrews*. Grand Rapids: Eerdmans, 1964.

_____. *The Epistle to the Galatians*. Grand Rapids: Eerdmans, 1982.

_____. *1 & 2 Thessalonians*. Dallas: Word, 1982.

Buchanan, George W. *To the Hebrews*. Garden City: Doubleday, 1972.

Burton, Ernest DeWitt. *A Critical and Exegetical Commentary on the Epistle to the Galatians*. Edinburgh: T. & T. Clark, 1921.

Cranfield, C. E. B. *A Critical and Exegetical Commentary on the Epistle of Saint Paul to the Romans*. 2 vols. Edinburgh: T. & T. Clark, 1975, 1979.

Davids, Peter H. *Commentary on James*. Grand Rapids: Eerdmans, 1981.

Dodd, C. H. *The Johannine Epistles*. London: Hodder & Stoughton, 1946.

Dunn, James D. G. *Romans*. 2 vols. Dallas: Word, 1988.

_____. *The Epistle to the Galatians*. BNTC. Peabody: Hendrickson, 1993.

Fee, Gordon D. *1 and 2 Timothy, Titus*. NIBC. Peabody: Hendrickson, 1984.

———. *The First Epistle to the Corinthians*. NIC. Grand Rapids: Eerdmans, 1987.

———. *Paul's Letter to the Philippians*. NIC. Grand Rapids: Eerdmans, 1995.

Fitzmyer, Joseph A. *Romans*. Garden City: Doubleday, 1993.

Fowl, Stephen E. *The Story of Christ in the Ethics of Paul: An Analysis of the Function of the Hymnic Material in the Pauline Corpus*. Sheffield: JSOT, 1990.

Frame, J. E. *A Critical and Exegetical Commentary on the Epistles of St. Paul to the Thessalonians*. Edinburgh: T. & T. Clark, 1912.

Hanson, Anthony T. *The Pastoral Letters*. Cambridge: Cambridge University Press, 1966. Rev. ed., with title change: *The Pastoral Epistles*. Grand Rapids: Eerdmans, 1982.

Hawthorne, Gerald F. *Philippians*. Dallas: Word, 1983.

Hays, Richard B. *The Faith of Jesus Christ: An Investigation of the Narrative Substructure of Galatians 3:1–4:11*. Chico: Scholars, 1983.

Héring, Jean. *The First Epistle of Saint Paul to the Corinthians*. Trans. A. W. Heathcote and P. J. Allcock. London: Epworth, 1962.

Hughes, Philip E. *A Commentary on the Epistle to the Hebrews*. Grand Rapids: Eerdmans, 1977.

Karris, Robert J. *A Symphony of New Testament Hymns: Commentary on Phil 2:5–11, Col 1:15–20, Eph 2:14–16, 1 Tim 3:16, Tit 3:4–7, 1 Pet 3:18–22, and 2 Tim 2:11–13*. Collegeville: Liturgical, 1996.

Käsemann, Ernst. *Commentary on Romans*. Trans. G. W. Bromiley. Grand Rapids: Eerdmans, 1980.

Kelly, J. N. D. *The Pastoral Epistles*. BNTC 14. Peabody: Hendrickson, 1963.

———. *A Commentary on the Epistles of Peter and of Jude*. London: Black, 1969.

Lane, William L. *Hebrews*. 2 vols. Dallas: Word, 1991.

Lightfoot, J. B. *St. Paul's Epistle to the Galatians*. London: Macmillan, 1865.

———. *Saint Paul's Epistle to the Philippians*. London: Macmillan, 1879.

Lincoln, Andrew T. *Ephesians*. Dallas: Word, 1990.

———. "The Theology of Ephesians." Pages 73–172 in *The Theology of the Later Pauline Letters*. Cambridge: Cambridge University Press, 1993.

Lohse, Eduard. *Colossians and Philemon: A Commentary on the Epistles to the Colossians and to Philemon*. Trans. W. R. Pohlmann and R. J. Harris. Philadelphia: Fortress, 1971.

Longenecker, Richard N. *Galatians*. Dallas: Word, 1990.

Marshall, I. Howard. *The Epistles of John*. Grand Rapids: Eerdmans, 1978.

———. *1 and 2 Thessalonians*. Grand Rapids: Eerdmans, 1983.

_____. *1 Peter*. Downers Grove: InterVarsity, 1991.

_____. *The Epistle to the Philippians*. London: Epworth, 1992.

Martin, Ralph P. *The Epistle of Paul to the Philippians*. London: Tyndale, 1959.

_____. *Colossians and Philemon*. Grand Rapids: Eerdmans, 1973.

_____. *James*. Waco: Word, 1988.

Mayor, Joseph B. *The Epistle of St. James*. London: Macmillan, 1892.

_____. *The Epistle of Jude and the Second Epistle of St. Peter*. 1907. Repr., Grand Rapids: Baker, 1965.

Michaels, J. Ramsey. *1 Peter*. Waco: Word, 1988.

Milligan, George. *St. Paul's Epistles to the Thessalonians*. London: Macmillan, 1908.

Mitton, C. L. *The Epistle of James*. London: Marshall, Morgan & Scott, 1966.

Morris, Leon L. *The First Epistle of Paul to the Corinthians*. London: Tyndale, 1958.

_____. *The First and Second Epistles to the Thessalonians*. Grand Rapids: Eerdmans, 1959.

Moule, C. F. D. *The Epistles of Paul the Apostle to the Colossians and to Philemon*. Cambridge: Cambridge University Press, 1962.

O'Brien, Peter T. *Colossians, Philemon*. Dallas: Word, 1982.

_____. *The Epistle to the Philippians: A Commentary on the Greek Text*. Grand Rapids: Eerdmans, 1991.

Perkins, Pheme. *First and Second Peter, James, and Jude*. Louisville: John Knox, 1995.

Pokorny, Petr. *Colossians: A Commentary*. Peabody: Hendrickson, 1991.

Reicke, B. *The Epistles of James, Peter, and Jude*. Garden City: Doubleday, 1964.

Robertson, A., and Alfred Plummer. *A Critical and Exegetical Commentary on the First Epistle of St. Paul to the Corinthians*. Edinburgh: T. & T. Clark, 1911.

Sanday, William, and Arthur C. Headlam. *A Critical and Exegetical Commentary on the Epistle to the Romans*. Edinburgh: T. & T. Clark, 1905.

Schweizer, Eduard. *The Letter to the Colossians: A Commentary*. Minneapolis: Augsburg, 1982.

_____. *Jesus Christ: The Man from Nazareth and the Exalted Lord*. Macon: Mercer University Press, 1987, esp. the chapter "The Hymns in the New Testament."

Selwyn, E. G. *The First Epistle of St. Peter*. London: Macmillan, 1946.

Thrall, Margaret E. *The First and Second Letters of Paul to the Corinthians*. Cambridge: Cambridge University Press, 1965.

Westcott, B. F. *The Epistles of St. John*. London: Macmillan, 1883.

_____. *St. Paul's Epistle to the Ephesians*. London: Macmillan, 1906.

Young, Frances M. *The Theology of the Pastoral Letters*. Cambridge: Cambridge University Press, 1994.

Chapter 4. The Synoptic Gospels and the Acts

Allison, Dale C. Jr. *The New Moses: A Matthean Typology*. Minneapolis: Fortress, 1993.

Best, Ernest. "Mark's Preservation of the Tradition." Pages 21–34 in *L'Évangile selon Marc: Tradition et Rédaction*. Ed. M. Sabbe. Leuven: University Press, 1974.

Black, Matthew. *An Aramaic Approach to the Gospels and Acts*. 3d ed. Oxford: Clarendon, 1967.

Bock, Darrell. *Proclamation from Prophecy and Pattern: Lucan Old Testament Christology*. Sheffield: JSOT, 1987.

Bornkamm, G., G. Barth, and H. J. Held. *Tradition and Interpretation in Matthew*. Trans. P. Scott. London: SCM, 1963.

Brown, Raymond E. *The Birth of the Messiah: A Commentary on the Infancy Narratives in the Gospels of Matthew and Luke*. Rev. ed. Garden City: Doubleday, 1993.

_____. *The Death of the Messiah—from Gethsemane to the Grave: A Commentary on the Passion Narratives in the Four Gospels*. 2 vols. Garden City: Doubleday, 1994.

Bruce, F. F. *The Acts of the Apostles*. Grand Rapids: Eerdmans, 1951.

Caird, George B. *St. Luke*. London: Black, 1963.

Davies, W. D., and D. C. Allison Jr. *A Critical and Exegetical Commentary on the Gospel according to Saint Matthew*. 3 vols. Edinburgh: T. & T. Clark, 1988, 1991, 1996.

Fitzmyer, Joseph A. *The Gospel according to Luke*. 2 vols. Garden City: Doubleday, 1981, 1985.

France, Richard T. *The Gospel according to Matthew*. Leicester: Inter-Varsity, 1985.

Guelich, Robert A. *Mark 1–8:26*. Dallas: Word, 1989.

Haenchen, Ernst. *The Acts of the Apostles*. Trans. R. McL. Wilson. Philadelphia: Westminster, 1971.

Hagner, Donald A. *Matthew*. 2 vols. Dallas: Word, 1993, 1995.

Hill, David. *The Gospel of Matthew*. Grand Rapids: Eerdmans, 1972.

Hooker, Morna D. *The Gospel according to St. Mark*. London: Black, 1991; Peabody: Hendrickson, 1993.

Hurtado, Larry W. *Mark*. NIBC. Peabody: Hendrickson, 1989.

Kingsbury, Jack D. *Matthew: Structure, Christology, Kingdom*. Philadelphia: Fortress, 1975.

Lane, William L. *The Gospel according to Mark*. Grand Rapids: Eerdmans, 1974.

Lemcio, Eugene E. *The Past of Jesus in the Gospels*. Cambridge: Cambridge University Press, 1991.

Longenecker, Richard N. "Acts." Pages 205–573 in vol. 9 of *The Expositor's Bible Commentary*. Ed. F. E. Gaebelein. Grand Rapids: Zondervan, 1981. Repr. in one vol., *Acts*. Grand Rapids: Zondervan, 1995.

Luz, U. *Matthew 1–7: A Commentary*. Trans. W. C. Linss. Minneapolis: Augsburg, 1989.

Marshall, I. Howard. *Luke: Historian and Theologian*. Exeter: Paternoster, 1970.

_____. *The Gospel of Luke: A Commentary on the Greek Text*. Grand Rapids: Eerdmans, 1978.

_____. *The Acts of the Apostles*. Grand Rapids: Eerdmans, 1980.

Morris, Leon L. *The Gospel according to Luke*. London: Tyndale, 1974.

Moule, C. F. D. "The Intention of the Evangelists." Pages 165–79 in *New Testament Essays: Studies in Memory of T. W. Manson*. Ed. A. J. B. Higgins. Manchester: Manchester University Press, 1959. Repr. as an appendix in *The Phenomenon of the New Testament*. London: SCM, 1967.

_____. *The Gospel according to Mark*. Cambridge: Cambridge University Press, 1965.

_____. "The Christology of Acts." Pages 159–85 in *Studies in Luke–Acts*. Ed. L. Keck and J. L. Martyn. Philadelphia: Fortress, 1980.

Munck, Johannes. *The Acts of the Apostles*. Rev. W. F. Albright and C. S. Mann. Garden City: Doubleday, 1967.

Nolland, John. *Luke*. 3 vols. Dallas: Word, 1989–1993.

Powell, Mark A. *What Are They Saying about Luke?* New York: Paulist, 1989.

_____. *What Are They Saying about Acts?* New York: Paulist, 1991.

Rese, Martin. *Alttestamentliche Motive in der Christologie des Lukas*. Gütersloh: Mohn, 1969.

Schweizer, Eduard. *The Good News according to Mark*. Trans. D. E. Green. Atlanta: John Knox, 1971.

_____. *The Good News according to Matthew*. Trans. D. E. Green. Atlanta: John Knox, 1975.

_____. *The Good News according to Luke*. Trans. D. E. Green. Atlanta: John Knox, 1984.

Soards, Marion L. *The Speeches in Acts: Their Content, Context, and Concerns*. Louisville: Westminster/John Knox, 1994.

Stanton, Graham N. ed. *The Interpretation of Matthew*. London: SPCK; Philadelphia: Fortress, 1983.

_____. "The Origin and Purpose of Matthew's Gospel: Matthean Scholarship from 1945–1980." *Aufsteig und Neidergang der römischen Welt II*. 25.3:1189–1951. Ed. H. Temporini and W. Haase. Berlin: de Gruyter, 1984.

_____. *A Gospel for a New People: Studies in Matthew*. Louisville: Westminster/John Knox, 1993.

Talbert, Charles H. *Literary Patterns, Theological Themes, and the Genre of Luke–Acts*. Missoula: Scholars, 1974.

Williams, C. S. G. *A Commentary on the Acts of the Apostles*. London: Black, 1957.

Chapter 5. The Fourth Gospel and the Johannine Apocalypse

Barrett, C. K. *The Gospel according to St. John*. London: SPCK, 1956.

Beasley-Murray, George R. *John*. Waco: Word, 1987.

Brown, Raymond E. *The Gospel according to John*. 2 vols. Garden City: Doubleday, 1966, 1970.

Bultmann, Rudolf. *The Gospel of John: A Commentary*. Trans. G. R. Beasley-Murray, R. W. N. Hoare, and J. K. Riches. Philadelphia: Westminster, 1971.

Caird, George B. *The Revelation of St. John*. BNTC 19. Peabody: Hendrickson, 1966.

Dodd, C. H. *The Interpretation of the Fourth Gospel*. Cambridge: Cambridge University Press, 1958.

Jeremias, Joachim. *The Central Message of the New Testament*. New York: Scribner's, 1965.

_____. *Abba: Studien zur neutestamentlichen Theologie und Zeitgeschichte*. Göttingen: Vandenhoeck & Ruprecht, 1966.

Ladd, George E. *A Commentary on the Revelation of John*. Grand Rapids: Eerdmans, 1972.

Longenecker, Richard N. "The One and Only Son." Pages 119–26 in *The NIV: The Making of a Contemporary Translation*. Ed. K. L. Barker. Grand Rapids: Zondervan, 1986.

Michaels, J. Ramsey. *Revelation*. Downers Grove: InterVarsity, 1996.

Morris, Leon L. *The Revelation of St. John*. London: Tyndale, 1970.

_____. *Commentary on the Gospel of John*. Grand Rapids: Eerdmans, 1971.

Mounce, Robert H. *The Book of Revelation*. Grand Rapids: Eerdmans, 1977.

Swete, Henry B. *The Apocalypse of St. John*. London: Macmillan, 1886.

Westcott, B. F. *The Gospel according to St. John*. 1881. Repr., Grand Rapids: Eerdmans, 1971.

▧ PART 3—The Contextualization of the Confessions Today

Allen, Diogenes. *Christian Belief in a Postmodern World*. Louisville: Westminster/John Knox, 1989.

Anderson, Gerald H., and Thomas F. Stransky, eds. *Third World Theologies*. Mission Trends 3. New York: Paulist, 1976.

_____. *Witnessing to the Kingdom. Melbourne and Beyond*. Maryknoll: Orbis, 1982.

Anderson, Gerald H. And Thomas F. Stransky, eds. *Third World Theologies*. Mission Trends 3. New York: Paulist; Grand Rapids: Eerdmans, 1976.

_____. *Liberation Theologies*. Mission Trends 4. New York: Paulist; Grand Rapids: Eerdmans, 1978.

Arbuckle, Gerald A. *Earthing the Gospel: An Inculturation Handbook for the Pastoral Worker.* Maryknoll: Orbis, 1990.

Bevans, Stephen. "Models of Contextual Theology." *Missiology* 13 (1985): 185–202.

Bibby, Reginald. *Fragmented Gods.* Toronto: Irwin, 1987.

Bosch, David J. *Witness to the World. The Christian Mission in Theological Perspective.* Atlanta: John Knox, 1980.

_____. "Evangelism: Theological Currents and Cross-Currents Today." *International Bulletin of Missionary Research* 11 (1987): 98–103.

_____. *Transforming Mission: Paradigm Shifts in Theology of Mission.* American Society of Missiology Series 96. Maryknoll: Orbis, 1991.

Comblin, Joseph. *The Meaning of Mission.* Trans. J. Drury. Maryknoll: Orbis, 1977.

Conn, Harvey M. *Eternal Word and Changing Worlds: Theology, Anthropology, and Mission in Trialogue.* Grand Rapids: Zondervan, 1984.

Cornille, Catherine, and Valeer Neckebrouck, eds. *A Universal Faith? Peoples, Cultures, Religions, and the Christ.* Louvain Theological and Pastoral Monograph 9. Essays in honor of Prof. Dr. Frank De Graeve. Grand Rapids: Eerdmans, 1993.

Costas, Orlando E. *The Integrity of Mission: The Inner Life and the Outreach of the Church.* San Francisco: Harper & Row, 1979.

_____. *Liberating News: A Theology of Contextual Evangelization.* Grand Rapids: Eerdmans, 1989.

Dyrness, William A. *Invitation to Cross-Cultural Theology: Case Studies in Vernacular Theologies.* Grand Rapids: Zondervan, 1992.

Geffre, Claude. "Theological Reflections on a New Age of Mission." *International Review of Missions* 71 (1982): 478–92.

Gilliland, Dean S., ed. *The Word among Us: Contextualizing Theology for Mission Today.* Dallas: Word, 1989.

Gittins, Anthony J. *Bread for the Journey: The Mission of Transformation and the Transformation of Mission.* American Society of Missiology Series 17. Maryknoll: Orbis, 1993.

Glasser, Arthur F. "Mission in the 1990's." *International Bulletin of Missionary Research* 13 (1989): 2–8.

_____, and Donald A. McGavran. *Contemporary Theologies of Mission.* Grand Rapids: Baker, 1983.

Haleblian, Krikor. "The Problem of Contextualization." *Missiology* 11 (1983): 95–111.

Hall, Douglas J. *Christian Mission: The Stewardship of Life in the Kingdom of Death.* New York: Friendship, 1985.

_____. *Thinking the Faith: Christian Theology in a North American Context.* Minneapolis: Augsburg, 1989.

_____. *The End of Christendom and the Future of Christianity.* Valley Forge: Trinity International, 1997.

Hauerwas, Stanley, and William H. Willimon. *Resident Aliens.* Nashville: Abingdon, 1989.

Hesselgrave, David J. *Communicating Christ Cross-Culturally.* Grand Rapids: Zondervan, 1978.

_____ and Edward Rommen. *Contextualization: Meanings, Methods, and Models.* Grand Rapids: Baker, 1989.

Hiebert, Paul G. "Critical Contextualization." *International Bulletin of Missionary Research* 11 (1987): 104–12.

Hood, Robert E. *Must God Remain Greek? Afro Cultures and God-Talk.* Minneapolis: Fortress, 1990.

Hunsberger, George R., and Craig van Gelder, eds. *The Church Between Gospel and Culture: The Emerging Mission in North America.* Grand Rapids: Eerdmans, 1996.

Hutchison, William. *Errand to the World: American Protestant Thought and Foreign Missions.* Chicago: University of Chicago Press, 1987.

Kinnamon, Michael. *Truth and Community: Diversity and Its Limits in the Ecumenical Movement.* Grand Rapids: Eerdmans, 1988.

Kitagawa, Joseph Mitsuo. *The Christian Tradition: Beyond Its European Captivity.* Philadelphia: Trinity International, 1992.

Koyama, Kosuke. *A Model for Intercultural Theology.* Frankfurt: Peter Lang, 1991.

Kraft, Charles H. *Christianity in Culture: A Study in Dynamic Biblical Theologizing in Cross-Cultural Perspective.* Maryknoll: Orbis, 1979.

_____. *Communication Theory for Christian Witness.* Rev. ed. Maryknoll: Orbis, 1991.

Kung, Hans. *Signposts for the Future: Contemporary Issues Facing the Church.* Garden City: Doubleday, 1978.

Longenecker, Richard N. *New Testament Social Ethics for Today.* Grand Rapids: Eerdmans, 1984. Repr., Vancouver: Regent College Bookstore, 1993.

Lotz, David W., ed. *Altered Landscapes: Christianity in America 1935–1985.* Grand Rapids: Eerdmans, 1989.

Luzbetak, Louis J. *The Church and Cultures: New Perspectives in Missiological Anthropology.* Maryknoll: Orbis, 1988.

Marty, Martin E. "From the Centripetal to the Centrifugal in Culture and Religion." *Theology Today* 51 (1994): 5–16.

Moltmann, Jurgen. "Christianity in the Third Millenium." *Theology Today,* 54 (1997): 75–89.

Neill, Stephen. *Christian Partnership.* London: SCM, 1952.

_____. *Call to Mission.* Philadelphia: Fortress, 1970.

Newbigin, Lesslie. *A Word in Season: Perspectives on Christian World Missions.* Grand Rapids: Eerdmans, 1974.

_____. *The Open Secret: Sketches for a Missionary Theology.* Grand Rapids: Eerdmans, 1978.

Nida, Eugene A., and William D. Reyburn. *Meaning across Cultures.* Maryknoll: Orbis, 1981.

Niebuhr, Reinhold. *Man's Nature and His Communities*. New York: Scribner's, 1965.

Niles, D. T. *Upon the Earth: The Mission of God and the Missionary Enterprise of the Church*. London: Lutterworth, 1962.

Oduyoye, Mercy Amba. "The Church of the Future, Its Mission and Theology. A View from Africa." *Theology Today* 52 (1995): 494–505.

Padilla, C. Rene. *Mission Between the Times*. Grand Rapids: Eerdmans, 1985.

Parshall, Philip. *Bridges to Islam*. Grand Rapids: Baker, 1983.

Rahner, Karl. *The Shape of the Church to Come*. Trans. E. Quinn. London: SPCK, 1974.

Saayman, William, and Klippies Kritzinger, eds. *Mission in Bold Humility: David Bosch's Work Considered*. Maryknoll: Orbis, 1996.

Scherer, James A., and Stephen B. Bevans, eds. *New Directions in Mission and Evangelization*. I. *Basic Statements 1974–1991*. Maryknoll: Orbis, 1992.

Schillebeeckx, Edward. *The Church with a Human Face*. Trans. J. Bowden. New York: Crossroad, 1987.

Schineller, Peter. *A Handbook on Inculturation*. New York: Paulist, 1990.

Shorter, Alyward. *Toward a Theology of Inculturation*. Maryknoll: Orbis, 1988.

Schreiter, Robert J. *Constructing Local Theologies*. Maryknoll: Orbis, 1985.

Smith, Donald K. *Creating Understanding: A Handbook for Christian Communication across Cultural Landscapes*. Grand Rapids: Eerdmans, 1992.

Smith, Wilfred Cantwell. *The Faith of Other Men*. Toronto: CBC Publications, 1962.

Stackhouse, Max L. *Apologia: Contextualization, Globalization, and Mission in Theological Education*. Grand Rapids: Eerdmans, 1988.

Stott, John, and Robert T. Coote, eds. *Down to Earth: Studies in Christianity and Culture*. Grand Rapids: Eerdmans, 1980.

Taber, Charles R. "The Limits of Indigenization in Theology." *Missiology* 6 (1978): 53–80.

———. "Contextualization." *Religious Studies Review* 13 (1987): 33–36.

Tracy, David. *The Analogical Imagination: Christian Theology and the Culture of Pluralism*. New York: Crossroad, 1981.

Ukpong, Justin S. "What Is Contextualization?" *Neue Zeitschrift für Missionswissenschaft* 43 (1987): 161–68.

Whitehead, James D., and Evelyn Eaton Whitehead. *The Promise of Partnership: A Model for Collaborative Ministry*. San Francisco: Harper & Row, 1991.

Willimon, William H. *What's Right with the Church*. San Francisco: Harper & Row, 1985.

Yates, Timothy. *Christian Mission in the Twentieth Century*. Cambridge: Cambrdige University Press, 1994.

Index of Modern Authors

Index of Ancient Sources